Making Moral Citizens

**Where Religion Lives**

Kristy Nabhan-Warren, *editor*

Where Religion Lives publishes ethnographies of religious life. The series features the methods of religious studies along with anthropological approaches to lived religion. The religious studies perspective encompasses attention to historical contingency, theory, religious doctrine and texts, and religious practitioners' intimate, personal narratives. The series also highlights the critical realities of migration and transnationalism.

A complete list of books published in Where Religion Lives is available at https://uncpress.org/series/where-religion-lives.

# Making Moral Citizens

How Faith-Based Organizers
Use Vocation for Public Action

......................................................

**JACK DELEHANTY**

The University of North Carolina Press  Chapel Hill

*This book was published with the assistance of the Authors Fund of the University of North Carolina Press.*

© 2023 The University of North Carolina Press
All rights reserved
Set in Charis by Westchester Publishing Services
Manufactured in the United States of America

Library of Congress Cataloging-in-Publication Data
Names: Delehanty, Jack (John D.), author.
Title: Making moral citizens : how faith-based organizers use vocation for
    public action / Jack Delehanty.
Other titles: Where religion lives.
Description: Chapel Hill : The University of North Carolina Press, [2023] |
    Series: Where religion lives | Includes bibliographical references
    and index.
Identifiers: LCCN 2022036512 | ISBN 9781469673158 (cloth : alk. paper) |
    ISBN 9781469673165 (paperback : alk. paper) |
    ISBN 9781469673172 (ebook)
Subjects: LCSH: Faith-based community organizing—United States. |
    Social justice—Religious aspects. | LCGFT: Ethnographies.
Classification: LCC HN90.C6 D43 2023 | DDC 303.3/720973—dc23/
    eng/20221007
LC record available at https://lccn.loc.gov/2022036512

Cover illustration: Continuous line drawing of people in conference room
© Ahmad Safarudin/Dreamstime.com.

*To Katy Kvale*
*and Jim Delehanty*
*with love and gratitude*

# Contents

# Acknowledgments

This book is the product of many people's work, support, care, and kindness. My deepest gratitude is to the people who make up the organization I call ELIJAH, particularly the ELIJAH core team at the church I refer to as St. Martin's. I am humbled by the trust they placed in me and their willingness to share their stories, motivations, and aspirations. Several people at ELIJAH and St. Martin's went out of their way to help me and push me when I needed it. I cannot name them, but they know who they are. Organizing is demanding, intensive work, and allowing an outsider into it is no small matter. I am more grateful than I can say to all who let me follow them as they poured their hearts into joining with others to improve the world for everyone. Special thanks to those who took additional time to sit with me for interviews.

The arguments in this book were developed through conversations and collaborations with mentors, colleagues, and advisers. Chief among these was Penny Edgell. Penny is a model scholar: rigorous yet caring, demanding yet affable, and intelligent beyond description. Besides being an incredibly productive researcher and a brilliant teacher, she is steadfastly devoted to helping young academics launch their careers, and extremely good at it. Without her, my research agenda would never have gotten off the ground. I was lucky enough to work with Penny only because of the generous wisdom of the late Erik Olin Wright, a giant in the field of sociology who, despite his stature, was willing to meet with me, a student he'd never met, to talk about graduate programs. When I told Erik I wanted to do research on religion and activism, he immediately said, "You should go to Minnesota and work with Penny Edgell." It was one of the most straightforward pieces of advice I have ever received, and one of the best. That a social stratification scholar like Erik knew that Penny was the best possible mentor for someone studying religion, a sociological world away from his own subfields, is evidence of how strong—and deserved—her reputation is.

A few other people deserve special mention. Elaine Maisner and Mark Simpson-Vos at UNC Press, along with series editor Kristy Nabhan-Warren, saw promise in my work and helped it come together as a publishable manuscript. Letta Page helped polish the writing, and Kate Weigand provided the index. Ruth Braunstein has always been eager to provide insightful commentary and sound professional advice. Michelle Oyakawa became my friend and collaborator at just the right time to help me understand and process what I was seeing and hearing in the field. Many of the key points herein developed in conversations with her. Richard Wood and Gerardo Martí each went out of their way to support this project and ensure it was as sharp as it could be. Patty Ewick and Shelly Tenenbaum read and reread drafts of each chapter and helped me navigate the academic publishing process. Along with Sarah Barry, Parminder Bhachu, Debbie Merrill, and Rosalie Torres Stone, they made me feel welcome at Clark University as I adjusted to a new job in an unfamiliar region. Ron Aminzade, Lydia Bean, Kraig Beyerlein, Tricia Bruce, Jonathan Coley, Kathleen Collins, Jennifer Cossyleon, David Forrest, Jacqui Frost, Todd Nicholas Fuist, Brad Fulton, Teresa Gowan, Yagmur Karakaya, Jaime Kucinskas, Amy Levad, Paul Lichterman, Wes Markofski, Liz McKenna, Rory McVeigh, Dana Moss, Margaret Post, Ryan Steel, Evan Stewart, Caty Taborda, and Grace Yukich all contributed in various ways to the ideas that became this book. Parts of this research were funded by the Institute for the Study of American Evangelicals at Wheaton College and the Society for the Scientific Study of Religion.

I owe my interest in the complexities of the social world to my parents, Katy Kvale and Jim Delehanty. It began when I was very young: no conversation, question, or book was off-limits. From the moment I could, they taught me to read everything in sight and to question why the text said the things it did. They sometimes told me that I would thank them later for banning cable and video games from our home when my brother and I were young. I am thanking them now. Later, my mom married Tom Schirz and my dad married Jo Ellen Fair, who have both provided love and support beyond measure. My brother, Tony, has always been ready with a laugh and a smile anytime anybody needs one. Long may he keep it up.

Above all, thanks to Tania, the source of my joy and strength and my partner in whatever life may bring us, and to Sylvie, who amazes and inspires me in every moment.

Making Moral Citizens

# Introduction

Broadway Apostolic, a large Pentecostal church in a poor urban neighbor-hood in the Midwest, welcomes a mostly Black congregation for worship every week, but on this Saturday in late January 2017, the faces were a roughly even mix: Black, white, and brown. Catholic nuns in habits sat alongside pastors in robes. Jewish and Islamic head coverings punctuated the rally's interfaith nature. Headsets translated remarks coming from the altar. As people settled in, a gospel choir sang, danced, and clapped in joy-ful rhythm, enthusiastically joined by large sections of the audience. Every seat in the massive sanctuary was full, as was every aisle and corner. Fif-teen minutes before the proceedings were to begin, more than 2,000 people, representing 171 different religious congregations, were crammed in. Not a single space to sit or stand was unoccupied.

The setting oozed faith, but this was not just a religious gathering. It was also a political demonstration. President Donald Trump had been inaugu-rated eight days earlier, and those assembling at Broadway had tasked them-selves with plotting ways the faith communities they represented could come together to resist the new administration's rhetoric and policies. Behind all this was ELIJAH, a faith-based community organization (FBCO) dedicated to uniting people across race, class, and religious lines to build power for social change.[1] FBCOs are local and regional networks of religious congregations that work together to confront racial injustice and economic unfairness. ELIJAH is one of more than 220 FBCOs in the United States.[2] Collectively, their member institutions represent more than 5 million people.[3] This makes the FBCO field one of the largest venues of grassroots civic activity in the country.

Though many people associate religious commitment with political con-servatism, these coalitions have long been at the forefront of a different kind of social movement. For at least the last forty years, they have been working to improve the lives of marginalized, working-class, and middle-class people. In the 1980s, the East Brooklyn Congregations spearheaded the Nehemiah Project, one of the most successful affordable-housing pro-grams in U.S. history.[4] More recently, FBCOs were at the center of grassroots coalitions responsible for the wave of paid sick time and $15 minimum wage laws that swept through cities from Seattle to Philadelphia in the 2010s. In these and many other instances, FBCOs have injected movements for socioeconomic and racial equity with the faith-inspired voices of everyday people organized through religious communities. ELIJAH, founded in 2000 in a large city in the Midwest, is among the largest and most effective regional FBCO federations in the United States.

The Broadway gathering was an impressive event, one of the largest rallies ELIJAH had ever put together. But everything about it except the size—the diversity, the focus on using the political system to advance an ambitious faith-infused social justice agenda, and the atmosphere of religious and racial unity emanating from the proceedings—was typical of what FBCOs across the country strive to do every day.

How does a movement like this come together? What makes it possible for FBCOs to not only unite people across race, class, and religious differences but also engage them in sustained, time-consuming, and complex political projects aimed at bettering everyday people's lives?

This book explains the strategies ELIJAH uses to engage religious communities in collective action for racial justice and economic fairness. During my three-plus years of research in ELIJAH, I observed how its leaders make solving big public problems into a matter of personal religious meaning for people of different backgrounds, using religious commitment in creative and unexpected ways to foster a sense of togetherness and commitment to action that can alter the terms—and sometimes even the outcomes—of policy debates, as well as transform religious identity and renew religious community for participants.

This book adds to a growing conversation about religion and progressive activism in the United States by revealing the mechanics of how religion works in this kind of social movement organizing. Scholars analyzing religion's contributions to social movements have typically focused on how it provides material resources, such as funds, meeting spaces, and communication networks; the beliefs and doctrines that provide fodder for persuasion about what is right, just, or godly; and the frames used for moralizing social problems—for example, connecting Jesus's status as a poor migrant to the challenges migrants to the United States face today.[5] Without denying the importance of these widely noted contributions, this book explains how some of the most influential activist leaders in the United States are doing something different with religion: something more intimate and personal, using emotional and sometimes confrontational interactions to make individuals' faith commitments into a basis for rethinking who they are, what they care about, the responsibilities their faith confers on them, and how they can live up to those duties. ELIJAH's organizing, I will show, leans on *personal transformation* to engender social change.

I did not begin this project intending to write about personal transformation, nor about emotions, introspection, or deep one-to-one conversations—all central in the analysis to come. In fact, early in my research I was taken aback by how many conversations I heard about emotions, especially pain, shame, and guilt. To my unaccustomed eyes and ears, many of these discussions seemed unnecessarily personal, unfriendly, sometimes even hostile. Often, facilitators of the meetings I was attending opened proceedings by demanding that participants relive some of their toughest moments, publicly recount personal stories of grief and distress, explain how their perspectives on past trauma had developed over time, and process what their experiences meant in view of others' stories. As meeting after meeting revolved around intense interactions like these, I wondered what the discussions had to do with the policy fights about issues like criminal justice, wages and worker protections, housing, voting, health care, the environment, and education that had drawn my interest to the FBCO world in the first place. Why was a group concerned with changing society spending so much time on how people *felt*? It was only with repeated exposure to and participation in this organizing model, the benefit of time to reflect on it, and a lot of guidance from ELIJAH leaders that I was able to see how the political action ELIJAH carries out, as well as the religious unity its participants display, depends entirely on the deeply personal, emotionally demanding practices its leaders have developed for channeling faith into commitment to social change—a process hinted at but not explained in depth in previous research on progressive religious organizing.[6]

*Making Moral Citizens* explains that religion's contributions to this kind of organizing hinge on the interplay between deep personal introspection and sweeping structural critique—dynamics that I call moral vocation and moral citizenship, respectively. *Moral vocation* is a person's ambition to enact a morally worthy self amid a chaotic social world. It is not just a sense of what is good but an ongoing, evolving life project that relies on probing reflection and interpersonal conversation to develop a sense of what a person cares about and how they can achieve it. In turn, *moral citizenship* is a sense that people's moral goals and aspirations are linked, and that achieving them requires collective action rooted in sound social analysis that identifies the public root causes of people's seemingly personal problems. Moral citizenship is a collective commitment to confront the racial injustice and economic unfairness that impede people's ability to live secure, prosperous lives—a shared commitment to fulfilling moral vocations through joint public action. When leaders bring people to perceive that enacting their moral vocations requires embracing moral citizenship, they can achieve things like putting more than 2,000 people in a room together to confront the Trump administration and, more importantly, keeping them engaged afterward.

Of course, people's moral vocations don't all look the same. Faith, race and class background, life experiences, and other factors intersect. Few would expect a Black Pentecostal mother, an immigrant Catholic father, a white Methodist grandfather, and a childless twenty-something white Protestant with fluid gender and sexual identities—all common in ELIJAH—to have identical or even substantially similar visions of what is good and how best to pursue it. Differences like these are meaningful, but they only obscure, rather than neuter, what people from different backgrounds often share: an underlying impulse to authentically live out their values by making good choices as an individual. This ambition to *choose to do good* is nearly ubiquitous in American religious practice, and it creates a cultural foundation that skilled leaders can tap into.[7] By asking people to reflect on their formative moments, traumatic experiences, and future ambitions, then showing how their stories are connected across different life situations, ELIJAH leaders make moral vocation into the religious fuel for an iterative process of deep reflection about what one's faith means, and what responsibilities it confers, in a society plagued by deep inequality.

When activist leaders link these personal and public ways of thinking, they make the collective embrace of moral citizenship into an appealing way for people of different backgrounds and faith commitments to live out their distinct moral vocations together—building the foundation for a powerful multiracial, multifaith social movement organization. This happens, I will show, through *relational practices*: intense, emotionally charged, and often challenging interpersonal interactions that reveal commonalities among different people's experiences and goals. While relational practices have drawn plenty of attention in prior research, this book focuses on the dynamics that make these practices central in forming people's identities, religion's role in supporting them, and how they enliven the particular style of political action FBCOs employ. In revealing these cultural undercurrents of faith-based organizing, *Making Moral Citizens* shows how religious activist leaders bridge social divisions to foster a sense of common moral purpose and fuel a movement for racial justice and economic fairness.

## The Personal, the Public, and the Practices in Between

The rally at Broadway, titled "For Such a Time as This: Building our Prophetic Resistance," provides some useful examples of how ELIJAH leaders synthesize the personal and the public. In one sense, my job at Broadway that day was to help things run smoothly. In the prior weeks I had spent evenings with people from ELIJAH working on turnout: sitting in church basements, hunched over laptops with spreadsheets, making calls and sending texts to people from congregations across the region. I spent the morning of the rally setting up folding chairs wherever they could be crammed in. As the crowd arrived, my job was to help parents find the childcare room. I did that until I was abruptly tasked instead with shooing people away from a block of seats in the front that had been reserved for members of a consortium of local mosques who would enter together ceremonially, wearing traditional dress, to visibly demonstrate ELIJAH's cooperation across religious, racial, and ethnic lines. But these tasks aside, I was there to watch and listen and learn. I had spent hundreds of hours in the field by this point, and interviewed more than two dozen of ELIJAH's leaders, but the stories I heard at Broadway that afternoon still stand out as a clear example of how moral vocation and moral citizenship come together through relational practices.

Just like nearly every other ELIJAH meeting I had attended, the rally, despite its size, was infused with a surprisingly intimate, emotional feel, as everyday people shared how the sources of shame, pain, fear, and guilt in their lives reflect structural problems that transcend any one person's situation. A Black man explained how stress over car detailing and his constant fear of being pulled over strain his day-to-day life. He maintains his car obsessively, at substantial cost relative to his meager income, to avoid putting his life at risk by being stopped for a broken taillight or some other minor problem. He described seizing up with anxiety every time he saw a police car near him on the road. His story made it clear that even though anxiety and stress can seem like personal problems, his struggles are not his alone. Rather, they are the result of a society that tolerates and normalizes police violence against people of color.

The stories continued one after another, different people with different backgrounds and experiences invoking the same themes. A white man explained how a prior felony conviction affects his confidence while look-ing for jobs, since he knows most employers will reject him. A white woman, a corporate manager whose company had recently been acquired, described the horror she felt when the new ownership team implemented a policy re-quiring all departments to fire 10 percent of their employees each year in order to "promote excellence," regardless of how the company was doing overall. A fifty-something immigrant from Mexico shared that over her thirty years of living and working in the United States, she had gladly paid more than $50,000 into Medicare and Social Security, even though undoc-umented people like her cannot benefit from these programs. Sniffling back tears, she relayed the emotional toll it takes when people tell her that she and the people she loves are drains on society's resources and should be "sent back" to countries they left long ago—or, in her children's case, have never set foot in.

These storytellers, only a few examples among many who spoke that afternoon, came from starkly different backgrounds. One could hardly find work; another was financially secure enough to quit her high-paying job in protest of corporate policies she found immoral. Often, differences like these impede cooperation in social change projects, as divergent life experiences make it hard for people to empathize and work together, even when they want the same things.[8] But in this case, these stories highlighted the per-sonal and emotional consequences of racial and socioeconomic inequalities and showed how these consequences impede the deep cultural ambitions that many people share, like wanting to live and work with dignity, free of fear and shame while supporting one's family. As people described these basic human desires and identified the barriers that stand in their way, their shared emotions fostered a sense of connectedness that transcended social boundaries.[9] Taken together, their stories exposed the mutual threats to their mutual desires.

Their ability to construct empathy across difference is why relational practices like storytelling and similar activities, much more than policy analysis or even theological discussion, are at the core of every ELIJAH event. Planning meetings of four or five leaders in coffee shops or living rooms, training sessions with twenty or thirty people in church basements, and press conferences and rallies at the state capitol all foreground the emo-tional consequences of structural inequities. As activities that encourage reflection about how one's life and challenges are similar to other people's, especially people from different backgrounds, relational practices are designed to identify concrete ways a person's life has been molded by structural forces, illuminate commonalities across different people's experiences of those forces, and use those connections as the foundations for relationships that can be transformed into collective power. Through storytelling and other relational practices, such as one-to-one conversations, collective lamentations, and interactive songs and prayers, people in ELIJAH learn to identify the deep human interests that drive them; recognize that others share these interests, even if their immediate situations are different; and name the structural impediments to achieving their personal goals. Technical conversations about policies and strategies, and even discussions of religious texts or beliefs, no matter how detailed or persuasive, can rarely match the connection-building power of relational practices.

This book uses the case of ELIJAH to show how relational practices can enliven moral vocations and anchor them to moral citizenship: a shared sense of moral duty to confront the systemic problems that put a life of prosperity, freedom, and dignity out of reach for tens of millions of Americans, especially but not exclusively poor people, members of the working class, immigrants, and people of color. Moral citizenship is not just my term; it is one ELIJAH leaders sometimes use to describe the ongoing act of taking responsibility for creating a just society for all. Although I borrow this term from ELIJAH's own language, I argue it has additional utility as a sociological concept that transcends my case study for two reasons. First, it plays a central but previously unrecognized role in social movement organizing by providing a shared cultural project with the capacity to span social differences while preserving participants' core personal commitments and respecting their roots in rich cultural and religious traditions. It is not hard to imagine that the diverse group of storytellers at the rally might not only have different goals but also have different ways of understanding and enacting what it means to be a good person, as well as different symbolic traditions for describing their goals and how to pursue them. Moral citizenship provides a shared language and vision that can connect these otherwise distinct moral vocations. It is commonly argued that the progressive sphere lacks powerful cultural visions of how society should work that have the potential to unify its diverse constituencies.[10] Moral citizenship is such a vision—or can be, when it is promoted skillfully and persistently through relational practices.

The other reason moral citizenship is sociologically interesting is that it is not a religious or political ideology but a shared social commitment that must be learned through interaction with others. No person, whether Catholic, Protestant, Muslim, or atheist, can become a moral citizen in isolation, no matter how much time is spent studying religious texts or reading political or activist literature. Rather, moral citizenship must be taught and learned cooperatively, and my long-term observations of ELIJAH and other organizations in the FBCO field suggest that relational practices are among the best ways to accomplish this teaching and learning. Relational practices can make ordinary people into moral citizens who see working with others to advance racial and socioeconomic equity as a core element of their broader moral commitments—whatever those commitments may be. Among ELIJAH and other FBCOs, these commitments are religious, but they do not necessarily have to be. As we will see, moral citizenship and the relational practices that engender it have roots in religious traditions, but they have the potential to be effective in nonreligious spaces, too.[11]

Ultimately, ELIJAH aspires to build a movement of moral citizens who work together to dismantle systemic racism and promote economic fairness. But my analysis reveals that achieving these political goals involves intense emotional work that drills deep into each participant's psyche and identity, which involves discussing the usually unspoken sources of anger, pain, and guilt that many people feel in their lives, and acknowledging fear, regret, and concern for potential loss. As sociologist Michelle Oyakawa explains, developing and telling personal stories can transform individual concern about an issue hampering one's life into engagement in collective work toward building power for change.[12] This is because interests are not static but culturally situated.

Before being exposed to others' stories through relational practices, many people understand their interests narrowly, thinking of their troubles as individual problems with individual solutions. Consider Marco, a Latino in his midthirties, a suburban Protestant who worked as a restaurant chef and had long been privately tormented by the strain his demanding but low-paying job put on his family life. He could rarely attend his child's evening teeball and soccer games, and his on-call schedule made it impossible to make weekend plans. He wanted to quit his job, but he couldn't. His whole family was dependent on the health insurance tied to it.

Relational practices reframe narrow personal interests like Marco's into broad cultural concerns. Through a series of one-to-one conversations with Lisa, a white woman in her fifties who attended his church and was a leader in ELIJAH, Marco learned to recognize that his personal troubles were not so personal after all. By revealing how the missed games and canceled weekend plans affected him emotionally, Lisa's probing questions helped Marco realize that his work schedule made him feel guilty and inadequate, like he is an unsupportive father, not just an overworked chef. With this revelation, Marco's interests transformed. He was no longer just a person unsatisfied with his job but someone whose work schedule prevented him from living a satisfying family life—and someone who was angry about it. In this regard, Marco realized, he was not so different from others whose experiences at work, whether related to schedules, low wages, insufficient health insurance, unsafe working conditions, sexual harassment, or anything else, make family life challenging.

A narrow interest, like Marco's original wish for a different job with a more predictable work schedule, can be pursued in isolation, through individual efforts whose benefits accrue to just one person or family. It might involve completing some additional training, learning to write a stronger résumé or cover letter, or building up the nerve to confront one's boss. The solo pursuit of change can also promote a zero-sum culture within a workplace, where one person's gain of more predictable hours means someone else has to pick up the on-call shifts. Relational practices teach that apparent solutions like these don't truly solve people's problems but merely pass them on to others, continuing the cycle of distress. In contrast, pursuing a broad cultural interest, such as wanting to better support one's family, involves recognizing that people in other life situations not only share that interest but can contribute to advancing it even if their immediate priorities or life situations are different. Organizers in FBCO federations strive to identify and politicize this kind of recognition, expanding the scope of analysis from the individual to the community.

Such transformations of how people understand their lives are at the heart of what groups like ELIJAH do. Yet important questions about relational practices and their role in faith-based organizing remain unanswered. Collectively, social scientists have learned quite a bit about how important these practices are for social change organizations, but we know much less about the specific cultural dynamics that animate them: what makes them work well in particular settings, how they help organizations advance certain goals, and what specific role, if any, religion plays in supporting them.[13] *Making Moral Citizens* provides a window into these less visible aspects of the organizing process, showing how relational practices take form, why they are effective (and sometimes not effective), and what they can tell us about the intersection of religion and social change work in the contemporary United States.

## Religion's Role: Providing Moral Vocations

If relational practices are so central in FBCOs' organizing, what role does religion itself play? At first, the answer may seem obvious: shared faith provides shared symbols and common rituals that foster mutual trust and understanding. People may believe different things, but being familiar with activities like prayer, song, and quiet contemplation makes it possible for organizations to use these common practices to bridge differences. This is the explanation offered by much of the existing scholarship on faith-based organizing, including work by sociologists Ruth Braunstein, Brad Fulton, and Richard Wood, which finds that the shared experience of being faithful, combined with effective use by leaders of "bridging cultural practices" like interfaith prayers and songs, helps people trust and relate to one another even when they have different beliefs and backgrounds.[14]

But if shared faith is such a powerful foundation for effective interaction across difference, why do people develop a strong sense of togetherness in some interfaith settings but not others? Research has found that lasting togetherness is much harder for interfaith groups to achieve than is often supposed.[15] What is happening among those groups that, like ELIJAH, actually succeed in bringing it about?

Answering this requires a subtle but important adjustment to the way scholars have typically thought about religion and social change work. Instead of asking *what religion does* or *what role religion plays* in social movements, we should instead ask *what people do with religion together*. This matters because religion doesn't do the same thing, or play the same role, for every person in an organization, especially a diverse one like ELIJAH. As sociologists like Melissa Wilde and Penny Edgell explain, religion alone usually can't provide the full picture of why people do what they do—even for the most devout.[16] Instead, what we often think of as people's religiously motivated action is based on the ways religion intersects with other elements of their lives and backgrounds, including their race, class, and gender. Certainly, faith matters for social action, but it operates as one among several sources of identity and meaning that contribute to people's overall dispositions and behavior. Asking what religion does means overlooking the ways it interacts with other social factors. Asking what people do with religion makes these interactions central.

This analytic frame is useful for understanding what happens in ELIJAH and similar groups because it helps us embrace, rather than write off, the variation in how people from different backgrounds combine faith with other parts of their lives—often at the same times and in the same places. We don't need to look for religion doing any one thing for everyone or for the group as a whole. Instead, we can look for points of convergence where people who may be doing different things with their faith nevertheless come together around similarities in what matters to them. We might hypothesize that organizations in which leaders can identify such convergences and make them the focus of relational practices will be more likely to foster meaningful solidarity than otherwise.

Moral vocation is the convergence point at the heart of what people do with religion in ELIJAH. As previously explained, moral vocation is my term for a person's sense of (a) having unique life experiences and goals that foster distinct attributes and capacities, and (b) possessing a moral responsibility to act out those attributes and capacities to do good in the world. Many of us, no matter our political leanings or cultural backgrounds, engage in social change projects as much to be a better person—however we might understand that idea—as to change the world.[17] As social theorist Erving Goffman famously argued, as we go through our days, we develop a sense of who we think we are, then choose paths of action that correspond with an idealized version of the self-identity we construct for ourselves.[18] Moral vocation refers to this ongoing personal project, honing and performing a moral identity through our daily activities and practices. People in ELIJAH do many things with religion, but reflecting on and refining their moral vocations through relational practices is one thing they can do with religion *together*. As we'll see in later chapters, practices that focus the group on this shared element of religious commitment not only show how different people's vocations are linked through social structure but also illuminate how collective action can be a means for advancing all of them at the same time.

Moral vocation is a powerful basis for organizing across difference because despite its roots in Protestant theology, it has diffused outward to become a flexible and wide-reaching cultural project, one that can be made meaningful to people of nearly any religious background. As sociologist Richard Madsen explains, across the many religious traditions in the United States, Americans use religion to envision a highly individualized self that is characterized by "self-reflexive (and somewhat self-righteous) voluntary choice."[19] More than believing in the divine or belonging to a religious organization, much contemporary religious commitment, especially in the United States, is about the ongoing construction of a moral self that is supported by religious *ideas and symbols*, without requiring the approval or judgment of religious *leaders or institutions*.[20] Sociologist John O'Brien points out that religious people often respond to the conflicting demands of modern life not by seeking formal, rules-based guidance from religious authority sources like clergy members or texts but by "mobilizing meanings of autonomy and agency to project a self differentiated from religious authority and routine religious behavior."[21] In other words, people don't only use religion to conform to institutional authority and divine guidance but also, and often more so, to cultivate a sense of personal mission and creed that can be defined as much by independence from institutional authority as by obedience to that authority.

The widespread shift from institutional to individualistic moral authority documented in the research of scholars like Madsen and O'Brien is the most important religious underpinning of ELIJAH's work and the dimension of religious commitment I'm most concerned with in this book. Astute organizers engage religious people across a wide range of traditions, denominations, and backgrounds by emphasizing meanings related to personal agency and autonomy—meanings that relational practices focused on personal stories and experiences are uniquely suited to tap. As we will see in chapters to come, people in ELIJAH value and prioritize different elements of religious commitment. Some prize continuity with historical traditions and religious institutions, while others have a stronger sense of individual spirituality. Moral vocation—the sense of having a unique, personal religious calling and mission—resonates across these and other ways of enacting religious personhood. One person's moral vocation might be about being a worthy, authentic member of a traditional community. Another's might involve developing the courage to critique cherished institutions or traditions. Thus, Black Protestants concerned with living up to the legacy of the Black church's role in the civil rights movement, Catholics who wish to make amends for their church's role in colonialism or its tolerance of sexual abuse by priests, immigration activists who aim to transform religion's role in politics, and United Church of Christ members whose goal is simply to "create a world where we take care of each other better," as Tricia, an ELIJAH leader, puts it, can *all* use the logic of moral vocation to pursue the personal religious projects that matter to them, at the same time and often in the same spaces.[22] While these people live their religion differently, they can live their distinct moral vocations together.

## From Moral Vocation to Moral Citizenship

Near the conclusion of the Prophetic Resistance rally, Alissa, a white woman in her forties and ELIJAH's executive director, rose to address the crowd.

She began by thanking the storytellers and invited the crowd to applaud them. Before everyone parted ways, Alissa wanted to offer those assembled a vision of what they were being asked to get into. They needed a practical picture of the tasks ahead: praying, marching, showing up to city and county and state level government meetings, calling legislators, and, most importantly, recruiting others from their congregations to join them in these activities. Equally important, they also needed a larger aspirational vision of what kind of movement they were being invited to join. This movement, Alissa said stridently, was about moral citizenship.

Alissa depicted moral citizens as people who draw on their moral commitments to confront, rather than acquiesce to or pray away, the "profound contradictions" between the promise of equality written into America's founding documents and the realities of inequality that have undermined that goal since the country's beginning. Alissa spoke for eighteen stirring minutes, bringing some audience members to tears. Moral citizens, she said, "never try to reconcile the irreconcilable. Freedom cannot be reconciled with slavery, liberty cannot be reconciled with state-sponsored violence, equality before the law cannot be reconciled with exceptions, for example, 'except for those people, because they are Black, or brown, or Muslim, or women, or poor.' Democracy cannot be reconciled with white supremacy." Moral citizens, she urged, recognize that a country that is not free for all people cannot rightly be called a *free country*. Conjuring powerful images of how America has fallen away from its egalitarian promise, Alissa depicted each member of the crowd as having the ability and the responsibility to help restore the nation's promise.

Alissa went on. Moral citizens are called to "pick up the mantle and demand that this nation fulfill its promise" of equality, dignity, and freedom for all. Moral citizens are those who "root out, anywhere we can find them, laws, policies, and practices that are predicated on the heresy that some people are less than human, less than American." She reached a crescendo:

> The story of where we are now is the story of the last 241 years, and we can choose right now to be part of a history of moral citizenship that has always pushed for the promise to be fulfilled, expanding and expanding the circle of who is free, who is seen, who is equal, who is a citizen. From the migrant farmworkers to the underground railroad, the women's suffrage movement, the Civil Rights Movement, the women's movement, the movement for Black lives, the water

protectors, and the movement here and elsewhere to provide sanctuary for so many others, this is moral citizenship.

This line drew a standing ovation.

Alissa is a remarkable orator, but the idea of moral citizenship that she so poignantly described is not hers alone. Instead, it is the sense of duty that all ELIJAH leaders invoke, through relational practices, to embed people's distinct moral vocations in a larger narrative of history that emphasizes the country's unfulfilled promises related to equality and democracy and each individual's potential role in helping to see to fruition its founding ideals. As Alissa hinted, moral citizenship draws on a logic of personal choice, not external authority. Rather than invoking universal commandments from God, it invites people to use their own moral vocations to challenge, rather than accept, the conventional wisdom that it is normal for some people to be more free, more dignified, and better protected under the law than others, and which acquiesces to the gradual erosion of democratic power in favor of corporate and elite dominance. Moral citizenship is a specific *political* application of the *cultural* platform that moral vocation provides. It calls individual actors into collective recognition of social ills, embeds those ills within a powerful story of sacred promise unfulfilled, and turns participants into characters in that story, assigning them responsibility for choosing to combat the problems they learn about together.[23] Making moral citizens requires stirring up moral vocations and guiding them intensively.

Moral citizenship may sound familiar to those who are acquainted with figures like Rev. Dr. William Barber II, the North Carolina pastor and leader of the Moral Mondays movement or those who have listened carefully to the morally inflected rhetoric of political figures ranging from Abraham Lincoln to Barack Obama.[24] Sociologist Ruth Braunstein argues that progressive leaders in the United States have steadily tapped this kind of language—nominally secular but infused with notable religious undertones—to situate individual actors within a historical trajectory, provide a sweeping sense of identity and belonging, and delineate citizens' responsibilities. This rhetoric acknowledges "that America's founding was far from perfect" and that our union remains imperfect and unresolved. It intentionally constructs a vision of America that includes, even depends on, people from historically marginalized groups, and it frames citizens' responsibilities as calls to rectify the problems of American society rather than to insist on its greatness while working to protect it from menacing outsiders, as conservative narratives tend to do.[25]

Braunstein calls this a "moral perfection" narrative, where *perfection* is a verb, encouraging citizens to perfect their imperfect society. She argues that it offers a compelling counterbalance to the moral decline narrative that Trump captured so well with his historically problematic slogan, "Make America Great Again," and which conservatives continue to use to frame the nation's problems. But there is a difference between *narratives*, the rhetorical tools that elites can commandeer for their chosen purposes, and *practice*, the domain of everyday action regular people undertake all the time. If moral perfection is a narrative that leaders invoke, moral citizenship is a program of daily practice that everyday people carry out. It employs sacred but nonsectarian symbols to call on people to accept responsibility for enhancing equity in U.S. society—and argues that individuals have unique contributions to make, contributions that come alive when they pursue their own moral vocations side by side.

This book argues that ELIJAH has become an effective vehicle for social change by using relational practices to channel participants' distinct moral vocations into a shared commitment to moral citizenship. Plenty of other research has noted the importance of phenomena similar to these three elements—relational practices, moral vocation, and moral citizenship— separately. But the full picture of how they come together to make effective faith-based organizing possible has been unclear until now. Existing research has prompted questions about what makes it possible to engage people in the tough conversations relational practices involve, how people can be moved to understand their moral vocations as embedded within a larger social project, and why the rhetoric of moral citizenship works for inspiring action, especially in multicultural contexts. This book argues that the answer to these questions hinges on the way relational practices, moral vocation, and moral citizenship combine. Relational practices ask people to develop effective moral vocations in the form of compelling stories of who they are, what they want, and why; to use these stories as the basis for building relationships among people of different backgrounds; and to collectively foster an understanding of community that emerges from the shared interests and experiences revealed in the process.

## How I Studied ELIJAH's Organizing

This book is based on qualitative research: primarily what sociologists call participant observation, interviews with thirty-one key informants from ELIJAH, and analysis of various documents, including emails, press releases, meeting agendas, and publicity materials.[26] From November 2014 to May 2017, I systematically observed ELIJAH's activities as a participant in its organizing process. I attended events ranging from small planning and strategy meetings to large rallies. I helped plan, and then often attended, visits with legislators and demonstrations at the state capitol and city hall; public meetings at schools, churches, and community centers, where ELIJAH participants grilled elected officials and corporate leaders about their policy goals and company procedures; and a few of the more contentious events, such as a dramatic disruption of the state chamber of commerce's annual breakfast with legislators and a confrontational occupation of a payday lending store.

Because congregations are the base units of faith-based community organizing, I did the bulk of my observation as a member of the core team of ELIJAH leaders at a Catholic parish I call St. Martin's.[27] I was not a member of St. Martin's or any other congregation before starting this project, but as an inclusive church that beckons people regardless of their prior religious commitments and one of ELIJAH's most active member congregations, St. Martin's welcomed me as a participant in and observer of the organizing process. Leaders at St. Martin's and others within ELIJAH were appropriately skeptical of my activities as a researcher, so to ensure that I got a full picture and not just a snapshot of their work, they asked me to commit to remaining active in both organizations for at least two years. Making this commitment helped me gain leaders' trust and access settings and documents that would not have been available to most outside observers.

My work with ELIJAH also occasionally brought me into other organizational spaces that helped me develop a fuller picture of faith-based organizing. Of particular importance are two national conventions I attended where FBCO leaders from across the country gathered to deepen relationships and share strategies. These meetings were crucial for my research because they provided confidence that what I was observing in ELIJAH also played out in other FBCOs. One of these was a clergy training session, where I had the opportunity to watch some of the country's top community organizing practitioners, theologians, and social justice movement leaders train clergy from many states and numerous religious traditions in relational practices. The other national convention was associated with Pope Francis's visit to the United States in 2015. At this gathering, where Latinx people significantly outnumbered white and Black participants, I got to see faith-based organizers from all kinds of religious traditions and every region of the country strategize together about how to capitalize on the election of a pope who was clearly supportive of social justice causes. Besides these national conventions, I attended numerous organizing trainings where leaders from ELIJAH worked with other, often secular groups, such as labor unions, neighborhood groups, and Black Lives Matter organizers, to streamline their activities and develop coalitions. Thus, while ELIJAH is only one organization, my research design provides confidence that what I observed in the field was not idiosyncratic but the product of social-structural factors that shape the activities of other organizations as well. I do not claim that this research is generalizable or nationally representative, but I can confidently say that it sheds light on processes that matter for understanding how religion and social justice organizing can come together in the contemporary United States.

## Plan of the Book

Chapter 1 summarizes the structural and cultural contexts surrounding faith-based organizing in the contemporary United States. Gaping socioeconomic inequalities are sparking changes in the ways people connect religion with civic life. As more people become financially precarious, fewer see themselves as empowered political actors. At the same time, changes in the American religious landscape are creating new possibilities for cooperation among religious groups that have historically kept distant. Meanwhile, the empirically dubious but culturally enduring association of religion with conservative politics subtly but persistently undermines religious progressives' perceptions of faith's efficacy for solving problems and their public legitimacy as religious actors. Moreover, the secular posture of the progressive Left often fails to affirm the values and traditions religious adherents cherish. In this context, moral citizenship has strong appeal for religious people concerned with inequality because it provides a language and set of symbols for publicly proclaiming their faith in a way that takes inequalities seriously.

Chapter 2 provides an in-depth profile of ELIJAH, using examples from my fieldwork to describe its organizational structure, explain key cultural dimensions, and discuss how these affect its work. I walk readers through a variety of ethnographic vignettes to demonstrate how various organizational features play out substantively in ELIJAH's day-to-day organizing. This chapter familiarizes readers with tensions between pursuing short-term minor victories or longer-term major struggles; broad recruitment versus intensive leadership development; sticking to principles versus political expediency; and technical political strategy versus sweeping moral framing.

Chapter 3 is about the way ELIJAH leaders gently—and sometimes not so gently—use relational practices to expand moral vocations toward racial justice and economic fairness. I provide detailed examples of how ELIJAH unites people across difference via moral imperative, drawing on diverse cultural-theological traditions to show participants new ways to think about religious identity that appeal across different combinations of race, religion, and class. Following several participants, I show how ELIJAH leaders use relational practices to foster moral vocations and link them with moral citizenship.

Chapter 4 gets into the practice of moral citizenship and how it transforms participants' understandings of self and community. I bring readers into the one-to-one conversations and emotional personal testimonies that locate individual experiences and commitments within broader social contexts and link them to widely shared cultural ambitions for family, dignity, and equity. Through these practices, leaders construct moral citizenship as a religious duty and use it as the foundation for explicating an alternative vision for society.

Chapter 5 moves to political work, particularly how ELIJAH leaders orient moral citizenship toward incisive, strategic political action. Case studies of events within campaigns to procure a municipal earned sick and safe time policy and a statewide bill permitting undocumented immigrants to obtain driver's licenses reveal how ELIJAH's background cultural work supports strategic action that is surprisingly broad in scope, flexible across issues, and capable of situating short-term issue campaigns within a broader long-term power agenda.

While moral citizenship holds promise for rejuvenating social movements, it is not a perfect model, nor has it been flawlessly implemented in ELIJAH or elsewhere. Chapter 6 discusses how relational practices can sometimes reinforce some of the same cultural divisions and structural disparities they aim to rectify. Storytelling, in particular, can amplify tensions by creating false equivalencies between life situations that are far from analogous, sometimes leading people from marginalized backgrounds to wonder what they have to gain by hearing the stories of people who are more privileged. Skillful leaders can manage this difficulty, but only when they invest considerable time and resources in these efforts.

The conclusion wraps up the book with the implications of my analysis for the study of religion and activism in modern life and our understanding of how civic groups work. I discuss the relationship between religious organizing and the secular left and how faith-based community organizing both reflects and seems poised to help drive further changes in the American religious landscape.

# 1  The Contexts of Faith-Based Community Organizing

· · · · · · · · · · · · · · · · · · · · · · · · · · · · · · · · · · · · · · · · · · · · · · · ·

The streets were full of police as I walked south through Philadelphia toward Center City. With the pope due to arrive in town later that day, security was tight, with officers on every corner, yellow rope blocking off streets, and National Guard troops roaming. Approaching Center City, I realized the street closures were funneling people into a small number of security checkpoints. It took me a while to find my way around the blockades, but soon enough I found a checkpoint, complete with metal detectors and bomb-sniffing dogs, and was allowed through.

The security clampdown was prompted by the arrival of more than 3 million people in Philadelphia for the World Meeting of Families, a triennial Catholic event traditionally headlined by the pope. I was there for a smaller subsidiary event called the Faith Matters in America summit, a national convention of faith-based community organization (FBCO) leaders from across the country. Gathering in the Sheraton Hotel, they hoped to use the energy sparked by the papal visit as a springboard for a nationwide revitalization of faith-inspired public action.

As I got my bearings inside the third-floor foyer in the Sheraton where the Faith Matters group was assembling, I ran into Rick, and we sat down on a sofa to chat. An athletic-looking white man in a red polo shirt, jeans, and tennis shoes, Rick had recently retired from a career teaching English as a second language. He was one of about a dozen parishioners from St. Martin's who had arrived on an overnight bus crammed with sixty people from ELIJAH-affiliated congregations. With every hotel room within thirty miles booked and seats on the ELIJAH bus in high demand, Alissa, the executive director, had told me I was welcome to join the group in Philadelphia, but I had to find my own way there and secure my own place to stay. Fortunately, I'd found a cheap plane ticket and a friendly graduate student from the University of Pennsylvania with a spare couch. Rick, still stiff after getting off the bus a couple of hours earlier, said I was lucky to have been spared the long, cramped, sleepless ride.

After hotel staff put out an early lunch buffet, Rick and I filled plates and wandered into the adjacent ballroom. About forty tables, each with eight places, were arranged in front of the stage. We sat down next to Cyrus, a Black man in his seventies, also a member of St. Martin's. Already sitting at the table were Armando and Tess, a Latinx couple in their forties who were also Catholics from ELIJAH but attended a different parish. Cyrus introduced them to us as his "new friends from the bus." As the tables around us began to fill, I recognized quite a few faces I knew from ELIJAH amid the visibly multifaith crowd.

As people settled in, they ate, talked, and paged through their welcome folders. Rick, Armando, and Tess were commiserating about the uncomfortable bus ride, so it wasn't long before Cyrus, who has little appetite for negativity of any kind, pushed his plate aside, picked up the large drum he takes with him everywhere—even on overnight bus rides—and started leading songs. Hearing the familiar spirituals, people across the room joined in. Soon, more than half the room had abandoned their lunches for singing and dancing. A group hopped onto the stage, grabbed the microphone, and started leading songs in Spanish. Cyrus climbed up to join them, joyfully drumming and doing his best to hum along despite not being able to sing in their language. About 300 people, well over half of Latinx descent, were in the room, enjoying the camaraderie under the watchful eye of a life-size cardboard cutout of Pope Francis. The atmosphere was full of excitement about the three days ahead. There would be trainings and group discussions; a protest march; a visit from Cardinal Peter Turkson, the president of the Pontifical Council for Justice and Peace (and a favorite for the papacy before Francis's surprise election); and all sorts of events associated with the World Meeting of Families. The weekend would culminate with the papal Mass on Sunday afternoon.

The singing and dancing continued for about half an hour until Kate, a Latina in her forties, took the stage for the welcome address. Speaking enthusiastically in Spanish, then repeating each phrase in English, she told the group that she was the chief of staff for People Improving Communities through Organizing (PICO), the national network of FBCO federations that had organized the gathering. She said she had begun her organizing career in Oakland, and asked if anyone in the room was from there. A group in one corner cheered loudly. Kate said that in Oakland, she'd grown up in a Latinx community, but at a young age she learned she was a little different from many of her friends. She remembered asking her mom why she didn't go to catechism on Wednesday nights like the other kids. Her mom told her, "Kate, it's because we're Protestant. We're not Catholic like they are." This was her first taste of religious difference, Kate said, and she had often wondered during her childhood why she was different from her friends in this way. Once she started organizing, she learned another lesson: how small that difference really was. Today, she added, she was honored and humbled, as a Protestant, to be gathered with faith leaders from different traditions and from all regions of the country to witness Pope Francis's message of love for the world.

It was obvious from Kate's words that despite the venue, this was not a Catholic gathering. Instead, it was a multifaith convention designed to augment a sense of unity and common purpose across geographic, racial, and religious difference, and turn this into a basis for action. Kate described it as "a once in a lifetime opportunity" to launch a national social justice movement in the presence of a pope who seemed deeply supportive of such causes. She explained that it was time for religious communities to "stand up for the ninety-nine percent, for our brothers and sisters at risk of incarceration and deportation, and for the people across this country who are being targeted by the systems of power that profit from our collective misery."

Yet this moment was about much more than the new pope. As this chapter explains, the mid-2010s were a period when a host of economic, political, and religious developments coincided to invigorate faith-based organizing. With costs for health care, housing, and college education skyrocketing; the post-recession economy slanting in favor of the wealthy; activists from Occupy and Black Lives Matter bringing public attention to economic inequality, police killings of Black people, and other forms of systemic racism; and political debates about immigration failing to produce workable solutions, conditions were rife for multiracial, multifaith cooperation. Other researchers have provided excellent accounts of the FBCO field's history, so there is no need to delve deeply into that history here.[1] Rather, my aim in this chapter and the next is to explain how key social-structural aspects of contemporary U.S. society are driving FBCOs' contemporary activities, shaping whom they recruit and how, the issues they take up and why, and the strategies they use to pursue their agendas. This chapter illuminates the cultural and structural contexts shaping faith-based organizing on a national level. Chapter 2 then looks to my case study, ELIJAH, to show how these features play out substantively in local organizing.

## A Bird's-Eye View of Faith-Based Community Organizing

The Faith Matters in America summit was organized by Faith in Action (FIA), a network of FBCO federations with forty-nine affiliates in twenty-five states.[2] Its guests included people from more than twenty of those federations, some from Philadelphia and other nearby eastern cities, others from as far away as Oakland and Seattle. Attendance was capped at three hundred, not due to space concerns but because this was as many people as organizers thought could meaningfully interact. Leaders hoped that by drawing on one another's energy, passion, and stories, participants would return home with enhanced drive and new ideas for organizing in their own communities. That 60 of the 300 hundred spaces were allocated to ELIJAH underscores its status as one of the most influential FBCO federations in the country.

FIA is one of four major national FBCO networks, along with the Gamaliel Foundation, the Industrial Areas Foundation, and the Direct Action and Research Training Center.[3] The networks have their own cultures and strategies but similar structures. Each one collects dues from local and regional federations and bolsters them with support from grants and foundations. In return, the national networks help local groups train participants, coordinate strategies, and share resources so they can cooperate on campaigns and learn from one another. The local federations, like ELIJAH, recruit dues-paying member affiliates, mostly congregations but sometimes other groups as well, like labor unions. They use the dues, along with money from grants, to hire professionals who train congregational leaders in community organizing strategies. Hence, FBCOs are organizations of organizations. Their federated, institution-based structure means they conceptualize communities, not individuals, as the base units of their work. This enables the groups to remain strongly rooted in and responsive to local communities even as they coordinate and strategize together on national-level projects.[4]

## Growth and Diversity among FBCO Federations

Over the last twenty years, the number of FBCO federations has grown considerably, even as rates of religious belonging have diminished during the same period. In a 2011 survey, Richard Wood and Brad Fulton found 189 FBCOs active in forty states, up from 133 federations in thirty-three states in 1999, and estimated that the congregations affiliated with these federations together comprised more than 5 million people.[5] Fulton's 2019 followup study identified more than 220 active FBCO federations.[6] This growth speaks to FBCOs' considerable ability to channel religious energy into the pursuit of racial and socioeconomic equity.

Besides being from different parts of the country, local FBCO federations vary significantly in size and in the makeup of their membership by race, religion, ethnicity, and religious tradition. Some federations have only a few member congregations, while ELIJAH, one of the largest, boasts roughly 120. Some—especially in Texas, the Southwest, and California—are made up mostly of Latinx-dominated member congregations, and some are mostly Black. Others, including ELIJAH, have majority white membership profiles and must work hard to recruit people from racial and ethnic minority backgrounds. Overall, as Wood and Fulton show, FBCOs represent the racial and ethnic diversity of their home communities better than any other kind of civic organization in the United States. This is true in terms of the makeup of their affiliate congregations as well as the personal characteristics of their paid staff and boards of directors.[7]

All this positions FBCO federations among the most internally diverse civic organizations in the United States today. Scholars have explained their strength by pointing to their roots in local community networks, their ability to marshal religious culture in a way that smooths divisions, and their use of relational practices to transform participants' understandings of self and community.[8] But key questions linger. Why does moral citizenship appear to have staying power, while other kinds of religious commitment are in decline? How are actors in FBCOs transforming religious practices and identities by framing moral citizenship as an inextricable part of what it means to be religious in contemporary society? And what do these transformations mean for the ways that religious practices infuse democracy and civic life in the United States today? Sociologists of religion argue that religious practices are both products and producers of social structure, and those who study social movements and civic life show how moral culture, emotions, and daily practices shape political action.[9] This chapter builds on both by showing how moral citizenship has emerged as a solution to the cultural problems that inequality and religious polarization pose today.

## Deepening Inequalities

At the Faith Matters in America summit, leaders frequently referred to Pope Francis and their hope that he would inspire people to confront problems like deportation, mass incarceration, climate risks, and the growing economic deprivation of all but the wealthy. Such allusions highlight one way that religious groups can respond to gaping racial and socioeconomic inequalities: by framing social justice goals as moral imperatives. There have always been religious groups concerned with justice and equality in the United States, but recent economic and political developments, along with the activism drawing attention to them, have made it easier for faith voices to articulate sweeping moral critiques of resource and power disparities. The appeal cuts across issues as well as racial, class, and religious constituencies. And the moral-imperative framing opens possibilities for enhanced collaboration with secular partners.

This story begins with increasing concentration of income and wealth among the elite since the 1970s, leaving other Americans to make do with less.[10] These days, many people work long hours and multiple jobs, often for low wages and in poor conditions. Many of these jobs are precarious and can disappear at any moment, as the 2008 recession and the coronavirus pandemic made abundantly clear. Even those who can support themselves with one job must often sacrifice luxuries to meet everyday expenses like housing, childcare, education, and health care, whose costs have all risen much faster than wages since the 1970s.[11]

These financial strains hit families of every racial and ethnic background, but they hit hardest in communities of color, who often cannot not rely on established wealth or even minor savings, having never had equal access to employment, housing, education, or credit.[12] Racial wealth disparities are growing deeper every day.[13] Credit card, medical, and student loan debt; home ownership; health-care access; and retirement savings all remain heavily stratified by race.[14] Labor unions provided a midcentury check on corporate power but have receded dramatically in recent decades, possibly *because* income and wealth inequalities are so racialized. Some researchers, inspired by W. E. B. Du Bois's work on how capitalism exploits race, have argued that racial hierarchies provide a "psychological wage" that assuages white people's anger about small paychecks and bad working conditions and tamps down their demand for union jobs.[15] Rising attention drawn to racial inequalities by social movement groups like Black Lives Matter has also sparked a push for social justice organizations to treat racism and white supremacy as serious problems in their own right, rather than as side effects of economic disparities.[16]

These changes in the structure of the economy have made it easier for social movement groups, including FBCOs, to cast inequalities of all kinds as moral problems rather than inevitable economic developments. In particular, the 2008 recession and the federal government's decision to bail out major banks focused the public's attention on structural inequity and unequal political power. The contrast between the millions who lost their jobs, homes, and savings and the flow of economic relief to big banks and their wealthy investors profoundly affected many Americans' understanding of how individuals' economic struggles relate to social structure.[17] The middle and lower classes incurred tremendous losses in the recession, and the recovery was slow and nearly meaningless for those whose wages stagnated at the same time the costs of health care, housing, and college skyrocketed.

The realization that inequalities are structural, sharply distilled in the Occupy movement's "We are the 99 percent" rhetoric, grew in cultural influence as the post-2009 recovery lurched along. Everyday people came to recognize how their economic fortunes were entwined with larger forces and that making sound financial decisions wasn't always enough to keep them out of trouble.[18] While the media heralded economic growth and corporate profits soared, the 99 percent was struggling with unemployment, poverty, rising costs of living, and government austerity measures that crippled already meager social services. Viewed in this context, it's no surprise that some Americans, particularly the young, were primed to embrace programs like free college tuition, student debt forgiveness, universal health care, a higher minimum wage, and rent control from the mid-2010s onward.

One particularly important effect of the recession is that it put major life course transitions, such as going to college, getting married, buying a home, having children, and retiring, on hold or even out of reach for many people and families. More than simply depriving people of resources, increasing debt and insecurity have made it clear that symbolic markers of achievement and success can't be taken for granted. Families organize their lives, hopes, and rituals around these symbolic transitions, and when economic conditions make them hard to achieve, things like high housing costs and student and medical debt stop being just numbers and instead become life-defining experiences that are easy to cast in moral terms, especially when contrasted with growing corporate profits and stock market gains that help only the wealthy. Critiques of inequality become deeply resonant when they show how family life is impeded by corporate excess.

When highlighted in relational practices, this framework can provide a compelling basis for making religious issues out of things that might otherwise be seen as merely technical or policy issues. For example, in September 2016, ELIJAH leaders at St. Martin's held an Economy Encounter, where they showed about thirty attendees from the parish a set of slides illustrating the dramatic rise in corporate profits since 2008. Included were things like how twenty-three locally owned banks had consolidated under the control of Wells Fargo and Bank of America, the many new fees these banks were charging customers and how they hit customers with the smallest bank balances the hardest, how government borrowing had increased in inverse proportion to corporate tax rates since the 1970s, and how student loan and medical debt had ballooned since the recession.

After the slides, leaders used a creative activity to illustrate how multiple issues are connected through corporate power. They handed out cards to twelve people seated around a table. On the front of each card was the name of a major corporation with a presence in the area. On the back was a photo of one of the company's executives, along with a sentence explaining some damaging business practice the company was engaged in, such as wage theft or lobbying against worker protections. Then Mallory, a white woman in her sixties from the core team, pulled out a ball of yarn and tossed it to the person holding the Target card, a professionally dressed white woman in her forties, and asked her to read the text on the back of her card. It was a statement about how Target contracted with a cleaning firm that had been accused of wage theft, and it concluded by pointing out how Target was connected to Wells Fargo—Wells Fargo's CEO was on Target's board of directors. Then, Mallory instructed the person with the Target card to hold on to one end of the yarn while tossing the ball across the table to the person with the Wells Fargo card, who then read a similar statement. The activity continued until the yarn crisscrossed the table in a fearsome knot, demonstrating the scale, complexity, and interconnectedness of corporate power across multiple issues.

With this activity, ELIJAH leaders aimed to educate parishioners on the structural roots of the economic challenges that they and people they knew were facing. The information could have fit right into a sociology course on stratification and power. But the relational practices that followed the slides and the yarn activity cast these problems in starkly moral terms. In a story-sharing session themed around how corporate power affects families' livelihoods and ability to live with freedom and dignity, parishioners recounted very personal details. One described her mother's foreclosure, which forced the older woman to move back in with an abusive, alcoholic ex-husband. A man shared his brother's story: Working as a restaurant server, he lacked access to paid time off and was struggling to care for his new infant son. The server and his wife had begun to bicker over income and childcare and how to be the parents their child needed. Seizing on elements of the social and economic structure; linking them to relatable cultural questions of family, love, and dignity; and juxtaposing those harms against rising corporate power and profits transformed economic problems into moral ones.

In this way, increasing public consciousness of the family effects of socioeconomic and racial inequalities has paved the way for FBCO leaders to talk about the need for change in a religiously convincing way. According to the moral worldview these leaders espouse, the people in the parishioners' stories are not individuals who have made bad choices but members of families and communities caught short by corporate excess. It says that their problems are *our* problems. Relational practices humanize social problems and hold empathetic space for those grinding through the consequences.

Correspondingly, ELIJAH and other FBCO federations consistently emphasize family and community in their work and communications. In 2015, ELIJAH and coalition partners called their proposed policy package for increased worker protections—including minimum wage, paid sick time, a fair scheduling ordinance, and paid family leave proposals—their Working Families Agenda. Sociologist Rebekah Peeples Massengill shows how Walmart uses themes like "working families" and "consumer choice" to dampen critiques of its labor policies.[19] Here, ELIJAH flips the script. Shifting the frame from "workers' rights" to a "working families agenda" moves the focus from individual workers to entire families, and from contracts to communities. It calls attention to how low wages, poor working conditions, unpredictable schedules, and job insecurity undermine families' ability to flourish and destabilize communities to society's detriment.

Similarly, one of the most powerful sequences at the Faith Matters summit in Philadelphia occurred when two mothers shared back-to-back stories about devastating family troubles they traced directly to corporate greed. Chloe, a Black woman in her early twenties, was fired from her airport janitorial job in the Northeast because she left work during a shift after learning that her sick daughter had been taken to the hospital. Chloe had asked for permission to leave; when it was denied, she left anyway. Juana was a mother, too—a Latina in her forties whose twenty-one-year-old son had died while incarcerated following a minor drug charge. After a for-profit firm took over health-care provision for the prison where he was housed and drastically cut back staffing and services, Juana's son developed an easily treatable health condition. The prison's skimpy new health staff ignored his repeated complaints, however, and the treatable condition became a deadly one. With assistance from FIA, Juana was suing the private prison operator and its health-care subcontractor. Her story was a powerful example of the human consequences of deregulatory government policies that give corporations a free reign to seek profits in contexts like prisons, hospitals, and nursing homes.

Like hundreds of other stories I heard during my fieldwork, Chloe's and Juana's distilled major structural changes, such as the increasing precarity of work and the privatization of public services, into clear examples of family and community suffering. Chloe was fired because her employer had adopted a bare-bones staffing model that could not accommodate basic human needs like leaving work to attend a sick child. For Juana, the combination of overpolicing minority communities, harsh drug sentencing, and profit-driven changes in the criminal justice system resulted in tragedy. Stories like these draw sharp moral distinctions between dominant economic structures and the families and communities that become entangled in them. They also highlight how corporate power's growth at everyday people's expense hits hardest in communities of color.

By bringing issues like these to the fore of public debate, activist movements including Occupy and Black Lives Matter have paved the way for faith-based social justice groups to articulate a morally compelling critique of current social conditions. Religious congregations provide networks through which people can be recruited into relationships, and religious traditions provide visions of family and community that can be employed in relational practices and oriented toward moral condemnations of the status quo. These critiques are not new, but they are evolving and growing more resonant as the effects of inequalities reach more and more families. Until recently, social scientists generally agreed that, in the United States, conservative politicians and pundits had been far more skilled than progressives at employing the language of family and community to frame their goals.[20] That may no longer be the case.

## Economic Insecurity and the Great Risk Shift

Direct experience or imminent threat of victimization by inequalities is not the only thing pushing people toward moral critiques of social systems. Another factor, especially important for bringing middle-class people into partnership with the marginalized, is growing economic insecurity even among families who seem to have enough. Political scientist Jacob Hacker describes a "great risk shift" in U.S. society, in which corporations and other powerful actors have gradually off-loaded economic risk onto regular families.[21] Tax cuts for top earners have made social safety net programs like

Medicare and Social Security less robust. Meanwhile, the costs of health care and housing have risen, and the responsibility to pay for higher education has shifted from the state to students and their families, often involving significant debt. These changes have made life less stable, even for people who appear to be middle class and identify as such. One major medical problem can bring on years of financial hardship. A family's college savings can be wiped out by an unexpected surgery or illness. For those who make it to college, dropping out or even failing a single course can be disastrous, as the loan bills will come due even if there is no degree awarded and therefore little hope of wages sufficient to pay them off. Those who succeed in school enter a labor market where wages are depressed and face higher costs for housing and other necessities than did previous generations.

These and other contingencies have helped collapse the structural gap between the middle class and the lower and working classes to a level not seen since World War II.[22] It is not that things have gotten better for the poor but that life has become more precarious for everyone except the wealthy. The great risk shift means that relational practices can easily transform middle-class people's instinctive feelings of sympathy for deprived families like Chloe's and Juana's into empathy—the shared, lived experience of unpayable debt, insurmountable bills, and the cascading effects of involvement with the justice system. Clearly, the degree of difficulty is steeper for those at the lowest ends of the socioeconomic scale, yet commiseration over seeing their lives shaped by the paired forces of corporate greed (the 1 percent) and government austerity (such that social safety nets are eroded) creates a foundation of empathy across the 99 percent that skilled organizers can exploit.

This is why relational practices are so important and effective for social change organizations. By facilitating story sharing and relationship building, leaders in community organizing—a social change model developed by and for poor and working-class communities—can develop constituencies that include people who currently face immediate deprivation and loss *and* those who are doing okay for now but understand they're at increasing risk. FBCO federations' organizing is driven by relational practices that use rhetoric about family and community to facilitate such cross-class, cross-racial, and cross-cultural solidarity.

## Changes in the Religious Landscape

Besides the deepening inequalities sparking morally driven interrogations of social structure, a second major contextual factor shaping the activities of FBCO federations today is the changing landscape of American religion. Developments since the 1960s have created both the structural possibility and the cultural imperative for groups other than conservative white Christians to form broad coalitions and engage in politics together. During the 1980s and '90s, for instance, as conservative Christians joined forces with the Republican Party and took over the national conversation about how faith should infuse civic life, there developed a cultural perception that abortion and gay marriage were the only issues that mattered to religious people. Though inaccurate, this stereotype brought about a politicization of religious commitment with cascading effects.[23] It drove large numbers of young people away from the religions of their parents and sparked a great deal of mistrust among some liberals for any public speech or action in which a religious influence could be detected.[24] While scholars argue that these trends have been damaging for American religion on the whole, their confluence also produced a cultural need for an inclusive religious community that seeks common features in the difficulties that various communities face and takes their social justice concerns seriously. Whereas past iterations of progressive religious activism tended to offer solace and representation for members of specific religious groups, this newer vision's emergence in direct juxtaposition to the Religious Right means hat it both relies on and can amplify a broader vision of what religion can be. It isn't about advancing the confessional goals or interests of Protestants, Catholics, or any other group; instead, it's about reclaiming the mantle of what religion means—which, to FBCO participants, involves advancing justice and equity for all people.[25]

## The Problematic Religious Decline Narrative

Rates of religious attendance and belonging are declining in the United States, suggesting a clear trend away from organized religion. The most recent national survey estimates from the Pew Research Center show 65 percent of American adults describing themselves as Christian, down from 77 percent only ten years prior, and similar, though less dramatic, patterns hold among other faiths. Meanwhile, the proportion who describe their affiliation as atheist, agnostic, or "nothing in particular" rose from 17 percent to 26 percent during the same period.[26]

Yet while the decline of religious affiliation, attendance, and belief are widely accepted by social scientists, the master narrative of religion's fading significance obscures important details. One is substantial variation by race and ethnicity. Christianity is no exception to the overall religious decline, but certain nonwhite Christian communities are stable in population share, and some are even growing. In particular, the proportions of Latinx and Asian Americans who identify as Protestant have been increasing in the last decade (the share of Latinx Americans who are Protestant increased slightly from 23 percent to 24 percent from 2009 to 2019).[27] Political scientist Janelle Wong finds growth among Latinx evangelical Christians as well: from 2010 to 2013, the proportion of Latinx in the United States who identify as evangelical or born-again rose, in her analysis, from 12 percent to 16 percent.[28] Wong also notes that evangelical Christian affiliation is rising among Asian Americans and concludes that nonwhite and immigrant Christians are the only growing segments of the American religious population. As religious communities that suffer disproportionately from racial disparities in wealth, income, and access to other resources, nonwhite religious groups are potentially powerful bases of support for faith-based social justice groups like FBCOs

Another significant trend obscured by the religious decline narrative is the decline's relatively slower rate among Black Americans, particularly Black Democrats. For example, the proportion of white Democrats who claim no religious affiliation rose from 24 percent to 42 percent in the decade between 2009 and 2019, while the proportion of nonaffiliated Black Democrats rose from 13 percent to 20 percent: still an increase in nonreligious identity but a much smaller one than among white Democrats.[29] These statistics hint that the Black Church will continue to inject a strong religious presence into the Democratic Party coalition—a presence that was evident in Black pastor Rev. Raphael Warnock's victory in the 2020 U.S. Senate runoff election in Georgia, fueled in large part by voter mobilization in Black Churches.[30] Beyond Black progressives remaining religiously affiliated at higher rates than their white colleagues, Black Church leaders have been central in supporting recent protests, including those in Ferguson, Missouri, in 2014; in Charlottesville, Virginia, in 2017; and across the country in the 2020 George Floyd protests.[31] The Black Church and its Civil Rights legacy is still a vibrant source of material support and cultural inspiration for today's Black activist leaders.[32]

The Black Church's persistent influence in Black communities and Black-led protest movements has two important consequences for progressive organizing. First, it means that religion can be a touchstone for movements to effectively engage Black communities. The Black Church retains a strong role in shaping many Black communities' visions of social responsibility and national identity, and faith-based networks can tap into these cultural veins in a way secular groups cannot.[33] Second, it means that faith-based social justice groups' ethical reasons for prioritizing racial diversity are also strategic, as stability or even growth among nonwhite constituencies can help buttress religious coalitions against the prospect of declining white religious adherence.

Increasing Religious Polarization

In his 1988 book, *The Restructuring of American Religion*, sociologist Robert Wuthnow observed that the late twentieth century was marked by growing acrimony concerning religion's role in public life, as earlier denominational divisions gave way to an all-pervading liberal-conservative split. Strategic incentives and cultural imperatives, particularly a need to push back against the Religious Right, accrued to motivate liberal religious groups to coordinate and cooperate across denominational and racial lines in ways they had not often done before. The fact that many FBCO federations include white and Latinx mainline Protestants and Catholics, Black Protestants, and members of other religious communities, including Judaism, Buddhism, and Islam, but rarely include many white evangelicals or conservative Catholics makes a bit more sense when viewed in light of this trend.

Wuthnow's argument, since echoed and refined by many other scholars, was that at midcentury, the American religious landscape was divided by denomination, but by the late twentieth century, those divisions had become political and cultural instead.[34] In postwar America, religious culture was strained by the tensions among three central religious groups: Catholics, Protestants, and Jews. Each had distinct, often conflicting ideas about how religion should infuse civic culture, and though none were completely homogeneous in terms of partisan affiliation, members of each tended to agree on politics more than they differed and to follow the political cues provided by clergy and denominational leaders.[35] In the 1950s and '60s, Wuthnow explains, "lawsuits, court decisions, voting, and political affairs frequently found Protestants and Catholics on different sides of the fence, while antagonisms between Christians and Jews simmered just barely beneath the surface."[36] Negative attitudes among Protestants toward Catholics and Jews were common, and religious prejudice boiled over in political debates ranging from birth control legalization to Zionism to the anti-Catholicism that threatened John F. Kennedy's 1960 presidential campaign.[37]

By the 1980s, however, the principal divisions in American religious culture were no longer denominational. Instead, they were mostly political, as religious groups split into camps that aligned, albeit imperfectly, with the categories we call conservative and liberal today. For example, Baptists in the United States first split over debates about slavery in 1845, creating separate Southern and Northern Baptist Conventions.[38] Yet while the elites of these separate denominations fought bitterly over slavery, until midcentury the political differences between their rank-and-file members were much less significant than those between Baptists and Methodists or between Baptists and Catholics. Denominational differences within the major religious traditions of Protestantism, Catholicism, and Judaism were much less divisive than the cultural differences among those traditions.[39]

The civil rights movement marked the start of a significant shift in this alignment, as the Republican Party strategically exploited racial backlash to shift the support of southern white Christians, including both Protestants and Catholics, from Democrats to Republicans, eventually seizing on abortion as a politically mobilizing issue following the Supreme Court's 1973 decision in *Roe v. Wade*.[40] First using thinly veiled racist messaging, then stoking outrage over abortion, conservative elites papered over denominational differences among southern white Christians by appealing to a sense of a broader white Christian culture under attack by racial equality, women's autonomy, loosening sexual mores, and the rise of secular humanism.[41] It didn't take long for conservative white Christians to perceive a common white Christian cultural project—preserving their social dominance—that transcended denominational divides. As Wuthnow noted in later studies,[42] the major turmoils of the 1960s, including debates over civil rights and the Vietnam War, made many southern and western white people feel abandoned by what they perceived as liberalizing influences in eastern cities and on college campuses. Their creeping disdain for the federal government and associated welfare and other social service programs facilitated the rise of a conservative white Christianity that was not only associated with resentment toward racial equality, women's equality, liberalizing social change, and federal social services but defined by it.[43]

As this transformation played out in cities and towns across the country, local institutions, including churches, became beachheads in cultural battles over how society should respond to questions about equality, race, gender, sexuality, and other divisive social topics. In this new cultural alignment, a congregation's political direction was not determined by its association with a major religious tradition but by the political and cultural preferences of its members—a body that was changing fast amid suburbanization. Some urban churches were nearly emptied by white flight out of urban cores throughout the 1970s, '80s, and early '90s, and many of those that survived, now populated largely by Black and immigrant families, became bastions of social justice activism.[44] As their neighborhoods were stripped of economic resources and social services, FBCO pioneers made their first forays into organizing religious communities in the poor neighborhoods of cities like Oakland, Chicago, Brooklyn, and San Antonio.[45] Meanwhile, in the booming suburbs, new churches sprang up to serve the influx of white families. Lacking historical neighborhood roots, these churches competed for members by developing their own distinct cultural and political atmospheres.[46] Unsurprisingly, since their flavors were designed to appeal to families fleeing diversifying cities, whiteness and white supremacy were pervasive.

For many families uprooting from an established urban neighborhood to a new subdivision, a potential new congregation's denomination mattered less than how it felt—whether the ministries, music, aesthetics, and even the parking lot aligned with a family's preferences and conveniences, which for many included an aura of white affluence that physically and symbolically distinguished the new suburban oases from the cities they left behind.[47] The result was a re-sorting of the faithful by political geography, as churches were distinguished by the degree to which their cultures reinforced the perception that cities and the poor and nonwhite people who lived in them were not just economically suffering but morally decrepit as well. While some urban churches became anchors of community organizing, suburban congregations distanced themselves, symbolically and physically, from the needs of poor communities and people of color.

## Contemporary Fault Lines

The realignment Wuthnow identified bears heavily on the ways people from different faith communities interact in public life and how they channel their faith into civic engagement today. Most scholars of religion agree that these days, conservative Catholics have significantly more in common with conservative Protestants than they do with liberal Catholics, and mainline Protestants are more similar to liberal Catholics than to conservative Protestants. In *The End of White Christian America*, Robert Jones argues that "after more than a century of uneasy and sometimes downright hostile relations, conservative white Protestants and Catholics realized in the 1990s that they needed each other."[48] Historical denominational tensions quickly receded as these groups teamed up to preserve white Christianity's place at the top of the American power structure and protect U.S. society from abortion, nontraditional marriage, women's liberation, and other unwanted social change. This alliance, which Jones labels the "White Christian Strategy," persists, as evidenced by the fervent white evangelical support for Catholic Supreme Court nominees like Samuel Alito in 2006 and Neil Gorsuch, Brett Kavanaugh, and Amy Coney Barrett more recently. Conservative white Protestant and Catholic leaders frequently join forces to support conservative movements—first the Religious Right, then the Tea Party, then Trumpism—and they fund lawsuits about things like businesses' rights to refuse service provisions based on race or sexual orientation and the Affordable Care Act's provision that employer-sponsored insurance packages must cover birth control.

Thus, late twentieth-century cultural and political realignment left a clear line between conservative white Christians and most other religious Americans—one that we can still trace in the makeup of FBCO federations around the county. As Wood and Fulton show, only a few have even a single white evangelical affiliate congregation.[49] ELIJAH has none. Even in the suburbs, research shows that FBCO federations can much more easily engage mainline Protestant and Catholic groups than white evangelical Christians.[50]

But if conservative white Christians make up one side of the major fault line in American religion, the other side is much harder to label neatly. It consists of large segments of the nonwhite Christian groups previously mentioned, as well as significant elements of the white Christian community, including liberal Catholics and mainline Protestants; majorities of American Jews, Hindus, Buddhists, and Muslims; and members of other non-Christian religious groups, such as Unitarian Universalists and pagans. While the exact demographic makeup of this "liberal" religious coalition has shifted with trends in immigration and religious disaffiliation, Wuthnow's initial account of the overall divide as "a division between self-styled religious 'conservatives' and self-styled religious 'liberals,' both of whom acknowledged a considerable degree of tension with the other side," remains apt.[51]

### Moral Citizens' Sacred Task

Back in Philadelphia, Pastor Michael McBride, a Black man in his forties, asked everyone he could see to touch another person.[52] It was now Friday evening, and he was standing in front of Independence Hall, where the Faith Matters group had gathered after their march from the Sheraton, with a couple of stops along the way. The first stop was outside a Dunkin' Donuts, where leaders prayed for equitable treatment for fast-food workers, especially the end of wage theft. The second was outside an Immigration and Customs Enforcement (ICE) detention center, where they had spent nearly an hour praying and chanting for humane treatment for immigrants and their families. In a deeply moving moment, detainees inside the facility, who could hear but not see what was happening outside, banged loudly on the walls in response to the prayers and songs drifting in from the streets below. It was a powerful representation of the symbolic bonds that these leaders were enacting with those on the verge of deportation. Now, Pastor Mike, as he is known—the director of FIA's national LIVE FREE campaign against gun violence and police brutality—was calling people into another representation of those bonds, reminding those assembled that "we are connected, our roots are connected, even if we can't see them."[53] He said it was time to "pray to our creator to remind us of the connectedness of our roots." There, standing in front of Independence Hall, Pastor Mike gave a stirring religious call to civic action and social justice:

> We are here as a small expression of a mighty network of people who are committed to be together to turn the world upside down. We call to you, the God of Justice, to be with us as we continue this sacred task. We thank you for the gift of this pope who has come with a message that resonates with every person, from every tribe and every country and every faith tradition. We think he is indeed expressing your heart. It's resonating with many of the words that we have in our hearts. Many words that we express with our own mouths. Thank you for the platform afforded to him, to amplify these words. We do not look to him to solve our problems; we look to him to give us the power to change the worst conditions in the city of Philadelphia, and the city of Chicago, and the city of Milwaukee, and the city of Oakland, and the city of New York, and the city of New Orleans, and the city of Baton Rouge, and the city of Los Angeles, and the city of Denver, and the city of Houston, and the city of Indianapolis, and the city of Albuquerque, and the city of Santa Fe, and the city of Las Vegas, and every city across the country![54] We look to you to give us the power to change the worst conditions that our loved ones are facing. We ask you to help us shake the systems of mass incarceration, and deportation, and police brutality. Empower us to shake them, Lord, so that *all* can live in freedom!

It was no accident that this stirring speech had followed visits to a fast-food restaurant and an ICE detention center—examples of two institutions through which inequalities are reproduced. The trainings and exercises that the FIA leaders had been engaged in throughout the day were designed to remind everyone that issues like wage theft and deportation were things that no individual could do much about alone, but that change remained possible if people united in movement activism motivated by their faith. Implicitly, the point was this: as individuals, our power is limited; but collectively, it has boundless potential. Achieving this potential, Pastor Mike argued, was their sacred task.

In the face of deep inequalities, many feel powerless and full of guilt. Amid political and cultural polarization, people feel isolated and hopeless, and those whose religious commitments center social justice wonder what they should do. Religious progressives' shaken confidence is at least somewhat assuaged by the language of faith and the ways it provides comfort, inspiration, and a sense of personal calling and purpose—as Pastor Mike said, they do not ask God to change things for them; rather, they pray to find the power to change things for themselves—that is, to become moral citizens.

Calling for community and emphasizing the universality of Pope Francis's social justice message, Pastor Mike reminded those assembled before him that across their substantial racial, religious, and geographic diversity, they were united by moral vocations. Other than generic invocations of a creator and a "God of Justice," McBride's prayer was devoid of theological specifics. He succeeded in identifying "being in community" as a solution, in depicting the practice of moral citizenship as a compelling moral vocation in a culture plagued by inequity and division.

This chapter has shown how the imperative to become moral citizens develops not from religious beliefs alone but from structural and cultural conditions that became increasingly hard for many people to ignore throughout the 2010s. In chapters 3 through 5, we'll see how relational practices help people situate their own lives within these broader contexts, develop connections with others from different backgrounds, and undertake collective political action to advance their goals. First, though, we need to understand the specifics of ELIJAH as an organization: its structure, some key cultural dynamics, and a few central tensions. This overview of ELIJAH is what chapter 2 provides.

## 2  Inside ELIJAH

ELIJAH was founded in 2000 when three separate interfaith organizations merged. Today it's composed of over 120 member congregations, most of them Christian, though it includes a few Muslim communities as well.[1] The congregations sit mostly within ELIJAH's core metropolitan region, with about twenty scattered in other cities and towns around the state.[2] Approximately sixty of these member congregations are white-dominated mainline Protestant churches; about twenty are Catholic parishes, including some with significant Latinx constituencies; and another twenty or so are Black-dominated Protestant churches, most of which are theologically conservative evangelical or Pentecostal congregations. Like most faith-based community organization (FBCO) federations across the United States, ELIJAH has no white evangelical member churches.

ELIJAH's religious makeup is largely a consequence of the demographics in its region, and I saw no desire to exclude people from other faith traditions. For instance, at the time of ELIJAH's founding, a strong Jewish community organization already existed in the region, and the leadership agreed with ELIJAH's that, rather than combining, they would remain separate but work closely on issue campaigns together. Today, the groups still work together closely but remain distinct entities. During my fieldwork, none of the local Muslim community's mosques had officially joined ELIJAH as dues-paying members, but partnership efforts were underway. The members of one mosque sporadically attended ELIJAH meetings, and ELIJAH staff were conducting outreach to set up voter registration drives and other activities in the local Islamic community. By summer 2020, ELIJAH had recruited roughly twenty mosques into its work.

Like most other FBCOs, ELIJAH is an organization of organizations, which means that individual participants must technically be members of affiliated congregations. In practice, however, individuals who find their way into ELIJAH meetings are welcomed warmly and invited to return. Still, there is no comprehensive individual-level participation data. ELIJAH's membership is more racially diverse than its state's population (also true of a majority of the country's FBCOs).[3] During my event attendance from late

2014 to mid-2017, I estimated that somewhere between half and two-thirds of ELIJAH's regular participants were white, with the remainder about evenly split between Black and Latinx people. People of other races, including East Africans, Hmong, Filipinos, Native Americans, and Koreans, were often present but were few in number at most events. The class composition is also diverse, with a significant proportion of well-educated middle- to upper-class white people and people of color; a sizable contingent of working poor, including a minority of ELIJAH's white membership and most of its Black and Latinx participants; and a small but active contingent of poor people who depend on government programs and aid from their churches to stay financially afloat.

### ELIJAH's Organizational Structure

ELIJAH's work and projects are divided along three main dimensions (geographic region, racial/ethnic caucuses, and issue-focused teams) and into six regions: East Side, West Side, South Suburban, Northeast Suburban, Northwest Suburban, and Outstate. Each region has an assigned staff organizer responsible for deepening relationships within member congregations in the area, recruiting new congregations and helping build leadership teams within them, training lay leaders in leadership skills, facilitating communication among regional congregations, and coordinating strategic plans both within the region and with organizers and lay leaders from other regions. These highly trained professionals' salaries are modest, commensurate with ELIJAH's nonprofit status, but they support something approximating middle-class living. Organizing staff in the FBCO field are better paid and stay in their jobs much longer than the poorly paid and often overworked staffers of political campaigns and other politically oriented nonprofits. Their work demands extensive training, and because it focuses on cultivating and maintaining strong long-term relationships with individuals and communities, it is important to minimize staff turnover.

Broadly, ELIJAH organizers' job is to train lay leaders to organize their fellow congregants to participate in and eventually lead social change projects. In practice, this means that organizers spend the bulk of their time holding one-to-one meetings with congregation members, coordinating congregational and region-wide meetings and training sessions that teach lay leaders to coach others on civic skills, developing relationships with clergy and congregational staff, and illuminating the complex dynamics of political strategy and the legislative process at all levels of government.

To effectively support these trainees, staff organizers hone their expertise in municipal and state political processes, the minutiae of the issue areas their teams are working on, the region's broader political culture and history, and the long-term strategic calculus that drives relevant lawmakers' decisions. Their skills must include adeptness at using social media and other technologies to facilitate online discussions, livestream meetings, and other technical matters, and they are expected to keep keenly abreast of the news, as well as magazine articles, books, and academic research pertaining to social justice and social change.

## Lay Leadership

Though almost always outstanding verbal communicators, paid organizers are very rarely the public voices of FBCOs. Instead, they are tasked with training lay leaders to fill this role. Staff organizers often lead internal trainings and strategy meetings, but they seldom speak at public meetings with politicians or at protest actions. At public-facing events, staff organizers defer to the volunteer participants and leaders they have coached, who take center stage while staff coordinate behind the scenes. At the Prophetic Resistance gathering discussed in the introduction, only two of the day's nearly two dozen speakers were on ELIJAH's payroll: Alissa, the executive director, and Samuel, a part-time associate organizer who, prior to being hired, was involved as a lay leader within an ELIJAH congregation.

There are two reasons that staff organizers rarely speak for ELIJAH in public. The first is that when organizers take public roles, they give the appearance that they are the people whom ELIJAH represents and exists to serve. It is better, from a community organizing perspective, to have community members speak for themselves than to appoint paid professionals to speak for them. The stories and interests of communities, not of organizers, are what matters most. The second reason for foregrounding lay and clergy leaders is that gaining experience speaking in public is a crucial step in leadership development. Every ELIJAH action, no matter the immediate stakes, is also an opportunity for emerging leaders to develop their civic skills and increase their capacity to influence public life by telling their own stories and asserting their own demands of the public and policy makers. In planning meetings, leaders thinking about the slate of public speakers for an event frequently consider both how each person's story or remarks will resonate with the audience and how speaking at the event will contribute to the speakers' leadership development.

Wendy, a white woman in her sixties, is a member of the core team at St. Martin's, a West Side parish and one of ELIJAH's most active congregations. She is not on ELIJAH's staff, but she has a long history as a community organizer in multiple organizations across the country and is among ELIJAH's most engaged and influential lay leaders. During a planning session for a public meeting on paid sick time, St. Martin's parishioners suggested that they invite congregant Janelle, a disabled Black single mother of three, to speak. Lacking access to paid sick time and good health insurance, Janelle had been unable to receive adequate health care and spiraled into a cycle of depression and addiction that hampered her children's success in school. Her story, they suggested, would effectively convey the point that paid sick time not only helps low-wage workers but also helps provide the conditions needed for healthy, successful children and families.

Wendy, however, wanted to use the meeting as an opportunity to cultivate new leaders. Janelle was already a seasoned leader, Wendy noted, and others needed to gain experience speaking publicly to elected officials. At the small planning session, Wendy told the planning team, "I'm an organizer and I want to win, but this is bigger, about building power in the long term, tying what we're talking about in this room to what's going to happen five years from now. That has to be the focus of every meeting that we have, or I don't want to go. There's no point in going through the mechanics of organizing if it isn't coupled with a laser focus on building a bigger, broader base for the power agenda we want. That means getting new people involved and building relationships with people we don't know yet."

Wendy envisioned the public meeting on paid sick time as an opportunity to build a more powerful organizing presence in the community. Despite the importance of paid sick time for many low-wage workers, and the symbolic and material gains that would come from winning a major labor policy fight against opposition from business groups, she insisted that ELIJAH's chief priority was building long-term power. That might mean the campaign's volunteer leaders would have to work harder to find and train new storytellers.

The group, agreeing with Wendy's summation, decided not to ask Janelle to speak at the public meeting. Instead, St. Martin's leaders worked through their neighborhood contacts to identify community members who had not previously been involved in ELIJAH but were willing to tell their stories to city council members at the paid sick time meeting.

## Core Teams

ELIJAH veterans like Wendy are always looking for opportunities to expand the organization's base by bringing new people into its work, but the bulk of ELIJAH activities within congregations is typically organized by core teams. These are dedicated groups of highly committed activists that range in size from a handful of members to approximately two dozen. Typically, the core teams hold monthly planning and strategy meetings in their congregations, and they organize and attend regional and organization-wide events. Core team members maintain regular contact with one another and with their assigned staff organizers. They are responsible for conducting outreach and recruitment within their congregations; planning meetings, protests, and other actions on specific issue campaigns with ELIJAH participants from other congregations; soliciting material and moral support from their churches' clergy and staff; and working with staff organizers to plan short- and long-term strategy. As part of my research for this project, I joined the core team at St. Martin's, attending its monthly meetings and other parish activities for two years.

Congregations within the same region work together on issue campaigns by holding joint regional meetings and strategy sessions. Often, these meetings of different churches' team members are devoted to planning actions and strategies within the context of a particular issue campaign. The agenda typically combines an overview of the political context surrounding the issue at hand with focused training on a particular skill, such as arranging meetings with elected officials, recruiting congregation members to attend rallies or protests, or organizing house meetings, in which small groups gather in a lay leader's home to share stories and commit to action together.[4] The typical regional meeting is two hours long. The first half includes an opening prayer or blessing, a grounding activity—typically a relational practice like storytelling or one-to-one conversations—and a "power analysis" of the issue, which identifies the power holders ELIJAH's actions should target, such as specific legislators, city council members, or corporate leaders. The second half is typically devoted to developing an action plan and training participants to carry it out. Action plans can include phone banks, door-knocking sessions, public demonstrations at businesses or corporate offices, coordinated visits or calls to city councillors or state legislators, public meetings with elected officials, one-to-ones or house meetings to broaden the organizing base, or more aggressive tactics, such as large rallies or hearing disruptions. Regional meetings are typically planned by core team members from multiple congregations working together with the help of the regional staff organizer. Hence, core team members from different churches within a region typically come to know one another well and work together regularly.

### Racial/Ethnic Caucuses

ELIJAH also works to ensure that members of racial and ethnic minority groups have opportunities to work together across regions. In particular, language barriers make it important that, in addition to working with ELIJAH's other participants in regional contexts, Latinx participants have dedicated spaces for working among themselves. To this end, ELIJAH has established a cross-regional Latino Caucus with its own designated staff organizer. At several points in its history, ELIJAH has also boasted a Black Church Caucus and dedicated organizer, though to the consternation of some of the organization's Black leaders, the Black Church organizer's role was left unfilled during my fieldwork.

Without a dedicated Black Church organizer, ELIJAH's Black churches tended to work with white-dominated churches in the West Side and East Side regions throughout my fieldwork. Until late 2015, the West Side region was staffed by Angela, a highly experienced, remarkably effective Black organizer in her thirties, who had previously been the Black Church organizer. During her seven-year tenure with ELIJAH, Angela worked tirelessly to wear down trust barriers that had long inhibited Black Churches' participation. She successfully brought several Black churches into affiliation with ELIJAH and facilitated the election of a Black pastor as president of the board of directors beginning in 2012.

Angela departed in 2015 to start a new FBCO federation in another part of the country and was replaced in the West Side staff organizer position by Maddy, a similarly experienced white organizer who had previously staffed the Northwest Suburban region. Samuel, a charismatic lay leader from New Kingdom, one of ELIJAH's most active Black Churches, was added to Maddy's team as a part-time associate organizer, helping to bolster her legitimacy among the Black Church leadership after Angela's departure. Working with Maddy also helped Samuel, who had not been formally trained as an organizer before being hired, to develop his organizing skills in hopes of being brought on full-time in the future. Indeed, when Maddy followed Angela's path, departing to start her own FBCO federation outside the region a year later, Samuel was hired as ELIJAH's full-time West Side organizer. As my research period concluded in late spring 2017, ELIJAH was reestablishing the Black Church Caucus, though a dedicated organizer had yet to be assigned.

## Central Leadership

ELIJAH's regions and racial/ethnic caucuses work somewhat independently, with the board of directors and central leadership team promoting cooperation and continuity across sections. The board is composed of four officers elected by ELIJAH's membership (president, vice president, treasurer, and secretary) and eight at-large members appointed by the officers and approved by the executive director. As is true on many dimensions, FBCOs nationwide have more race, gender, and class-diverse boards than nearly any other field of civic organizations.[5] Of ELIJAH's twelve board members in mid-2020, three were Black, two were Latina, one was East African, and six were white; seven were women and five were men; and eight were from ELIJAH's core metro area and four represented outstate congregations. The board included three Black Protestants, four white Protestants, four Catholics (two white, two Latina), and one Muslim. The larger central leadership team of approximately thirty lay leaders hails from across ELIJAH's regions and meets regularly to plan leadership assemblies, determine issue priorities, and advise the executive director and the board on important decisions.

## Issue Focus and Flexibility

Attending any given ELIJAH event, one is unlikely to get a representative picture of the organization as a whole. Instead, the attendance will provide a snapshot of people who are active in a particular region or on a particular issue at a certain moment in time. ELIJAH emphasizes the deep connections between its many issue areas, encouraging all participants to work on multiple issue areas concurrently, but a given region's teams typically focus on one or two key issue campaigns at a time. Issue priorities are ostensibly determined by regional lay leaders, based on their perceptions of the most salient issues for the communities they represent. In practice, however, strategic input from ELIJAH's executive director, its political director (who also works as its sole legislative lobbyist), the board, and the central leadership team figures heavily in the allocation of time and resources to one issue or another. Issues can gain or lose priority based on developments in the state legislature and local governments.

The balance between communities' needs and political opportunities means that ELIJAH is most effective when its participants can easily change focus from one issue to another. For example, during most of my fieldwork period, congregations in the South Suburban region worked on issues related to ELIJAH's Working Families Agenda. This comprised a range of discrete issues, including campaigns to increase the minimum wage, pass a state-level mandatory paid family leave policy, and push local municipalities to compel employers to provide paid sick time to workers. But in early 2016, the state legislature abandoned its consideration of a statewide paid family leave bill. Suddenly, the only progress being made on the labor issues that constituted the Working Families Agenda was happening at the municipal level in the central city. All of a sudden, ELIJAH's South Suburban leaders were not direct constituents of the politicians making the decisions, making them ineffective lobbyists on the issue. The district group's progress on labor policies was temporarily but unmistakably stopped in its tracks. The Working Families Agenda was still important to people across ELIJAH's regions, but for the time being, only those living in the central city could make immediate progress on the issue.

At the same time, under heavy lobbying pressure from a private corrections firm, the state legislature had begun to consider reopening a previously closed private prison in a rural area where unemployment was high. Rural legislators argued that in addition to easing overcrowding in existing prisons, reopening the private facility would provide needed jobs in an economically depressed area.

Pivoting from labor (now playing out in the central city) to criminal justice issues, Shannon, the South Suburban organizer, quickly refocused ELIJAH's core teams in area churches to attend rallies and hearings related to the prison issue. Specifically, in regional meetings, she partnered with lay leaders to advance the argument that jobs that depended on incarcerating people were neither equitable nor sustainable. Since those who would be incarcerated in the new prison would be predominantly people of color, they also argued that the proposal was rooted in white supremacy. Drawing on arguments from Michelle Alexander's book *The New Jim Crow*, the team pointed out that using the language of job growth to justify reopening the prison was akin to codifying that the economic prosperity of rural whites mattered more than the freedom of people of color.[6]

Meanwhile, East Side and West Side leaders continued pushing city council members to enact paid sick leave and higher minimum wage policies. Both efforts were ultimately successful. The central city passed a strong paid sick time policy (as chapter 5 explains in more detail), and the private prison remained shuttered. South Suburban leaders pledged to take up the Working Families Agenda on a statewide basis again the following year.

The pivot from labor issues to criminal justice in the South Suburban region was only possible because Shannon and a small group of lay leaders were able to marshal an underlying set of critiques of white supremacy and capitalism that ELIJAH had been developing across issues for many years. This flexibility is one of ELIJAH's most important strengths. Whereas the U.S. civic sector is composed largely of organizations focused on narrow groups of issues or even single issues, moral citizenship asks people to become attuned to—and eager and able to become involved in—many issues at once.[7] It requires a holistic approach, so at quarterly all-ELIJAH leadership assemblies, organizers and lay leaders conduct exercises and training sessions to demonstrate and reinforce the ways that various issue campaigns are connected. Using highly detailed social and political analysis, leaders at these meetings emphasize two themes: how society's wealthiest members benefit from the status quo across issue areas, and how racial and ethnic hierarchies are used to justify and maintain policies that preserve or deepen economic inequalities. Explicit discussions of greed and white supremacy, often informed by or focused on popular books or films (like *The New Jim Crow* or Ava DuVernay's *13th*), illuminate intersections between the multiple issues that most directly affect different parts of ELIJAH's membership and animate their practice of moral citizenship.

For instance, over the course of a series of meetings in 2015, Shannon had worked hard to impress upon the South Suburban congregations that there were many connections between the Working Families Agenda and ELIJAH's other ongoing issue campaigns throughout the state. Shannon wanted to show how the payday lending industry, one of the Black Church Caucus's chief concerns, benefits from low wages and the lack of paid sick time—problems for workers of all races but that hit Black communities especially hard. She pointed out how low-wage workers who often take out high-interest payday loans would be less likely to need these loans if they had paid sick time. It was no wonder payday lenders vigorously opposed such policies; their business model depended on an economically precarious underclass. In desperate need of short-term loans, unprotected low-wage workers had no bargaining power to negotiate the exorbitant interest rates payday lenders charged, usually above 300 percent in ELIJAH's region. Armed with charts and figures, Shannon was a relentless presence in congregation meetings. Her research revealed that the chief executive of a local payday lending chain was also a major donor to several organizations involved in the statewide lobbying effort against paid sick time—and that lobbyists for these organizations, in tandem with the state retailers' association and chamber of commerce, had shut down state-level consideration of the paid family leave bill in 2016. Usually discussed as distinct issues in the media and by other area social movement groups, ELIJAH effectively taught its constituents that paid sick time and payday lending reform were elements of the same underlying moral project, and that moral citizens needed to be concerned with both. While ELIJAH's activities on the issues were being driven by different leaders in different regions, the two campaigns depended on each other for long-term success.

In my time researching ELIJAH, I mostly attended South Suburban and West Side events, along with all-ELIJAH gatherings. The South Suburban events were dominated by white Protestants, with the occasional participation of white and Latinx Catholics. This region's leadership was primarily working on issue campaigns related to the Working Families Agenda. They coordinated with Latino Caucus leaders as well as labor leaders affiliated with a long-standing Latinx workers' collective. The collective had been pushing for tighter regulation of the large contracting firms that hire primarily immigrant workers to clean big-box stores, warehouses, and factories after hours. According to Latinx community members, wage theft and poor working conditions ran rampant, and workers with undocumented status had particularly little recourse. Despite the obvious overlap between the projects of the Working Families Agenda and those of the workers' collective, I noted that it was rare for significant numbers of Latinx people to attend South Suburban events. Instead, Latinx people at ELIJAH churches in the region worked primarily through the Latino Caucus, which frequently organized joint actions with the workers' collective and was running a concurrent campaign to make driver's licenses available to undocumented immigrants. Latino Caucus meetings were typically held in Spanish, with partial translations offered for any non-Spanish-speaking attendees (at two of the meetings I attended, I was the only person benefiting from this service).

West Side meetings were typically more diverse, often split about evenly between white and Black attendees. West Side leaders were working on both the Working Families Agenda and a push to enact tighter regulations on "poverty profiteers"—an umbrella term ELIJAH uses to describe payday lenders, predatory auto and medical lenders, and for-profit prison operators. The unifying theme, according to ELIJAH's analysis, is that all these industries have a strong incentive to keep poor people poor. Their revenue streams depend on widespread economic insecurity. Accordingly, Shannon's astute discussion of the links between payday lending, poor benefits packages, and the corporate lobbying money that was stymieing the Working Families Agenda in the state legislature was often echoed by Maddy, the West Side organizer.

ELIJAH's federated structure means that while the group describes itself as "multi-racial, anti-racist, and interfaith," an attendee at any given meeting is unlikely to see its full diversity on display.[8] Participants who do not attend the quarterly all-ELIJAH leadership assemblies or large public meetings where the entire organization gathers, like the Prophetic Resistance event, might have few opportunities to interact with racial or ethnic others within ELIJAH.


Issue Teams

In addition to geographic regions and racial/ethnic caucuses, ELIJAH supports issue teams dedicated to specific policy areas, which during my fieldwork included a criminal justice task force, an education equity team, a citizenship team focused on immigrants' rights, a sanctuary response team quickly put in place after Trump's election, a renewable energy task force, a domestic violence task force, and a health equity team. At geographic region and racial/ethnic caucus meetings, leaders tend to avoid technical discussions and plans, keeping the work approachable for nonexperts in attendance. Gary, a veteran staff organizer who left ELIJAH to run for public office, was fond of saying at regional meetings, "We don't care how the sausage gets made; that's for the experts to worry about. Our job is to provide a clear moral voice, and you don't have to be an expert to do that." The issue teams, in contrast, are highly concerned with understanding and influencing the "sausage making." Their members (often but not always members of their congregations' core teams) are typically experienced experts with extensive local connections. At an education equity team meeting I attended, I could barely follow the conversation, as about fifteen ELIJAH veterans discussed ways to influence the school board's selection of a new superintendent. In attendance were current and retired teachers, a retired attorney whose firm had been retained by the state teachers' union, several people who had professional experience in education policy, and one participant who lived down the block from a school board member, a sort of incidental access that could nonetheless be useful.

The team was getting involved in the superintendent pick because of a controversy in which the school board had adopted elementary school curricular materials that contained racist text and images. Though it would cost the district considerable money, the team was committed to ensuring that the new superintendent would void the district's contract with the firm that had supplied the racist content. Angela had previously organized West Side and East Side congregations to disrupt school board meetings and attend community protests against the new curriculum. But at this education equity team meeting, discussion focused on personal connections to stakeholders, detailed strategies for lobbying specific school board members, and other fine-grained, technical, high-demand strategic work. I left the meeting bewildered, having struggled to follow the discussion as team members talked about leveraging their contacts and honing the strategic conversations they planned to have with key players.

Since the issue teams' members have extensive experience and connections in the areas they work on, it can be difficult for them to manage the tension between working within elite networks to influence policy in the short term and recruiting a broad base of participants to build longer-term power. Just as I was bewildered by the education equity team meeting, many people felt confused and frustrated after a meeting organized by the renewable energy task force in early 2017. A utility company was petitioning the state for subsidies to build a new coal-fired power plant at the edge of the metro area, and renewable energy task force leaders wanted to use the debate over the plant as a springboard to push local and state governments to bolster their commitments to renewables.

Leaning on congregational core teams from the East Side and West Side regions, Steve, a staff organizer, planned a weekday evening meeting at St. Martin's. He encouraged everyone to spread the word, advertising the meeting widely in other ELIJAH congregations as well as churches that weren't ELIJAH affiliates. Eager for civic engagement in the wake of Trump's victory, environmental advocates came from churches across the city. Steve planned to initiate an action plan in which ELIJAH leaders from the central city and the surrounding suburbs would pressure their municipal governments to formalize renewable energy goals, such as committing to 100 percent renewable energy by 2040. Steve also saw the campaign as having the potential to expand ELIJAH's organizing base among churches in the city that were not yet affiliates.

About seventy people attended (mostly middle- to upper-class whites from affluent West Side churches), many of whom were from non-ELIJAH-affiliated congregations. Based on a show of hands, over half were attending their first ELIJAH event of any kind. During the first half of the two-hour meeting, Steve and renewable energy task force leaders built a compelling moral case for religious people to take up the renewable energy issue. Citing Pope Francis and Bible verses, they argued that caring for creation is a fundamental part of God's intention for humans on earth. Further, they made a strong case for renewable energy as an equity issue, since vulnerable communities more commonly bear the brunt of pollution and climate change's effects. Copies of ELIJAH's Liberation Narrative, a ten-point document distributed at many ELIJAH events, were handed out, with an emphasis on its fourth point (bold in the original): *"Creation is God's gift for all life, not just humans.* The gifts of creation support our lives and we have an obligation to be stewards of creation in return. Business and public institutions have an obligation to protect and preserve creation's animals, land, and water."

Steve shared a personal story as he talked through the inclusion of environmental issues within ELIJAH's larger social justice project. He said he'd always cared about the environment but had long considered his environmental activism a hobby, mostly unrelated to his day job organizing on economic justice issues. But two years earlier, he read Naomi Klein's book *This Changes Everything: Capitalism vs. the Climate,* and it felt like an epiphany. The basic relationships and structure of the economy, which were currently failing to protect the environment, were not just a technical problem but also a spiritual one. Klein had helped Steve recognize how environmental activism fit into his moral vocation.

Attendees need not be energy policy experts to develop personal moral positions on energy policy, Steve pointed out. He argued that a major part of the faith community's responsibility regarding climate change was making sure the issue was framed as a moral and spiritual problem, not just a technical one. When an audience member interrupted to ask whether the solar technology needed to eliminate fossil fuel dependence was in place, Steve responded,

> That's a good question, and maybe somebody here can answer it, we'll find out. But I just want to say, that's a question about science, and

even if we respect science, we're not here to have a conversation about science. The other side doesn't care about science, so why should we have to know the science perfectly to have a position on this? We have to adopt a moral framing. We have to make it simple and emotional, instead of complicated and intellectual. And we can do that by articulating one simple goal: 100 percent renewable energy in our state. That's a goal that sends a clear moral message.

Echoing Gary's preference to stay out of the sausage making, Steve skill-fully deflected a technical question that he couldn't answer to pivot back toward moral concerns. And he clearly told the audience that faith actors like themselves bring a unique kind of agency to bear on political debates. The technical worlds of scientific research and its policy implications were important, he understood, but would necessarily operate in tandem with the world of moral claims inhabited by faith actors.

Further, by claiming the moral dimension of politics as these individu-als' domain, Steve affirmed attendees' responsibility to keep focused on the moral conversation and constructed a clear political statement tying eco-nomic and racial justice to climate change. Immediately after saying he was setting scientific problems aside for the moment, Steve began listing off economic barriers to seeking environmental protection. He said that only financially secure people can currently move toward renewable energy. Things like hybrid cars and solar panels are expensive, the local utility charges more for wind power than for standard gas and coal power, and even community solar farms require those buying in to prove strong credit histories. "It's a problem that people have to be privileged if they want to take a stand and act on this issue," he said, "and we're going to make sure people hear that we think that's a problem. So, in the course of healing the planet, we'll be working on racial, economic, and social justice, too." The ELIJAH newcomers in the room responded enthusiastically to this dis-cussion, nodding and murmuring their assent. They appreciated being told that they had a special kind of moral agency that gave them the power to shape future conversations about climate change and the environment.

Yet in the meeting's second hour, the discussion turned back to techni-cal considerations and political strategy, and I saw the people who had got-ten excited during the first hour's morally invigorating discussion grow quiet. As Steve and the lay leaders worked out their action plan, they dis-cussed strategy and laid out the intricate political calculus at hand. When the meeting split into neighborhood-based breakout groups, each group was tasked with identifying people who would set up meetings with city council members from their districts to push for stronger renewable energy commitments.

Pointing out that utility companies had enormous lobbying influence in municipal and local governments, Steve argued that ELIJAH leaders needed to go straight to their elected representatives and act as their own lobbyists. But this was easier said than done. Few attendees even knew who their city council members were. Others were understandably intimidated about requesting meetings with elected officials, especially regarding an issue about which they had little technical knowledge. Asking unseasoned activists to arrange these meetings may have seemed an effective strategy to Steve and the renewable energy task force leaders, but it was a huge leap for the average person attending a meeting in a church basement on a Tuesday night. To my knowledge, only one city councillor meeting resulted from the evening's event (organized, unsurprisingly, by a core team member from St. Martin's). Hence, not only was little concrete progress made on the renewable energy issue pursuant to this meeting, but Steve's astute, inspiring analysis of the renewable energy issue as a moral crisis was largely wasted. At the close of the evening, a few dozen potential new ELIJAH leaders left with the sense that ELIJAH was a technical organization for political experts rather than an accessible group of regular people acting on their faith.

Recruiting people into ELIJAH's mission and building energy around it requires skillful cultural work that marshals the logic of moral vocation. Steve's nimble dismissal of concerns about the science of renewable energy was well suited to this, but the rhetoric he used to "excite" attendees about meetings with city councillors was, in hindsight, a poor fit for recruiting them into carrying out the political tasks that can bring about short-term change.

## Benefits and Drawbacks of ELIJAH's Structure

As this chapter has illustrated, ELIJAH's organizational structure offers important strengths but also comes with certain challenges. It enables core team members to develop strong relationships with staff organizers and present ELIJAH's work to their congregations in ways that align with the congregations' local cultures.[9] The combination of geographic regions and racial/ethnic caucuses balances racial inclusivity with focused attention on particular communities' needs, while still allowing ELIJAH to enhance its power by coordinating campaigns and strategies across its region rather than conducting them piecemeal, one municipality at a time.[10] Ample space and time are devoted to identifying different communities' needs, and regional meetings and leadership assemblies bring together many constituencies and foster spaces for cross-cultural interaction that are otherwise rare in U.S. civic life.

Then, in quarterly organization-wide leadership assemblies, ELIJAH participants who may have become involved because of their interest in a particular issue, such as criminal justice reform, payday lending, or renewable energy, are taught about how corporate greed and white supremacy connect all these issues. Payday lending is linked to paid sick time, and economic disparities are reflected in the market for electric cars and solar panels. By structuring its work like this, ELIJAH ensures that each congregation can develop action strategies that fit its own culture and priorities, while also fostering opportunities for people to interact across congregations, regions, and racial/ethnic subgroups. The issue teams provide dedicated spaces for intricate planning, minimizing the frequency of occasions (like the renewable energy meeting) when new participants become overwhelmed by details or intimidated by ambitious action plans.

At the same time, this structure illuminates several key tensions that ELIJAH must manage as it organizes within congregations that have different class, racial and ethnic, and denominational compositions and whose members bring different degrees of enthusiasm and political acumen into social movement participation. The aforementioned education equity and renewable energy meetings speak to one of these tensions: balancing broad recruitment and sweeping moral framing with technically astute and strategically incisive political action. As sociologist Todd Nicholas Fuist points out, these modes of political action—moralized and performative on the one hand, technical and strategic on the other—are the poles of a continuum along which civic organizations like ELIJAH must plot their activities.[11] Effective social change work requires both, and balancing them within particular issue campaigns and larger political and cultural contexts is an ongoing challenge.

This tension lies at the heart of a larger question about what kind of organization ELIJAH wants to be. Social movement groups contribute to change partly by achieving direct results like policy changes or concessions from corporate leaders and partly by contributing to deeper alterations in the cultural contexts of political action.[12] The ways people define concepts like poverty, the economy, good jobs, and racial equity are not written in stone but created through the institutionalization of moral messages and cultural meanings.[13] Does poverty mostly reflect individuals' bad choices or social-structural conditions? How does the legacy of slavery affect Black Americans' life chances today? What are society's responsibilities for accommodating those who immigrate to the United States? The answers to these questions are contested, and social movement organizations across the political spectrum strive to make their answers appear credibly correct and moral. When ELIJAH leaders talk about speaking with moral clarity, they are talking about this realm of social movement activity: using their collective moral voices to transform the norms and narratives that give meaning and institutional backing to the concepts on which policy is built. Hence, much of ELIJAH's culture is focused on empowering individuals to set aside their concerns about knowledge, experience, and technical competence and speak loudly and clearly from a moral perspective, regardless of the issue at hand. It is precisely why Wendy elected to ask newcomers, rather than Janelle, to speak at the meeting on paid sick time. Janelle already had a voice that could contribute to this work, and Wendy wanted to cultivate more of these voices.

Yet FBCOs also see themselves as having a responsibility to marginalized communities and thus motivated to pursue necessary improvements in their living conditions. Saul Alinsky's legacy still runs deep in the FBCO world, shaping the training that staff organizers and lay leaders receive. Alinsky prioritized incremental, short-term gains on quality-of-life issues, arguing that the skills people develop by coming together to demand that cities fix streetlights and potholes not only help them improve their lives in the short term but are scalable and can eventually give birth to nationally influential people's organizations.[14] Running through Alinsky's philosophy was the conviction that communities should determine their own needs and act to meet those needs through whatever means necessary, including intentionally humiliating politicians and corporate leaders.[15] Changing the deeper moral calculus of policy making, Alinsky argued, was a desirable side effect of community organizing but should never be its main goal.

Pursuing short-term change is a complementary but distinct ambition to reshaping the moral narratives that give meaning to politics. At the renewable energy meeting, it was evident that the mostly white, mostly affluent attendees were hungry for work that would do the latter but lacked the impetus and the skills to do the former. Among economically insecure people whose needs are immediate, the situation is often reversed: they are eager to do whatever is necessary to procure needed reforms quickly, even if it means doing something uncomfortable or risky and even if the effort comes at the cost of working on a larger moral project. These differences in the cultural meanings that people bring into civic action mean that while all social movement organizations must negotiate tensions between morally performative and strategically incisive action, this tension is particularly keen in ELIJAH—and sometimes even a proxy for race and class relations within it.

This was in evidence at the education equity meeting focused on the appointment of a new school board superintendent. A team of highly experienced, well-connected activists had to decide how to prioritize competing modes of action in their effort to supplant the racist curriculum. Would they carry out their plans themselves, knowing that this would likely be the most efficient and effective approach given their connections and experience? Or would they use this issue—first reported in a Black-focused West Side community newspaper, now gaining attention in the city's main paper, and proving contentious in social media discussions—as a basis to recruit new education activists, help develop their moral voices, and teach them leadership skills? The latter more clearly aligned with ELIJAH's overarching goal of empowering people to speak with moral clarity on issues that affected their lives. It also addressed racial equity concerns, given that the team comprised predominantly white activists working on issues of deep concern to communities of color. At the meeting, team members lamented not having more Black representation and briefly discussed the importance of making sure the Black community had a voice in their undertakings. Leaders knew they would be able to develop more effective long-term relationships with school board members and with the poor, nonwhite communities most affected by problems in the schools if they spoke with the moral voice of dozens or even hundreds of nonexpert community members.

Yet in this instance, the education team chose to do the work themselves, sacrificing long-term relationship building and the potential expansion and diversification of their team in favor of short-term political expediency. It was deemed acceptable for this issue, but in most cases, ELIJAH leaders prefer the alternative. For instance, during the campaign for paid sick time, ELIJAH elected to forgo efficiency for the sake of bringing other West Side congregations into the planning. As Wendy told me, "I could make a bunch of calls next week and get a hundred people to this meeting myself if I wanted to. I have the relationships where I could make that happen. But that's not the point. We need to get other people in this church to be building relationships with the community around us. If I do all the work myself, we'll get the people to the meeting, but how's that going to change our standing in the community? How's it going to help people in our church learn how to build the relationships that we want?"

Thus, as I'll explain in detail in chapter 5, Wendy organized phone banks and recruited St. Martin's parishioners to spend significant time making calls to community members. Many of these parishioners were unskilled in the art of getting strangers to commit to attending a meeting over the phone, and the meeting fell short of its turnout goals. But Wendy's larger goal of facilitating church-community relationships and framing paid sick time as a moral issue that called for input from the St. Martin's congregation was advanced along the way.

For Wendy, long-term relationship building is worth sacrificing short-term expediency in almost every case. But in view of what happened at the renewable energy meeting discussed earlier, the education team's decision to keep its work contained to the group of experts seemed understandable. In the first half of the renewable energy meeting, task force leaders had effectively linked religious faith with climate issues and a range of other racial and economic justice concerns. Steve had attuned newcomers to one of ELIJAH's biggest emphases: that the underlying structure of the economy and the political scene are not intractable structures but products of humans' decisions, which can be revisited and influenced by moral arguments. Focusing on narrative and culture rather than the mechanics of the political process, Steve had given about sixty people a language for thinking and talking about climate change as a significant moral problem and a lens for understanding progress toward it as a way to address other issues along the way. He got them excited to act. But when it came time to propose action steps, what he suggested was too technical and demanding to appeal to anyone who was not extremely well versed in the political process already. As quickly as he'd built engagement, he alienated potential partners.

ELIJAH leaders manage the tension between the cultural and technical demands of politics and the imperative to make its work accessible to large numbers of people of different backgrounds by emphasizing moral vocation and moral citizenship and training all participants to speak with a moral voice. Meanwhile, the issue teams, core teams, organizing staff, and political director carry out the bulk of the technical work. But helping participants overcome the cultural and practical barriers to more intensive political participation is also a major point of emphasis. Staff organizers often tell participants that the seemingly high barriers to entry that they encounter when trying to engage in politics are no accident—they are designed to reduce everyday citizens' political involvement. Part of moral citizenship, the group stresses, is recognizing that such obstacles serve the interests of those currently in power. Overcoming—and inviting others over—the hurdles is a moral mission unto itself.

### Power for What? Power for Whom?

ELIJAH's organizational structure begs questions about power. Power for what? And power for whom? As indicated by the analyses of renewable energy and payday lending offered by Steve and Shannon, respectively, ELIJAH's organizers are deeply attuned to these considerations. They think carefully about the underlying structure of the economy and the political sphere. They identify the actors—politicians, corporate leaders, wealthy campaign contributors—who collectively hold the power to determine whether, when, and how to reinforce or alter this structure. And their conversations about injecting a moral voice into such deliberations reflect their ambition to make everyone (including but not limited to ELIJAH's participants) part of these decisions. Their overarching aim is to build power to steer the course of democratic decision-making in directions that benefit everyday people across races, religions, social classes, and immigration statuses.

This approach to power, focused on the deep workings of the political system and the structural underpinnings of the economy, provides a cultural pathway into activism for people recruited through congregational networks. It also makes the case that the various issues and problems that affect different sections of ELIJAH's membership are all connected. Lax regulations on payday lenders, low wages, and continued fossil fuel dependence could all be resolved, ELIJAH leaders argue, if moral citizens could develop the power to wrest control of the political system away from those who currently hold it. But the specific manifestations of this understanding of power in any given setting are subject to various other considerations, particularly the pressing needs of marginalized constituencies who do not always enjoy the luxury of taking a long-term view to politics. ELIJAH's work to cultivate moral citizenship and empower participants to act out this model across issues is deeply contoured by the ways participants' own lives are embedded in social structure.

For similar reasons, the issue flexibility that ELIJAH cultivates through its attention to social structure is not always appealing to all of its constituencies. Marginalized communities have strong incentives to focus on issues most pressing to them in the short term, rather than pivoting to the issues that offer the best chance for gains in any given political moment or those that provide the opportunities to expand a base. Some members of the Latino Caucus, for instance, grew frustrated when, in early 2015, legislative developments spurred ELIJAH to divert resources from the campaign to procure driver's licenses for undocumented immigrants into criminal justice campaigns. In that moment, ELIJAH's long-term focus on building power to transform the democratic process and redefine civic concepts like the economy did not seem to align with the Latinx community's immediate needs.

Finally, debates over how to define and build power will always carry tensions related to race and social class, no matter how far below the surface. Organizations pursuing social reform that spans issues and communities must find ways to align the interests and identities of the communities they wish to involve in their work.[16] Cultural sociologists argue that this is accomplished by creating distinctive group styles—collective representations of what a group is and why it exists. As sociologists Nina Eliasoph and Paul Lichterman explain, group styles lay out members' shared group bonds, speech norms, and symbolic boundaries and form a foundation for defining what kinds of action are or are not appropriate for the group.[17] We saw such a process in action when Steve diverted conversation about science toward moral claims-making. He suggested that faith actors can speak with unique moral clarity, and that as a result, they should focus on moral messaging more than technical concerns.

But research has shown that organizations with stable group styles tend to also have stable collective identities on which those styles are built. Shared status markers like race, class, urban or rural identity, sexuality, and immigration status can provide scaffolding for group styles. Class, as in Eliasoph and Lichterman's study of bar patrons; political commitments, as in Lichterman's analysis of Green party activists; or racial or ethnic bonds, as in Laura Enriquez and Abigail Saguy's study of immigrant student activists, can function as a base from which a group style can emerge.[18] In ELIJAH, the only unifying strand is religion—not shared beliefs, shared ideologies, or even a shared set of historical traditions but the shared pursuit of moral vocation. As we'll see in chapters 3 and 4, it takes a great deal of intensive cultural work to make this platform into a shared understanding of moral citizenship.

"Do you have the courage to overturn the tables?" Reverend Andrews stared intently into his audience members' eyes, probing for signs they understood how seriously he meant the question. Their answers—a few timid yeses— suggested they didn't, so he asked it again, his eyes now burning even more fiercely. He had to repeat himself a few more times until he got the loud, confident collective "Yes!" he was looking for.

Reverend Andrews, a friendly, fiery big man in his forties, is a father of ten, the head pastor of a Black Pentecostal church in a small city about an hour outside ELIJAH's main metro area, and the newly elected president of ELIJAH's board of directors. Wearing a flashy pin-striped suit, his shoes polished to a brilliant shine, he was winding up to finish a rousing sermon addressed to about a hundred people of many different Christian faith traditions and nearly evenly split among white, Black, and Latinx backgrounds. The group was seated around him in a circle of folding chairs in the windowless basement of a suburban Lutheran church in spring 2016 for an ELIJAH leadership assembly, an all-day Saturday affair. ELIJAH holds leadership assemblies quarterly, bringing together people from across the organization to deepen relationships and plan strategies. They are cognitively and emotionally demanding sessions that blend political analysis and strategy with religious ritual and leadership training. For many participants, they are also cathartic and spiritually rejuvenating. More than once, I heard people joke that when there was a leadership assembly on Saturday, they could skip church that week, having filled their spiritual cups before Sunday arrived. Listening to Reverend Andrews's intense "spiritual welcome and reflection," as the agenda called it, it was easy to see why.

To open today's assembly, Reverend Andrews spoke about one of ELIJAH's favorite stories from scripture: the one in which Jesus arrives in Jerusalem, walks into a temple, finds people counting money on tables inside, and angrily flips the tables over, sending the coins flying and the money changers scurrying. In the preceding few minutes, his sermon had moved from scripture to civil rights to skyrocketing corporate profits. He now linked those hefty profits back to scripture, comparing today's financial elite to the lenders and merchants of Jerusalem whom Jesus had confronted. His audience captivated, Reverend Andrews roamed the middle of the circle as he spoke, occasionally approaching and staring straight into the eyes of an observer from a foot away. His manner was charismatically confrontational. He wanted everyone in the room to know that he was asking them to do something hard and expecting them to do it anyway. He was demanding that they stop making excuses for themselves and those they knew.

As he neared the end of his sermon, Reverend Andrews approached me. His gaze pierced my comfort zone like a drill bit as he said, "You're going to be asked to do several things today. You're going to be put to task. Put to work." I was relieved when he moved on to stare down someone else. "Because faith without work is not actually real. You have to put together what you believe with the work that has to be done. In doing this work you are going to be ridiculed, you're going to be talked about. You are going to be not somebody's best friend. They are going to disagree with you. They might even say some really nasty things about you. But do you have the courage to turn those tables over? Because when Jesus went in, this was the beginning of the setup. Okay? This is the moment when they started to frame him for being an enemy of the state. But we're all right with being an enemy of the state as long as we're a friend of God, aren't we? Come on, say Amen!"

People did, loudly. Reverend Andrews's tone was brightening a little now as he described channeling discomfort into confidence. "Say to yourself that it's okay if people don't like me. Get yourself ready to tell this to people: 'You do not have to like me, but we will accomplish our goal.' When we go to the state capitol, and we've been there a lot this year, I tell the legislators that. I say, 'I am not your friend. You do not have to like me. But we will accomplish our mission.'"

Reverend Andrews's sermon was part theology, part political analysis, and part psychology, but mostly, it was about courage—specifically, courage amid discomfort. Reminding his listeners that civil rights protesters risked physical discomfort and worse, he asserted that activism by definition brings distress, because it means pushing back, not just against politics and policy but against taken-for-granted cultural assumptions and ideas. People take risks when they talk with their friends and family about race and white supremacy, ask people to share their deepest feelings and most painful moments, critique their congregations' responses to social problems, and tell or listen to traumatic stories, like the one from Juana about her son's death in prison (see chapter 1). In talking about courage, Reverend Andrews emphasized that moral citizenship means taking all these risks and more, putting one's friendships, comfort, and pride on the line.

This chapter explains the cultural project at the heart of ELIJAH's organizing: identifying the major points of discomfort in one's life, learning to understand the social causes of that discomfort, and channeling one's spiritual and moral energy—one's moral vocation—toward not only overcoming discomfort but also remedying its causes by working collectively with others. ELIJAH participants learn to construct life stories that situate past and present discomfort within a framework of shared struggle. Through relational practices, they affirm that their unique experiences have common root causes and dedicate themselves to working together to disrupt the social processes that bring pain into everyday people's lives.

Following a brief discussion of the ways risk and discomfort shape participation in activism and how this relates to moral vocation, I present the stories of three ELIJAH leaders who have learned to identify and channel their past discomfort in this way, developing moral vocations focused on turning personal stress into public engagement. The chapter then concludes with an example of a compelling relational practice that illuminates the commonalities among people's fears, stress, and discomfort and solidifies the importance of collective action for overcoming them.

## The Risks of Moral Citizenship

ELIJAH leaders acknowledge that their work is not easy or comfortable. But instead of minimizing this fact in their training and leadership development processes, they emphasize it. They build up their mission's importance by playing down how easily it can be accomplished, depicting moral citizens as courageous leaders who are called to lead others away from accepting the status quo. As they do this, they make embracing risk—getting comfortable with being uncomfortable—a key part of the identity they share as moral citizens.

Mostly, they don't mean physical risk, though that might occasionally be involved for those willing to accept it. Instead, as this chapter explains, leaders in ELIJAH create shared meaning around the need to embrace a different kind of risk: interpersonal risk. To be what ELIJAH leaders would call a moral citizen—courageous in the face of corporate greed and white supremacy and the public's acquiescence to these forces—means having tough conversations about topics that some people find distasteful or even threatening. It means inviting scrutiny and skepticism about one's work and motives, and being willing to risk judgment from one's friends, family, and others. It means being unafraid to tell people things they don't like to hear, asking others to do hard things and not taking no for an answer, and putting one's own comfort aside and asking others to do the same. Social change scholars explain that organizing is different from mobilizing.[1] *Mobilizing* means getting people who agree with you to do something. *Organizing* means doing the work to change how people feel and then getting them to act even though they're not sure about it yet. This necessarily involves putting oneself in uncomfortable positions, all the more so in religious life, since talking about race, politics, and social issues in general can be especially divisive in many congregational settings.[2] ELIJAH and its peer groups are not satisfied with faith-based mobilizing; what they do is faith-based organizing, and this involves interpersonal risk.

In recent years, researchers have been rethinking risk and its role in social change projects. Scholars used to argue that physical and financial risks—like being beaten or arrested; running out of money; or being retaliated against by government officials, police, or corporations—were the most important deterrents to potential involvement in social change efforts. Doug McAdam's classic study of recruitment into civil rights activism distinguished between high and low risk forms, pointing out that signing a petition, for example, typically invites much less risk than confronting police officers, which civil rights protesters often did.[3] In McAdam's telling, the kind of activism typical in ELIJAH is low risk, because it does not usually involve the threat of arrest, beatings, or other physical harm. But newer work by social movement scholars Michelle Oyakawa, Elizabeth McKenna, and Hahrie Han complicates the risk calculus by drawing attention to "the intramovement relational risks involved in recruiting and organizing peers and allies."[4] These risks are largely interpersonal, not physical. They are created by the potential for conflict or mistrust among activists with different life experiences, priorities, and preferred ways of doing things, and they are especially significant in organizations with a diverse membership. More than risking violence or retribution, activists in diverse coalitions risk embarrassment and discomfort when they share their stories openly, ask others to do the same, and make these stories the basis of the group's analysis and action. They risk being labeled insensitive, selfish, angry, uncooperative, or even racist.

In an organizing space like that of ELIJAH, these interpersonal risks are unavoidable. People are less accustomed to interacting with people from different backgrounds than their own and are often anxious about how to do it. But the interpersonal risks that Oyakawa and colleagues discuss are internal to the group, referring to the discomfort that participants might encounter while interacting with other group members. These risks are significant in ELIJAH, but they are not the only kind of interpersonal risks I observed shaping people's actions. People in ELIJAH consistently told me that organizing work brings *external* interpersonal risks—that is, potential consequences in their lives outside ELIJAH. They fear what their friends and family members might think of their activism. They also worry that people in general might judge them for what they do—that they might be lumped into a category of "ungrateful malcontents," told they are "bringing too much politics into church," or accused of "always playing the race card." In this context, "turning over the tables," as Reverend Andrews encouraged, means shaking things up in ways that make other people uncomfortable. Sometimes those people are fellow activists, but equally often they are friends, family members, neighbors, or people one knows from church, maybe even one's pastor. Training people to overcome such fears is not only a crucial step in moving them to action but also a key way of developing a sense of shared commitment and community as people who are unafraid to risk scorn from those who are satisfied with the status quo. In ELIJAH, as in the feminist movements discussed by sociologists Verta Taylor and Nancy Whittier, collective processing of personal distress is at the heart of collective identity.[5]

Oyakawa, McKenna, and Han explain that effective organizations cultivate "habits of courage" that help people push past interpersonal risks. These habits include "(a) overcoming powerlessness, (b) mastering vulnerability, and (c) holding themselves and others accountable to commitments."[6] In ELIJAH and other faith-based community organizations (FBCOs), such habits of courage are emphasized as well. What has not been previously explained—and what this chapter will show—is how religious symbols and commitments, filtered through moral vocation, can powerfully support both the habits themselves and the practices that foster them. Relational practices teach participants to see discomfort as normal and surmountable, simply part of what it means to answer a call to justice. They use the language of moral vocation to extend religious precepts outside their sectarian roots, showing, for example, how one person's motivation to adhere to scripture can dovetail with another's impulse to live out Catholic social teaching or some other set of symbols. In this way, leaders marshal moral vocation—an aspect of religious culture that different racial and religious groups share—to frame specific religious commitments as elements of a larger shared moral project rather than points of division. As Reverend Andrews stated, people have to "put together what you believe with the work that has to be done." What he didn't say but what ELIJAH's practices teach is that it doesn't matter what, specifically, people believe as long as those beliefs are capable of inspiring them to overcome the risks that impede organizing.

## The Elements of Moral Vocation

In the introduction, I explained that moral vocation combines three cultural impulses. The first is a sense of having a unique set of life experiences and goals that endows one with particular attributes and skills. The second is a perception of having the responsibility to use those skills for good, however one defines it. These impulses are widespread in U.S. society, and they transcend divisions like race, class, and religion. In ELIJAH's relational practices, they cohere to enliven the third part of the recipe: a sense of having a unique personal story that charts one's spiritual and civic growth over time, tracing one's development into a powerful leader with the capacity to influence society.[7] Thus, moral vocation is a sense of sacred personal empowerment and responsibility whose political and civic implications are not fixed but develop through repeated interaction with others. Ultimately, moral vocation is the sense of tying the pieces of one's life together with one coherent thread, creating a strong sense of *who I am, what I care about, and what I do*. It is given political meaning through practices that frame particular social goals as the "right" ones.[8] This makes moral vocation an ideal cultural foundation for organizing across constituencies whose members have different commitments and different ideas about how to advance them.

In FBCO federations, relational practices steer individuals' moral vocations toward the collective practice of moral citizenship. But as Reverend Andrews hinted in his sermon at the leadership assembly, and as ELIJAH leaders emphasize at every opportunity, developing a moral vocation oriented toward racial and socioeconomic equity, and persisting in that vocation over time, under pressure, and across major life changes, is hard. It is time-intensive, emotionally draining, and interpersonally risky. Aside from the significant time investment that good organizing requires, moral citizenship means resisting the temptation to acquiesce to cultural norms that sometimes impede organizing, such as being unwilling to ask others to think about painful details from their lives, avoiding talking or thinking about race (for a white person), or suppressing one's anger or tokenizing one's self for fear of being labeled angry or uppity (for a person of color). Developing such courage is not possible overnight; it requires persistent and habitual practice.[9]

## Vocation Stories

At the core of moral vocation is the idea that people have a responsibility to grow over time in their understandings of the world, their commitments to improving it, and the skills they can marshal to pursue those commitments. This way of thinking is not unique to participants in faith-based organizing or even in organized religion. Classic social movements theorizing by Joshua Gamson as well as by David Snow and Doug McAdam argues that "identity work"—intentional work done by leaders to make movement participation a core part of participants' identities—is central to contemporary activism.[10] More specifically, Braunstein found that a sense of spiritual duty to grow personally in service of political goals was common among Tea Party activists, and Lichterman observed similar dynamics among Green Party members. One person's moral vocation might call for steadfastly praying for an end to abortion, while another's might encourage meeting with city council members to demand commitments to renewable energy.

Yet two key themes run through these distinct examples—themes that skilled organizers can capitalize on. First, each of these hypothetical vocations can't develop innately but is learned socially, through interactions with others. Second, in each, the journey is as important as the destination. People feel they are called to an ongoing personalized life project, and dedication is what counts. Sociologist Christian Smith explains that from the 1960s onward, this kind of individualist moral authority came to replace more traditional institutional moral authority among Americans of nearly every religious background, as people plot their progress through life based on how well they are living up to standards they have set for themselves instead of moral absolutes dictated by religious leaders or institutions.[11] This mode of religious commitment, which Smith calls "moralistic therapeutic deism," makes it easy for activist leaders to frame the interpersonal risks of organizing as personal challenges that stand between participants and a full, meaningful life—challenges that people can learn to overcome and thereby grow in their faith.

Smith argued that moralistic therapeutic deism's rise was a threat to religious culture, a claim often repeated by religious conservatives concerned with the replacement of orthodoxy by what they pejoratively call "cafeteria" or even "counterfeit" Christianity, in which, they argue, people can pick and choose which rules to follow and which traditions to embrace. With individual moral projects proliferating at the expense of shared moral precepts, these writers fear that sacred community is giving way to a cult of the individual as people choose to chart their own spiritual paths instead of joining in collective devotion.[12] These concerns be logical from a fundamentalist perspective, but for activist leaders, this individualistic mode of religious commitment provides something very important: a way to frame the interpersonal risks involved with moral citizenship as surmountable challenges that people are called by their moral vocations to overcome. In ELIJAH, leaders capitalize on this opportunity by training people to chart their progress in life temporally, contrasting a sense of *who I was before* with *who I am now* and *who I am becoming*.[13] An organizational focus on the process of becoming, specifically shaking off one's hesitation to become a fearless, authentic agent of change, casts different personal goals as elements of the same larger project, allowing multiple distinct kinds of moral vocations to cohere in the shared language of moral citizenship. In the sections that follow, I show how three people from very different backgrounds invoke their own understandings of moral vocation, with roots in distinct religious traditions, to support their involvement in the same larger collective project. I then conclude the chapter with an example of how collective practices cement this logic as the foundation of solidarity in ELIJAH.

Kristin

Kristin is a thirty-year-old Presbyterian who immigrated to the United States from Canada at age six and had given birth to her first child a few months before our interview. She is white and speaks English as her native language, so during her childhood she didn't think much about what, if anything, she had in common with nonwhite immigrants. Her family entered the country legally but with a provisional immigration status tied to her father's work. A technology consultant, he lived in constant fear of disappointing his clients, knowing that unfavorable reviews would get back to his boss and could end with nonrenewal of his work visa. As a result, Kristin says, he lived at his clients' beck and call. He never said no to a late-night summons and was often absent from the family as his company exploited his legal vulnerability.

Kristin recalls that by the time she was a teenager, she had come to understand that immigration laws and corporate exploitation were the main reasons for her dad's stress, but she still didn't identify with immigrants from Latin America, Africa, or Asia, or think of her family as like theirs. She identified more with other white people, but she went to a largely affluent high school, and she didn't think many of her classmates shared her family's insecurity. This made her feel uneasy among her friends, ashamed of her family's precarity and uninterested in talking about it with anyone. It was easier to pretend that everything was okay than to talk about what wasn't.

These social challenges in Kristin's early life were compounded by personal difficulties. Since the family was constantly stressed during her childhood, Kristin put pressure on herself to be "a perfect daughter." She never talked about her challenges with her family, since they seemed trivial in comparison to her father's. Thanks to the shame she felt around family and friends, she internalized the premise that her problems were her own affair, not something she should discuss with others. This led to anxiety and depression throughout her adolescence. From an early age, Kristin learned that telling others about problems in her life was risky. It invited others' scrutiny and made her feel ashamed. Instead, she told herself that she should feel grateful for what she had.

These challenges from the past are a major driver of Kristin's commitment to ELIJAH. She and her husband, Victor, an immigrant from Mexico, attend All People's Church, an ELIJAH-affiliated, inner-ring suburban, multiracial Presbyterian congregation that is heavily steeped in anticolonial and antiracist theology. They, along with many other people from their church, are deeply involved in ELIJAH. In our interview, Kristin remarked, "I pretty much have experienced the truth in that scripture where Jesus says, 'Ye shall know the truth and the truth will set you free.'" She chuckled as she explained, "I grew up with a lot of Bible knowledge, unlike my husband, which is okay . . . but yeah, a lot of Bible knowledge."

After mentioning her Bible knowledge, Kristin immediately moved on to describe how all that knowledge didn't end up meaning much until she found her current church after graduating from college. "For me over the last, I'd say, ten years really, there's been a lot of transformation of my understanding of what those scriptures are saying." Kristin says she has grown into a fuller understanding of scriptures' meaning through her involvement in a congregation that takes race seriously and her marriage to a person of color. Notably, it is through *personal* work, learning to share openly and truthfully, rather than hiding her problems, that this transformation has come about. Kristin explained how, unlike in childhood, she now finds meaning in confessing her troubles to others. "Confessing even those really uncomfortable and hard things is freeing. It makes space for a greater transformation as well as a more helpful future, so being able to be like, "Oh yeah, I am dysfunctional," or "I'm anxious," or "My family has benefited from white supremacy because people don't judge us, don't exclude us based on how we look even though we are immigrants."[14]

Through exposure to new theology, new social perspectives, and a culture focused on relational practices that encourage being open about her troubles, Kristin learned how to make sense of her past and envision a "helpful future" in which she is unburdened by the interpersonal risks she previously associated with sharing details about her life. Since they reveal her family's earlier precarity, its hidden but shared struggle with nonwhite immigrants, those details are key to Kristin's ability to empathize with others and make them empathize with her. The act of confessing helps her broaden her interests and form meaningful relationships with people who are different from her, rather than hiding in a shell like she used to. Without sharing her struggles, she could not be an effective organizer or, as she now says, an authentic, biblically minded Christian.

Thanks to her church and the practices of testimony and confession she learned there and in ELIJAH, Kristin now recognizes how she has been harmed by immigration policy but also has benefited from white supremacy. She can acknowledge that her own struggles matter even though others may have struggled more. Instead of ranking different people's problems—what she calls "playing oppression olympics"—she focuses on their shared sources: white supremacy and corporate greed. She aims her religious passion at these sources and asks others to share their stories so they might learn to do the same. The life story that Kristin recounts is a sophisticated sociological biography that answers C. Wright Mills's famous call to "make the familiar strange."[15] Teachers in introductory sociology courses often ask their students to think of their lives like this, but Kristin has never taken a sociology course. Neither, she explains, could her Bible knowledge support this kind of nuanced thinking on its own. Kristin needed Bible knowledge *and* immersion in the culture, theology, and practices of her church to reach a point where she could make sense of her past, present, and future in a way that felt right. Her moral vocation was seeded in scripture, but it sprouted in relationships with other people and the relational practices she learned as a young adult.

This journey of personal growth, learning to negotiate conflicting feelings of victimization and guilt and channel them into productive work with others, forms the backbone of the future Kristin envisions for herself and others. When I asked her what she hoped ELIJAH might achieve in the future, she turned the conversation back to her own development, explaining her ambition to keep growing as an authentic moral actor willing to take risks and be uncomfortable. In particular, she mentioned becoming even less afraid to acknowledge white people's role in sustaining racial hierarchies. "Success would be continuing to hone my own voice and not being afraid to interrupt a conversation that is . . ." She trailed off as she considered how to say what she meant. When she picked up again, she connected her *personal* ambition to interrupt problematic conversations to a *shared* project of racial consciousness among white people. "I think what I mean is to stop not taking responsibility for our own shit, kind of thing." Switching from "my own voice" to "our own shit," she revealed that her personal moral vocation has become inextricably entangled with a collective project that involves challenging other white people to see race and racism better.

It is telling that when I asked Kristin what she hoped ELIJAH would be like in the future, she pivoted back to the personal, suggesting that success depends on individuals like her pushing past interpersonal risk. Her moral vocation centers her ambition to continue pushing against white people's impulse to "not take responsibility for their own shit." This involves developing the personal courage to interrupt conversations in which white people fail to acknowledge their own roles in perpetuating social problems or the ways they have benefited from white supremacy. Kristin wanted to keep learning how to better support her husband and other people of color without failing to acknowledge how, even as a white person, she too has been affected by dehumanizing immigration policies. She explained, "There are times where my inclination, being a white woman married to a man of color . . . is to try and step back. . . . In some environments, people are really more inclined to say, 'Oh, let's have Victor speak about this,' or 'Let's have Victor be here participating in this thing, in leadership.' Which I affirm. But I think I want to not be afraid of also speaking strongly about these things because I don't think it's just people of color that need to be speaking about racism." She sees ELIJAH's collective success as dependent on the continued personal work done by her and other white people to take racism seriously.

In explaining her personal growth as a Christian and an activist, Kristin started by talking about Bible knowledge and ended by discussing racial justice in language similar to what one might hear in an antiracism primer: language focused on acknowledging and being willing to answer for one's whiteness and making sure people of color don't bear the burden of dismantling white supremacy. Her moral vocation is deeply rooted in her own faith and centered on scripture, as one would expect from a Protestant. But in Kristin's case this vocation has pushed past the cultural barriers to thinking critically about race and social structure that white Protestant culture often imposes.[16] Kristin's experiences—her childhood as a white immigrant, her marriage to a man of color, her participation in her church and ELIJAH—combine to support an attachment to moral citizenship that for her is deeply rooted in the Bible but for others may come from various authority sources. Her focus on personal moral growth, based in her own unique experiences and capacities—that is, her moral vocation—both affirms her personal faith and connects her with others who think differently about what social justice means and how to achieve it. It empowers her to take on the interpersonal risks that Reverend Andrews spoke of in his sermon: confronting others and interrogating her past.

## Margaret

Like Kristin, Margaret is a white woman, but their similarities end there. Margaret is Catholic, childless, divorced, thirty years older than Kristin, and lives alone in a suburban townhouse. Unlike Kristin, she does not readily talk about race (she never mentioned it in our interview), and she has had to work hard to avoid instinctively backing away from ELIJAH, where she deals with significant interpersonal risks on a regular basis. I met her on the day of her first activity with ELIJAH, a voter turnout "deep canvass" before the November 2016 election. In most voter turnout drives, canvassers simply tell residents where and when to vote and ask them to commit to showing up on election day. But in this case, ELIJAH canvassers had been told to ask neighborhood residents why they did or didn't plan to vote, what issues they had been dealing with in the neighborhood lately, and whether they had any stories they wanted to share about finances or debt. The idea was to infuse traditional voter turnout operations with the relational practice of exchanging stories so that the people involved—both the door knockers and the residents in the poor neighborhood they were visiting—would get the sense that they were being engaged as humans, not mere tallies in a vote column. Ultimately, ELIJAH hoped to follow up with some of the residents and get them to tell their stories publicly at upcoming meetings about payday lending and predatory auto and medical loans.

This deep canvassing was more than Margaret had bargained for. Eager to help elect Hillary Clinton, she had signed up thinking this was a normal voter turnout operation, like those she'd been part of with other organizations. Instead, she was given a detailed script that was much more demanding. It involved lingering at people's doors for several minutes instead of only a moment, asking people about their experiences and stories and sharing hers with them. She was visibly fatigued and overwhelmed during the debrief afterward. When I struck up a conversation with her in the parking lot as we headed back to our cars, she told me she was glad she'd come but wasn't sure she'd be back.

Margaret did come back for more work with ELIJAH (though no more deep canvasses), but it wasn't easy for her. In an in-depth interview a few months after we met, she told me that it had been hard to get used to ELIJAH's emphasis on sharing deeply personal details and experiences. She has long been involved with liberal political causes, particularly gun violence and climate change, but the interpersonal risks involved in ELIJAH's work continue to shake her. She explained, "I don't have a problem meeting new people, or talking to people; I enjoy that, but I have this thing, nervousness or apprehension I guess, doing phone banks, and with doors, like especially that first day when we met, I don't know who's on the other side of that door. I don't mean in a fearful way, like they're going to do something to me, but more in a they're going to reject me way, before they have a chance to listen to what I have to say. . . . I guess that's my fear, that rejection component of it."

A few minutes later in the interview, when I asked what challenges she dealt with in ELIJAH, Margaret returned to interpersonal risk. She said she worries about imposing on people when she tries to recruit them for an ELIJAH task. "That's been the biggest challenge for me, that in ELIJAH they want you to not just show up yourself but reach out to other people, too. I don't even know that many other people in the first place, so that's one issue, but even if I did reach out to other people, if I had the opportunity . . . I probably wouldn't, because I feel like I'm imposing on them." ELIJAH wants her to be an organizer, but Margaret would prefer to be a "worker bee," as she described it. She is eager to attend meetings and do some tasks herself, but not thrilled about taking the interpersonal risks involved with asking others to join her. ELIJAH leaders consistently push her for more, arguing that real power cannot arise from individuals doing things independently but depends on inviting others into the work and forming lasting relationships.

Similar to Kristin, Margaret manages these risks and pushes through them by thinking of her work with ELIJAH in reference to challenges that have plagued her throughout her life, though her challenges are different from Kristin's. Margaret conceptualizes her moral vocation on the basis of her objection to the ways churches she attended in the past avoided engagement with social problems. She described having "been to a lot of Catholic churches over my lifetime, and I've been involved in a church in different aspects, but it was mainly just, oh, we're having a food drive, or we're having this or that. . . . It was very removed from what people really needed. There was not a human connection; it was mainly just donating things."

This experience of parish cultures that, in her opinion, ignored Catholic social teaching left Margaret with an empty feeling that grew throughout her life as she realized how ineffective charity and donations were for addressing society's systemic problems. Now, she sees working in ELIJAH as a way to feel better about the relative lack of engagement with social justice in her past. She explained, "You know, this is very, like, un-Christian of me, but the goal [of being part of ELIJAH] is to make me feel better first, because I've, it makes me feel better to know that I'm really making a difference, compared to the stuff I did in churches I went to before. And then only secondary to that is the feeling that I am doing something good for other people." Aligning with Christian Smith's assessment of much of contemporary American religion as therapeutic, Margaret reveals that ELIJAH is part therapy for her, helping make up for a past in which she and her churches didn't do much to confront social problems.[17]

Yet it is ironic that Margaret describes this approach to ELIJAH as un-Christian, because such an approach is foundational to the philosophy of faith-based community organizing. While Margaret's interest in making herself feel better is not the same as Kristin's interest in raising racial consciousness among white people to combat white supremacy, their interests nevertheless align and support working on the same kinds of projects. Moreover, this feeling of being driven by one's own story, not just concern for others, is precisely the attitude that ELIJAH leaders want to cultivate among people like Margaret, as chapter 4 will explain in more detail. When people are motivated by altruism, it is easy for them to dip in and out of social justice work according to whim and convenience. Lacking a personal stake, people can easily slide into bad organizing habits, like promising more than they can deliver, backing out of commitments, or failing to interrogate their own biases and assumptions.[18] Organizing scholar Mark Warren argues that only when there is something on the line for them personally can white people become true partners to those engaged in struggles for racial equality.[19] Rather than thinking of racial justice work as "the right thing to do" for other people, they must embrace the cause as their own. Margaret, in a roundabout way, has done this, even though her language for it is inexplicit.

Margaret's moral vocation, geared toward overcoming and accounting for what she sees as a past in which she was insufficiently socially engaged, centers her own personal growth in the work, gives her a stake in it, and moves her to push beyond the interpersonal challenges involved. She is not an antiracist firebrand like Kristin. She never will be, and that is okay, both for her and for ELIJAH. One does not have to be fluent in the language of activism to be welcome and effective in the group. One must only be willing to put one's self on the line, dedicated to growing and learning through relationships with others. By skillfully tapping Margaret's moral vocation and teaching her to orient it toward justice work, ELIJAH leaders have brought her to this point.

## Samuel

Samuel is an infectiously friendly Black man who grew up in South Chicago in the 1980s. These days, he owns a barbershop and works as an organizer for ELIJAH, having joined the staff in 2017 after several years as a volunteer leader. He meandered into religious life beginning in the mid-2000s, when he finally opened up to a longtime barbershop client, a pastor who came in twice a month and sometimes brought his kids in for haircuts, too. Samuel's past included time in prison, "boozing and womanizing," and other details he thought might send a pastor looking for a different barber, so he had never shared too much about his personal life with this particular customer. But one day that all changed. As Samuel described it to me, "I was having a tough time that day and he sat down and I just started venting like, man . . . [he paused] my life is, I'm not happy. I got a brand-new home, I got a brand-new vehicle, good job, good income cutting hair, but me and my wife . . . My son, half the time I don't know where he's at, he's been disobedient, I had to discipline him a few times, doesn't seem to be working, his grades are slipping." Samuel didn't know it at the time, but he had just revealed the first seedlings of his moral vocation—seedlings that would be carefully cultivated by ELIJAH leaders in the coming years. A dissatisfaction with his family life and a feeling he was failing as a father led him to reflect on how markers of material success—a good, stable job; a new home; a new car—had given him only an illusion of happiness. He needed something more.

The client in the chair that day was Pastor Al, head pastor of New Kingdom Church and an ELIJAH stalwart, a man who would later serve as ELIJAH's president. Pastor Al saw an opportunity in Samuel's venting. Samuel recalled, "So he said to me, 'You said all of these things, but you never mentioned God.' And then he said, 'You know what I'm gonna do? Come Friday I'm gonna come by your house; can you make sure that your wife and your younger son is there?' I said, 'Yeah, I can.' From that point on, and I tell you no lie, he introduced me to God, officially introduced me to God . . . and there was a change that started very slowly, gradually, but noticeable, as far as what my understanding of manhood was, what my understanding of being a husband was, what my understanding of fatherhood was."

Under Pastor Al's guidance, Samuel regained a sense of control in his family life through his conversion to Christianity and engagement in the congregation at New Kingdom. The meanings of family began to expand for him as he developed new understandings of his roles as husband and father. But after a few years, he still felt confused and conflicted about his past, unsure how to reconcile his now peaceful, prosperous, suburban lifestyle with the pain he knew his childhood friends from Chicago were still experiencing as they popped in and out of prison and struggled to support themselves and their families. These conflicted emotions were still bothering him in 2013, when Steph, a Black leader in ELIJAH who also ministered at New Kingdom, gave him a copy of Michelle Alexander's *The New Jim Crow* and invited him to attend a discussion she was leading on it.

As Samuel recalled, "[At that time] I'd been, you know, following Pastor Al around ELIJAH a bit, going to the capitol, going to a few meetings, but really not engaged yet. But this book shot off so many different epiphanies in my head about the validation of what the narrative was, around my neighborhood where I grew up in Chicago, that me and my guys, you know, we were being targeted [by the police], you know, things didn't seem to be fair. Well, actually they were unfair, and we just didn't have the language for it at the time. So what that book did was give validation to the narratives that we heard around our neighborhood, you know, just the talk on the corners." Samuel continued, "Well, we would dismiss it because we never had any references to go to. And now I had documentation of the things we felt and what we talked about. This book validated the fact that there are systemic oppressions out there, there is a setup going on, we are being targeted . . . and so I really got grounded in the fact that this is the work that I need to be doing."

Reflecting on his youth, when Samuel and his friends suspected they were being targeted unfairly by the police but lacked a language for explaining how this might work, Samuel found validation and a call to action in the combination of New Kingdom's culture, his sporadic work with Pastor Al in ELIJAH, and Steph's invitation into Alexander's analysis. Captivated by his growing understanding of the systematic oppression of people of color through the criminal justice system, he was recruited by Pastor Al and Steph into deeper engagement in ELIJAH's work on criminal justice reform, which at the time was focused on opposing the expansion of private prisons and restoring voting rights to the formerly incarcerated. His conversion to Christianity was the start of his path into activism, but his increasing involvement was not driven directly by religious beliefs or ideology. Instead, it was a product of how his membership in the community at New Kingdom intersected with his lived experience growing up poor and over-policed to illuminate possibilities for transforming his understandings of fatherhood, marriage, and masculinity.

Like Kristin and Margaret, Samuel had to overcome numerous interpersonal risks to become a full-fledged ELIJAH leader. First, he had to share his troubles with Pastor Al in the barbershop. This snap decision ignited his transition into a culture where sharing was seen as strength, not weakness. Even now, Samuel regards the moment when he gathered the courage to open up to Pastor Al as providential, the turning point in his life, and he takes it as a lesson that one should never feel ashamed about sharing one's troubles. Yet even after his religious conversion and his initial foray into ELIJAH, Samuel was plagued by guilt about his childhood—not the criminal behavior he'd engaged in but the fact that so many of his friends had not escaped the cycle of incarceration like he had. He managed this guilt at first by thinking about it as little as possible and using sex, alcohol, and material items to salve his pain. Even as he shed his addictions and regained control of his family life following his conversion, he struggled with the stark contrast between his success and his friends' struggles. It took skilled leaders, Steph and Pastor Al, and an inspiring text, The New Jim Crow, to kindle a sense of empowerment within Samuel to do something about the conditions that had kept him down earlier and were keeping his friends down now. Before he could become an activist leader, and subsequently an

ELIJAH organizer, he had to learn to take the risk of grappling with his past instead of ignoring it.

## Bringing Distinct Vocations Together

Besides being leaders in ELIJAH, Kristin, Margaret, and Samuel have almost nothing in common. They come from different faith traditions—white mainline Protestantism, Catholicism, and Black evangelical Protestantism. They have different economic backgrounds: precarious but mostly manageable for Kristin, privileged for Margaret, poverty for Samuel. They are different ages. Kristin was thirty at the time of interview, Margaret was sixty-three, and Samuel was forty-five. Their pasts are different, and their present identities are, too. Kristin is a full-fledged activist. She embraces the languages of intersectionality and racial justice and pushes others to do the same. Margaret, in contrast, is a quiet woman who gives no signs of being attuned to activist culture or language. She believes in Catholic social teaching but has not translated her core religious precepts into contemporary progressive activist language like Kristin has. Samuel, meanwhile, embraces activism but arrived there in an unconventional way compared to many of today's movement leaders. His commitment to social change is firmly rooted in his spiritual rebirth as an evangelical Christian. He is theologically and culturally conservative but sees activism for economic fairness and racial justice as completely in line with the precepts and traditions of his faith, to such a degree that he now works for ELIJAH. Yet across these differences, these three ELIJAH leaders not only cooperate but identify as members of the same community of moral citizens. This is only possible because these individuals have each developed a religiously inflected—but not religiously exclusive—story about how they came to be involved in ELIJAH and what motivates them to continue. The stories blend seamlessly across their different cultural contexts because they highlight how each has fought to overcome interpersonal risks that previously prevented them from seeing the world as it really is and getting involved in work to change it.

The life stories that ELIJAH leaders like Kristin, Margaret, and Samuel have developed are prime examples of what Oyakawa calls "politicized personal narratives."[20] They construct moral citizenship as a means of fulfilling a moral vocation to which one feels powerfully called, even if that call was partially obscured until ELIJAH's relational practices illuminated it. Because they are powerful ways to connect faith symbols—Bible knowledge for Kristin, Catholic social teaching for Margaret, conversion and the Bible for Samuel—with broader public ambitions, such personal life stories are central to the work of FBCO federations.

Previous research highlights the role personal stories like these play in motivating people's involvement in activism, but my argument goes further.[21] Moral vocation is not just a matter of *personal* identity work, charting and evaluating one's own life. It is also the foundation for *collective* relational practices that spark reflection, discussion, and ultimately solidarity about how difficult it can be to push past personal and interpersonal risks. Stories like Kristin's, Margaret's, and Samuel's matter because they can form the basis for public, collaborative discussions of what each person has at stake in social change work, providing a means of moving past altruism and revealing that different people's life projects depend on the struggle for a more just society. Relational practices can also demonstrate, publicly and convincingly, that people's distinct self-stories are linked through social structure. When done well, such practices make the ongoing project of pushing past one's fears, risks, and hesitations—whatever those may be—into a cornerstone for group solidarity, as people in the group come to recognize one another as fellow travelers on the path toward enacting moral vocations through shared embrace of moral citizenship.

"My Pain Is Your Pain"

A powerful example of how relational practices that invite people to publicly discuss their vocation stories can foster solidarity took place a couple hours after Reverend Andrews's stirring sermon at the leadership assembly. Kristin teamed up with Cyrus, the Black Catholic man with the drum from chapter 1, and Ariana, a Latina Catholic in her twenties, to lead an exercise designed to make people think about their moral vocations and how they were connected with one another. As with the earlier sermon, the theme was overcoming personal and interpersonal risks.

The group was again seated in a circle when Kristin began introducing the exercise. Returning to elements of the story she had raised in our interview, she said, "When I think about disruption, there's two struggles and challenges that I face. As a white woman, first of all, I'm afraid of being a patronizing do-gooder. Perhaps it would be better if I sit silently by, because then I'm respecting others' leadership, right? To overcome that lie, I have to take a good hard look at my own life and recognize the ways the systems of our society have hurt me and hurt those I love. And that's painful. It's hard. My family migrated to the U.S. from Canada when I was six years old. Throughout my childhood, I saw the exploitation of my father as a worker. Time and time again."

Kristin continued, crying by now, the pain of publicly processing her shame and guilt written on her face as tears trickled down it. "Our status in this country, and our livelihood, was dependent on one contracting company leasing my father's labor to different computer companies, and those companies didn't care if the pager interrupted our family dinner, or when overtime went unclaimed because my father didn't want to rock the boat. My father had no control outside of our household, so he poured his identity into being the best father that he could. Which was a pretty great dad. But seeing how much he needed that, I absorbed for twenty-odd years the responsibility of being the perfect child. Because maybe, by being perfect, I could save my dad's dignity, which had been taken away from him over and over. And I'm not successful! And I'm convinced . . . Still I struggle with being convinced that I have already failed my dad and myself. There's been a lot of reflection in my life that has helped me kind of overcome that and release myself from that responsibility, because it's too much for me to carry alone. But this self-reflection is hard and painful, and recognizing my own pain quickly leads into a second lie. A lie that my struggles aren't as hard as fill-in-the-blank's. So I should be grateful that I had it so easy."

Kristin was moving from sadness to anger, her voice morphing from regretful to righteously acerbic. "It is a *lie*," she shouted vehemently, stressing key words, "that I should be *grateful* for the ways that I have *benefited* from white supremacy in this country, and not make a fuss about how this system is *tearing us all apart*. Following the rules quietly was how my family coped with this indignity, even though the rules have always been unjust." Her voice quieted again a little as she channeled her anger into a more reflective mood. "But I'm done following these rules. Because these rules, they oppress us all. And though it's scary, I know that my freedom is dependent on all of our freedoms. And when I can take responsibility and speak clearly about the ways it has hurt me, that makes me a more honest ally with my friends, with my colleagues. So each of us has to do this work ourselves, and not compare it to each other, but say how my pain is your pain. It's manifested in different ways, but we can work together to bring healing."

Often during speeches and stories at ELIJAH events, people nod along or interject "Amen" or "That's right," encouraging the speaker with their words and bodies. But the room was dead silent and perfectly still as Kristin wrapped up her moving narrative. In less than three minutes, she had told her life story and how her moral vocation had evolved over its course; situated her own struggles in a context that linked immigration, socioeconomic challenges, and racism; and passionately argued that the "rules" so many people fear breaking are really key elements of the structures that uphold injustice in the world. Kristin, as a white woman, had long struggled against the idea that disruption was not what people like her should be doing. She said that even now, disruption gave her pause, that it was "painful" and "hard," because if she avoids it, she can take the easy way out, accepting the appealing but ultimately damaging premise that people like her should "sit silently by" and let others lead. But deep down, she knows it is a fiction that white people can sit out of disruption, and she asserts that living according to this fiction increases the burden on people of color and upholds a "system that is tearing us all apart." Thus, a life without disruption abdicates her true religious calling, and by pushing past the risks associated with disruption, she can live up to her moral vocation.

After Kristin had finished speaking, still trembling with emotion, she handed the microphone to Ariana, who had been standing next to her the whole time. As Kristin caught her breath, Ariana told the group it was time for some silent reflection. She handed out pens and sheets of paper with three questions printed at the top. Each was designed to prompt respondents into thinking about how disruption—both the fear of it and the need for it—fit into their own moral vocation.

1. What will I lose if we do not disrupt the system?
2. What am I afraid of in participating in disruption?
3. I believe in disruption because . . .

Once the materials had been distributed, people sat in silence, thinking and writing, for what seemed like a long time but was really only about six minutes. When they had finished, Kristin led a sharing session that asked people to state how disruption fit into their own life stories. She said, "As people of faith, we come from a long tradition of testimony and prophecy, calling out the empire and calling out ourselves. And we also come together through song. So we're going to mix the two together and do a call and response sharing session using the song 'Wade in the Water.' I chose this song because in my Christian faith tradition there's an idea of baptism providing cleansing and purity. And in our history there's a metaphor, with this song as a spiritual, of water providing freedom. So we're going to call each other to wade into the water and know that we are not alone in this process. So pick one of your thoughts and share one sentence at a time. . . . When you feel called, you'll stand up and read your response to one of the prompts you just reflected on. And then in response, Ariana will lead us in singing 'wade in the water, God's gonna trouble the water.' We're gonna sing the chorus one time to start, and Cyrus will help us out. So please share your truth with this group, so we can all testify together."

Cyrus, sitting in his chair in the circle, began playing his drum. Ariana and Kristin, still standing in the center, joined him as he sang, "Wade in the water, wade in the water, children, wade in the water, God's gonna trouble the water." Nobody spoke up after the first refrain, so the three leaders sang another, beckoning for people to join in. After the third refrain, people started speaking their responses to the questions Ariana had distributed, hesitantly at first, then with more confidence. Each statement was followed by a refrain of "Wade in the Water," the collective voices providing reassurance and solidarity to help people overcome the challenges of speaking publicly and sharing their stories.

Nearly two dozen people spoke in all during the exercise, and their statements provide a compelling illustration of how people in ELIJAH build solidarity by emphasizing how each person's moral vocation leads to a need to disrupt unjust social systems. I provide many of the statements here, grouping them into themes and then explaining how the themes cohere in ELIJAH's larger project. What is important here is how, as in the vocation stories of Kristin, Margaret, and Samuel, the statements reflect different belief systems; different racial, ethnic, class, and cultural backgrounds; and different political priorities. Yet by making personal courage in the face of fears about disruption the center of the exercise, Kristin and Ariana streamlined the group across all these dimensions of difference and oriented everyone present toward the shared goal of embracing moral citizenship by disrupting business as usual in the region's economic and political spheres.

LOSS

With Cyrus drumming and humming in the background, the first person to speak up was a Latino who spoke in Spanish through an interpreter. He said, "If we don't disrupt, immigration laws are going to be tightened and enforced in unjust ways and our children will be deported." This statement reflects the first key theme: loss. Besides him, four others spoke about threats of loss or actual losses, suggesting that if they don't engage in disruption, there will be consequences for them or those they love. A Black woman chimed in, "I need to disrupt because if I don't I will lose out on my grandsons accomplishing out of life what they deserve." Another Latino man lamented the difference between what he had been told about the United States and how it actually worked, saying, "I was afraid of disruption because as an immigrant I was told, You came to this country, love it or leave it. So I loved it for a long time, but then it ruined my life and my family's life and took away everything we had." A white man said, "I believe we need disruption because without it, we will continue to feel oppressed and be oppressed." Finally, a Latina woman asserted, "We need to be disrupting because if we don't, we lose our freedom as self-sustaining people."

These speakers conceptualized disruption as a way to prevent loss. Notably, they were not the same kinds or degrees of losses; potential deportation of one's children and the experience of everything being taken away are more imminent and tactile things than, say, "losing our freedom as self-sustaining people." But amid the statements' variations, the same logic underpinned all of them: personal engagement in the risky practice of disruption was important to prevent people and communities from losing the things they valued.

## TRADITION

Other speakers envisioned disruption as a way to align themselves with tradition. The specific types of tradition they mentioned varied: some spoke about racial and ethnic traditions, others about religious traditions, others about passing on values to their children. A Black woman stated, "I believe it's so important that we disrupt things according to our stories, to what we've experienced." Clearly, she valued the tradition of disruption in the Black community and wanted to finish the task that Black leaders from earlier periods in history, such as slavery and the civil rights era, had started. A white man also nodded to prior courageous figures, saying, "We need disruption in order to honor the countless people who have gone before us and created a path where we can create a system that's better." A white woman invoked a more explicitly Christian understanding of tradition: "I'm not afraid of disruption if it holds to eternal values and eternal truths. We have to disrupt human things so that we can bring the eternal things, the kingdom as God wills it to exist on earth as well as in heaven." For another white woman, disruption was about preserving tradition into the future: "I have to be courageous in disruption in order to teach my young boys to be better, to do better, and to make the world better."

## PERSONAL INTEGRITY

For a third group of speakers, disruption was a way to preserve personal integrity. An Indian American woman in her early thirties said, "If I do not help disrupt the system, I will lose my integrity as someone who believes in Catholic social teaching." A Latina used similar logic, declaring, "I believe we need disruption because this is the only way for my soul to be pure and for me to be seen." Both of these speakers felt that a failure to disrupt would compromise their integrity as religious actors. Steve, a white man and the Northeast Suburban organizer we met in chapter 2, echoed their logic, but for him, it was racial equality more than religious authenticity that was at stake: "If I don't participate in disruption, I'm reinforcing a lie. For the white suburban leaders I work with and for my daughter. That if you're white, you're all right, and the best thing to do is just go along. And that's what put me in a spiritual hole for a long time." By suggesting that disruption is necessary for living up to Catholic social teaching and for keeping one's soul pure, many speakers framed it as an inextricable element of their moral vocations. In contrast, Steve (who is also Catholic) asserted that participating in disruption is essential to avoid upholding white supremacy by "just going along" with unjust social structures and patterns. But for all these speakers, disruption was a way to preserve personal integrity amid the cultural challenges of modern life.

## BEING SILENCED

A fourth theme among speakers' remarks was the fear of being silenced or not having one's voice heard. A Black woman proclaimed, "My fears around disruption is that it won't work, nothing will change, or my voice won't be taken seriously and it won't be heard." A white man agreed, saying, "We need disruption because no one will pay attention to you unless you raise your voice and the intensity of your actions." A few speakers later, another white man expressed something similar: "I believe in disruption because it's the only way we're going to be able to get the people in power to listen to us."

## UNITY

Finally, a fifth group of speakers explicitly saw disruption as necessary for achieving some form of unity across races, faiths, or cultures. A Black man expressed this as follows: "I believe in disruption because we all suffer in some kind of way, and what's not best for everyone needs to be changed to be best for everybody." For him, achieving good for everyone required acknowledging that everyone suffers, a disruption of the status quo idea that life is secure for many people, especially whites, as Steve had said earlier. A white woman similarly declared, "We need disruption because it's a nonviolent way to bring about change and justice for all." A white man sitting next to her—he might have been her husband—elaborated. He said, "We need disruption because we need to provide a political space that allows mutual fairness and dialogue for all of us." Finally, a Latina explicitly addressed racial unity, stating, "I believe in disruption because I feel like we cannot continue to be a threat. Not white people, not people of color, not Latinos, we have to raise our voices so that doesn't happen."

Nearly an hour had passed from the start of Kristin's passionate speech until the end of the exercise, when everyone who wanted to speak had done so. People in the circle looked tired but encouraged. Remarkably, the drumming and singing had continued the whole time. In fact, the collective act of singing was essential to the exercise. It drew on a familiar song, one with Christian roots but culturally associated with Black emancipation, to bolster the uncomfortable act of testifying about one's fears with the comfortable aura of shared engagement and collective reassurance. The ostinato of Cyrus's drum and the repeated collective voice made this more than a sequence of individual stories; it was an immersive, shared experience.

With this ritual, Kristin, Ariana, and Cyrus were trying to get people to reveal their fears, desires, motivations, and struggles, so that the whole group would see that everyone present had challenges to overcome and could benefit from disruption in some way. They achieved this by fostering an atmosphere that got people talking about different kinds of cultural commitments and framed them as equally valid reasons to care about disruption. People's remarks revealed distinct moral vocations rooted in different ways of understanding religious commitment. Shared religious commitment and an immersive religious practice facilitated overcoming these differences, but crucially, it was not religious belief that mattered. Instead, it was the shared cultural project of moral vocation. Who were the people in this room? During this exercise, they were first and foremost people working together to overcome their own personal risks and live out their own personal stories. By realizing this collectively, they could also become people embracing moral citizenship together.

## Constructing Vocation Together

ELIJAH leaders believe that collective power for social change can only develop when there is shared meaning at its heart. Creating such meaning requires overcoming deep interpersonal risks: the risks of sharing deep feelings, talking about hard subjects, and shaking off cultural schemas that divide people. Cultural practices focused on moral vocation, like the "Wade in the Water" exercise, provide a mechanism for doing this. Previous literature on organizing among constituencies as diverse as ELIJAH's largely argues that the primary task is to bring members of different social groups to see similarities in their economic and political interests. The case of ELIJAH, however, demonstrates the importance of moral vocation and relational practices in this process. Such practices, more than discussion of beliefs or texts, are what makes its work feel religiously authentic and meaningful across multiple traditions; this, more than discussion of economic or political interests, is what makes its social change work possible.

This chapter has provided answers to some key questions about how FBCO federations like ELIJAH use religion to support their social change projects. Focusing on vocation more than belief, they foster a cultural atmosphere that acknowledges different kinds of motivations for involvement, portrays them as equally valid, and depicts them as calls to push past the interpersonal risks that inhibit broadening one's interests and fostering relationships. But important questions still remain. How do leaders tie this sense of group solidarity, rooted in individuals' vocations and collective affirmation of these, to a collective understanding of what it means to be religious in a world plagued by deep inequalities? How does this way of building solidarity shape the practical political work that ELIJAH is able to do? And what challenges, both foreseen and unforeseen by organizers, might it bring? Chapters 4–6 take up these questions in turn.

"Activism is still not my niche. It's just not really my thing."

It was a bracingly cold January afternoon, and I was surprised by what Lydia, sitting with me in a small café overlooking a frozen lake, was saying. A tall thirty-four-year-old white woman with a piercing gaze, Lydia had been a frequent presence at ELIJAH events throughout my research. She had spoken at each of the half dozen or so Northeast Suburban meetings I'd been to, along with some leadership assemblies and strategy sessions. I had made sure to set up an interview with her because from the start of my time with ELIJAH, she had seemed like a central figure, particularly in climate justice work. I had started the interview expecting to hear why she embraced being an activist, not that it wasn't her "niche."

Her niche or not, Lydia does a lot of social justice work. The thing is that she doesn't see it as activism. Rather, she sees it as a religious duty—not something set apart from her spiritual life but a routine at the very core of it. The word *activism* typically connotes being different from the mainstream, rejecting at least some components of a normal life to take principled stands that go against conventional wisdom. By this standard, though, Lydia's involvement in ELIJAH barely qualifies, if at all. For her, engagement in social change work is a set of normal activities—not unusual or irregular extensions of her faith but regular religious practice.

As we drank our coffees, Lydia told me about her life and the evolution of her faith through a series of personal crises. She described a process of gradually coming to see moral citizenship as a religious duty—something she needed to do for herself, not for other people. She had learned, gradually, that her identity as a Christian, as a woman, and as a member of a democratic society depended on working with others to advance common interests—interests that she, while privileged in certain ways as a middle-class white person, shared with those who were harmed more directly by economic and racial inequalities. In this regard, Lydia is a prime specimen of the kind of activist that ELIJAH trains people to become because she has come to view struggles for racial and socioeconomic equity as her own. But Lydia did not always see these projects as being part of her self-interest. She had to learn this perspective through sustained engagement in relational practices in ELIJAH and in her home congregation.

Expanding from Lydia's example, this chapter explains the construction of self-interest in ELIJAH through relational practices. Through one-to-one conversations, storytelling, and other activities, people in ELIJAH learn to see their interests broadly, becoming collaborators in moral citizenship and pursuing projects whose benefits accrue to all.

Lydia was raised as a conservative evangelical in a small, almost entirely white Midwestern farming town. Her parents divorced when she was young, and religion soothed her resulting loneliness. "Early in high school, I really started to pursue my faith, and an evangelical kind of faith, which was compelling to me because it was said Jesus can be close to you. God can be close to you. You can have an intimate relationship." She described being uneasy about the teaching that some people were bound for hell, but she took comfort in her personal relationship with God and decided to spend her days "making sure as few people end up going to hell as possible."

In hopes of continuing her growth as a Christian, Lydia chose a small Bible college about two hours from her childhood home, but while there, doubts about her faith deepened. Concern about the idea of hell ate away at her, and she struggled to find joy and excitement in her religious life. "I just couldn't feel what I was told I should be feeling about salvation and faith. I was like, 'I'm supposed to be really happy about this and excited, but I feel like I'm fabricating it, and I don't see the fruit of the spirit in my life.' So I was kind of pursuing that, didn't know what to do with it, was going to different churches trying to figure it out, trying to find mentors. And it was about that time that I went to South Korea to teach English. I had graduated college, still asking the same questions, still trying to pursue this intimacy with God that I didn't quite know how to have."

When she got back from Korea, Lydia was still searching for religious confidence. "I thought, 'I have to find out how the good news is good news to me, because it doesn't feel like good news right now.'" She returned to the city where she'd gone to college and started looking for a church that could help her resolve the doubt that had now been plaguing her for years. She found it at All People's Church, an ELIJAH-affiliated Presbyterian congregation in an immigrant-heavy inner-ring suburb, the same church Kristin, from chapter 3, attends. Lydia was first attracted to All People's because it had a significant Korean American community and a Korean American pastor. She wanted to continue the connection she had made with Korean culture and language while abroad. But All People's turned out to be not just a Korean church. Korean Americans were the largest part of its membership, but no one ethnic group made up more than a third of the congregation, and there were significant numbers of Native Americans, Latin Americans, and immigrants from Africa and other parts of Asia, as well as a few white people. Unlike every other church she'd tried, this was a place where racial and ethnic difference was not only visible all the time but also a constant topic of discussion and analysis. The Korean influence, diversity, and joyous atmosphere drew her in.

Lydia took quickly to her new church environment. She found the diversity stimulating and felt appreciated and welcomed in a way she had never been in her previous all-white evangelical congregations. But the first significant conversation she had with her pastor at All People's surprised her. "I was telling him about my doubts. I was like, 'I don't feel close to God, and I don't know how to get there.' He said two things. First thing he said was, 'Tell me about your family.' I was like, 'That's dumb. I'm trying to have a real conversation with you here that's deep, and you want to make small talk about my family.' The other thing he said was, 'When I look at you, I see hundreds of years of Western civilization.' For someone like me who didn't know anything about history or my own culture or background, I had no idea what he was talking about."

Lydia was taken aback by her pastor's questions about her family and then his mention of Western civilization. This oblique reference to her whiteness was the first taste of a message that goaded her at first but that she would come to hear regularly and eventually embrace: to really understand herself and God, she needed to make sense of how whiteness had shaped her and how other people's racial and ethnic backgrounds had shaped them. Lydia had grown up learning that once a person came to know God, it didn't matter what kind of family they came from or what their culture or background was. Hearing her new pastor insist on the opposite was jarring. "I was like, 'Huh, that's weird. That's not how it's supposed to work. You're talking about subjective experience, but one's understanding of God should be objective.'" The idea that a person's racial background mattered for how they experienced God ran against everything she'd been taught in childhood but became more evident the more time she spent at All People's.

Nearly ten years after that conversation, Lydia remembered it as a formative event in her religious life, one that set her on a path toward a different kind of faith commitment than she had grown up with. "That was kind of the precipitating event that brought me to be curious and to understand for the first time that, wow, I am particular in a certain way. I began to unpack some of my background and to see how the events of my family have shaped who I am, and then also my culture. I was seeing people with a different background than mine who understood God differently, who just embodied themselves differently than I did, and who were happier than I was, frankly. It was really out of my own need that I began to explore what it meant to be from my particular family, from my particular culture, to be white, Western, American. For me, it was a process of liberation finding out those things."

It was freeing for Lydia to see that people from other racial and religious backgrounds not only knew God but appeared more confident and happier in their faith than Lydia had ever been. Years spent with inner turmoil, racked by a sense that she was supposed to be more confident in her faith than she really felt, had made Lydia thirsty for a kind of religion that valued connections between humans as much as those between individuals and God. Her childhood faith communities insisted that one is supposed to know with complete certainty that God is active in the world and in one's own life. The problem was that Lydia didn't know how to connect her own life story, from her parents' divorce onward, with her faith's messages. When distressed as a child, she was told the answer was to pray harder, study the Bible more, and question her faith less. But these solutions only deepened her confusion. In contrast, the relational practices of her new church, rooted in conversations and rituals that brought out people's stories and identified connections between them across cultures and backgrounds, "fits in with what I described before, that for me it was a real loneliness growing up. The small town I grew up in, there's certainly a sense of community there, but I was hungry for a different way to be and live and engage with each other. I wanted closer community than I had. And the economic system we have set up in this country makes it really, really hard. I want to get at the roots of that. That's where it intersects with my story."

## Faith in Connections

Lydia's experience is typical of how religious faith and self-interest can develop and transform in tandem through the relational practices community organizing groups like ELIJAH employ. Her story identifies significant emotional moments and patterns from her past, assesses how those feelings have shaped her life, and orients her current religious practice toward identifying connections with other people on the basis of emotional struggles that are rooted in but can also transcend each person's particular background. But more than this, Lydia's religious development reveals a change in how she understands religious commitment. Through relational practices, like her initial one-to-one conversation with her new pastor, and other practices she is regularly part of at All People's and ELIJAH, she has come to see the connections between people as religiously meaningful. She used to conceive of faith as an individual relationship with God. Now she understands it as a web of connections with others and sees sacred value in the bonds people form with one another by collectively processing their experiences and developing systems of mutual care and support. Understanding her own life story helps her see how her background has shaped her world, fostering a degree of empathy with others whose backgrounds have also shaped their worlds.

This empathy would not have developed had Lydia not been prompted by her pastor to think about what whiteness has meant in her life by asking about her family and mentioning "hundreds of years of Western civilization." She used to understand religious duty as the need to evangelize, to "make sure as few people go to hell as possible." Now she sees her duty differently: it is to serve God by understanding, empathizing with, and caring for other people. Moreover, she recognizes how blindness to white supremacy, colonialism, and "the economic system we have set up in this country" stand in the way.

This is ELIJAH's central religious claim: racial hierarchies and unjust economic systems inhibit sacred human connections and prevent people from living secure, prosperous, dignified lives, so moral citizens are called to tear down and rebuild these systems together. Relational practices spark this process by pushing participants to reflect on their deepest emotional challenges and most salient goals and identify their roots in social structure, including race. As parallels between different people's moral vocations become evident, empathy develops and recognition grows regarding how systems of socioeconomic and especially racial injustice prevent members of society from understanding other people's experiences and caring for one another as their faith commitments call them to do. In this way, ELIJAH's organizing process takes things people don't share, like backgrounds, beliefs, and short-term economic and political goals, away from the center of the group's activities and analysis and replaces them with something they have in common: a drive to grow in one's spiritual and religious practice—to advance one's moral vocation—by identifying and collectively pursuing social changes that can empower people to better connect with and care for one another.

In explaining how all this comes about, this chapter shifts the focus from individuals' own moral vocations to the collective commitments they develop through powerful interactive encounters. Especially central is the link relational practices forge between people's understandings of their own motivations—referred to in community organizing parlance as self-interest—and the bonds they share with one another. In the analysis that follows, we'll see how practices like one-to-one conversations and storytelling embed self-interest within frameworks of community and the common good. By emphasizing the roots of personal troubles in public issues, to borrow C. Wright Mills's language,[1] such practices help people broaden their perceived interests and see that they cannot be pursued in isolation. In turn, as the importance of group bonds for each person's interests becomes evident, religious meaning develops around those bonds, making each person's contribution to the collective project of social reform an outlet for individuals' moral vocations.

Understanding how relational practices fuse personal moral vocations to collective moral citizenship helps us better appreciate how religion works as a foundation for social justice projects, and offers hints about how secular organizations might be able to capitalize on similar cultural dynamics. Until relatively recently, scholars of social change movements typically thought of religious commitments as bundles of beliefs that people either possess or don't, leading to certain kinds of action and precluding others: because people believed X, they did Y.[2] But as I explained in the introduction, more and more researchers are finding that this "beliefs-driven actor model," as sociologist Paul Lichterman calls it, is an oversimplification.[3] For one thing, reducing religion to the presence or absence of beliefs ignores the substantial amount of cultural work that people do with their religious commitments: how they use faith practices and symbols creatively to make sense of who they are, what they value, and what they should do.[4] Moreover, a focus on beliefs fails to consider the ways that religious commitments are themselves co-constituted with other interests, identities, and concerns in a person's life, which themselves can shift and change as people go through life, especially when group dynamics and social cues portray them in a different light, as Lydia's example shows.[5]

Sociologist Ruth Braunstein calls attention to the importance of religious inclusion as a basis for solidarity among religious progressives, arguing that when groups embrace diversity, inclusion becomes a project worth pursuing for its own merits rather than a means to a political end.[6] Here I show how people in ELIJAH collectively develop inclusive religious meanings and attach them to their own ambitions and stories. In doing so, they expand their understandings of what religious people are called to do in the world even while they retain core beliefs and commitments they may have already held, providing stability and endowing the reconceptualization of faith that happens in organizing settings with a sense of growth rather than a rupture with one's past. For many people in ELIJAH, this process creates and continually cements an expanded sense of what it means to be religious in a society plagued by deep inequality and systemic racism. As religious meaning is attached to the ideas of community and mutual care, moral citizenship becomes a religious duty.

## Who Am I and What Do I Want?: The Importance of Self-Interest

As we have seen already, individual emotions and experiences are central in ELIJAH's work, far eclipsing both theological and political analysis in terms of time spent and resources allocated. Though this surprised me early in my fieldwork, the reason for it gradually became evident: the sense of collective religious commitment ELIJAH inspires is not only, or even primarily, rooted in beliefs, texts, commandments, or other sources of external religious authority. Of course, many participants are deeply motivated by such factors as individuals, but they are not the key drivers of what happens at the group level. Instead, collective religious commitment emerges out of *individualistic* religious authority: the importance each person ascribes to knowing and being able to describe their formative experiences, deepest motivations, and grandest aspirations.

This means that the core of collective religious behavior in ELIJAH is the idea that involvement in social change work should not be altruistic but motivated by one's own life story and the goals that emerge from it: what community organizers call self-interest. In organizing, self-interest does not refer to pure concern for one's own bottom line, as economists would use this term, but a culturally situated kind of self-interest that captures people's desire to live secure, dignified lives free of guilt and shame.[7] It may seem ironic that self-interest is so central to faith-based organizing, because we often think of religious actors as being motivated by sincere concern for others' welfare rather than their own. In many cases, they are. But moral citizenship is predicated on the assertion that everyone involved in social change work must have something on the line themselves, even if it is not immediately obvious what that something is. They must develop, and learn to proclaim to others, a story about why achieving change matters to them personally.[8] Only then can deep connections, especially between people of different backgrounds, emerge.

Of course, people's self-interest varies with their backgrounds, values, identities, and goals. For people living in poverty or deprivation, or who are victims of systemic racism or discrimination, self-interest is often tangible, immediate, and pressing. It might include a need for better working conditions, more affordable housing, lower interest rates on loans, stronger public schools, or protection from deportation for one's self, friends, or family. For others, particularly those living with some degree of privilege, self-interest can be more symbolic, akin to what Max Weber called value rationality—for instance, people feeling that they might fail to fulfill their religious calling if they don't immerse themselves deeply in social change work.[9] Of course, many people combine elements of both. But whatever a person's self-interest looks like, ELIJAH teaches that it cannot be pursued in isolation. To make moral citizenship into religious duty, ELIJAH executes an ongoing iterative process of (a) pushing participants to identify and continually refine their self-interest; (b) showing that no matter what that interest is, achieving it requires empathy, relationships, and collaboration with others; and (c) using relational practices to attach sacred meaning to this need for collective awareness and action. Through this process, people come to understand that fulfilling their moral vocation depends on recognizing and acting on the connections between different people's and different communities' interests and confronting the systems of power that keep those interests from being realized.

Identifying Self-Interest

I first experienced the importance of self-interest in ELIJAH during my second week of field research. Arriving about fifteen minutes early to a planning meeting within a campaign to restore voting rights to people who had previously been incarcerated, I hovered awkwardly in a corner of the church basement meeting room, hoping somebody I already knew would show up for me to talk to. Before long, a woman I hadn't met beckoned me with a smile and a wave to a table where she was sitting alone. She said her name was Anita and asked me to introduce myself. Later, I found out she was a Filipina American Catholic in her sixties who'd been part of ELIJAH since it was founded, among its most experienced and influential lay leaders. I told Anita I was a researcher studying faith-based organizing, and she seemed genuinely excited. But this didn't let me off the hook. As we waited for the meeting to start, Anita grilled me about my self-interest in the voting rights campaign: "It's great that you're doing a research project, and I hope I can help you out, but I want to hear more about what is driving you, why you're here." I told her I was just trying to attend any ELIJAH meeting that fit into my schedule while I got a sense of what the organization was like. But Anita's probing look told me I had missed the point. She wasn't just curious about why I had chosen that particular meeting to attend. She wanted to know what personal stake I brought to the work at hand. "Okay, but let's talk about you as a person and why you care about restoring the vote. Why does this matter to you?"

I grasped at straws to find an answer. I remember feeling relieved when the meeting began, saving me from my stumbling. But Anita's questions stayed in my mind throughout the next few days and returned often throughout my research. They were one of the first hints I'd get that most people's reflexive answers to questions about motivations—"I'm here because I want people's lives to be better," "I think it's terrible that people have to live like that," or even "My faith tells me things shouldn't be this way"—aren't sufficient for ELIJAH's purposes. These altruistic statements aren't wrong or bad, but in the view of ELIJAH leaders they reflect a type of truncated moral thinking that fails to consider the ways *all* people—not just the poor or the formerly incarcerated or immigrants or people of color—are damaged by systems of injustice.

Self-interest is so central in ELIJAH's culture for two reasons. First, it creates something closer to equal footing between privileged and marginalized people. People motivated by altruism, even sincere altruism couched in religious beliefs, inherently occupy a position of power relative to those they want to help. They are benevolent interveners in other people's problems, making the very structure of the relationship unequal. Second, self-interest helps ensure that more privileged people stay involved over the long haul in struggles whose effects on their own lives are not immediately obvious. Researchers have often found that no matter how firmly altruists may believe a problem is worth addressing, they have increased risk of dropping in and out because they have no skin of their own in the game.[10] This dynamic often leads to unequal organizational cultures, with members of marginalized communities, especially people of color, typically taking on the bulk of the work, while well-intentioned but naive altruists, often middle- to upper-class white people, swoop in at their convenience to make important decisions, take over publicly visible leadership roles, and take credit for hard-earned victories.[11]

Identifying and developing people's self-interest—their sense of what is on the line for *them*, not just for other people—is a step toward solving these problems and fostering a more equitable and sustainable organizational culture. People motivated by self-interest come to see the problems they are addressing as their own. More than kind do-gooders who assist how and when it suits them, they become "co-conspirators"—a favorite term of Alissa's—in the fight to restore equity and dignity for all people. The power imbalance diminishes, the motivation to stay involved heightens, and people become real long-term partners who would otherwise be temporary allies at best. Instead of a charitable side project, involvement in organizing becomes one's moral vocation. As Alissa fiercely proclaimed at a leadership assembly while introducing an exercise that asked people to reflect silently on their motivations for ten minutes, "If we don't know ourselves . . . we can't walk into this chaos and keep together, stay grounded, and advance our own design."

Over time, ELIJAH's training and leadership development process pushed me to develop my own self-interest and learn to explain it. If the conversation with Anita about restoring the vote had happened a few months later, I would have replied with something like this: "I understand that a society where people's right to vote can be taken away just because they were caught with drugs as a teenager isn't really a democracy. Things my family needs, like better health care and more reliable public transportation, might be within reach if those who hold power couldn't strip people of their right to vote. Our country only puts up with this because it mostly affects people of color, which means those who hold power are using racism to keep everybody else from coming together and making change. I see voter suppression as part of an intentional strategy to keep communities apart and stop them from using the democratic process to combine their power to get what they need. That dilutes my voice in our democracy and our society."

An answer like this would have told Anita that my self-interest is rooted in my concern with how the erosion of others' voting rights also strips me of my ability to use the democratic process to make life better for me and my family. More importantly, developing this understanding of my own self-interest and telling others about it over the course of my research cemented my own commitments and invited others to hold me accountable for following through. But even as a sociologist who is trained to think about interests, systems, and how they intersect, this understanding of my own self-interest didn't come about easily or immediately. I had to learn to think this way. Only through consistent involvement in relational practices was I able to develop a real self-interest in the voting rights struggle and learn to explain this self-interest to others.

Of course, my particular self-interest is unusual in ELIJAH, because it does not involve religious faith. But it is in this very flexibility that the power of moral citizenship lies. People can, with training and practice, develop a self-interest that is rooted in their own commitments, values, and identities, whatever those are.[12] For the vast majority of people in ELIJAH, these are religious, but my secular commitment to democracy constituted an equally worthy basis for self-interest that never invited scrutiny even though most people around me were religious.

Thus, while people can be *personally* motivated by many factors, including, of course, their religious beliefs and commitments, ELIJAH's *collective* analysis and culture develop on a different kind of religious foundation, one rooted in each person's ongoing pursuit of moral vocation. Relational practices prompt people to reimagine who they are, what they want, and who they are in community with and therefore accountable to. Recall Christian Smith's argument about moralistic therapeutic deism: across religious traditions in the United States, religious commitment has morphed from a source of external authority to a wellspring of internal motivation.[13] That dynamic undergirds what happens in ELIJAH. Rather than a set of explicit commandments for the group as a whole, religion operates as a source of parallel individual motivations, allowing people to draw on nearly any set of beliefs and traditions, potentially including secular values, to develop and explain their goals. As a nonreligious person, I usually spoke about self-interest from the perspective of one concerned about how the disempowerment of others undercuts the people's collective ability to determine how society should be run. But most people were explicit about their faith, asserting, for example, that they could not feel they were "right with God" if they stood by while others took on the mantle of combating inequality. Others, like Lydia, infused democratic language with religious precepts, asserting that God intends for people to love and care for one another, and that such care becomes impossible when some people are stripped of their dignity or their political power. The difference between this kind of self-interest and altruism is subtle but extremely important. People concerned with society's collective ability to develop systems of care for one another, and who therefore commit to tearing down social structures that make such care impossible, acknowledge that their own lives are also harmed by the marginalization of other people. Making this kind of connection not only fosters empathy but embeds moral citizenship more deeply within a person's ethical commitments than is possible with a purely altruistic concern.

## One-to-Ones

While developing self-interest is the goal of many kinds of relational practices, the most important is a type of personal conversation known in community organizing as one-to-ones. One-to-ones are two-person conversations in which one person asks the other about their personal history and probes for memories, experiences, and concerns capable of motivating lasting, committed involvement in social change work. Lydia's initial conversation with her pastor, in which he asked about her family and helped her identify how her whiteness had shaped her past experiences, is an example. Many studies of community organizing discuss one-to-ones as a means of strengthening social networks: by engaging with one person at a time, organizations enhance their strategic capacity by drawing more people into leadership development and collective action.[14] But one-to-ones also play a crucial role in attaching religious meaning to social justice projects. By encouraging people to identify and articulate the motivations that draw them into social justice work and thus expand their moral vocations, these conversations begin the process of endowing social change work with personalized moral meaning and thus accountability.

Many community organizers say one-to-ones are the single most important practice of effective organizing, and it is easy to see why.[15] As I began my research, Alissa told me, "The biggest thing you need to understand about our work is that it's not a political resource that people consume. This is not legislative advocacy, and we're not just asking for people's time and money. What we do is try to bring people to understand how they can advance as powerful citizens, which means we have to grapple with our own lives and stories."

One-to-ones are typically the starting point for this grappling and therefore play an important role in recruitment and ongoing relationship building. Lisa, a suburban white Protestant who helped push her congregation into affiliating with ELIJAH in the mid-2000s, recalled that the process began with her and a staff organizer "doing about fifty one-to-ones with people in the congregation, because we needed to find out what pain was out there that we could start to address." In 2015, when the mostly white education equity team was working on a campaign to eliminate suspensions as punishment in the local public schools, its chairperson worked with the pastor of a Black church to connect every education equity team member with a member of the Black congregation for a one-to-one. Since school suspensions primarily targeted children of color, it was essential to understand the cultural contexts of Black families' experiences with the public school system. One-to-ones are crucial for bringing new people into ELIJAH's work and for fostering and growing relationships among veterans. More than any other practice, they prompt people to identify and develop their self-interest and share it with others so common experiences, goals, and impediments can be found.

In one-to-ones, unlike in casual conversations, people are encouraged to take risks by asking difficult personal questions. This was emphasized during a one-to-one workshop at a three-day training for clergy from multiple faith-based community organization (FBCO) federations that I attended. Led largely by ELIJAH staff and affiliated clergy, this was a condensed version of the weeklong leadership training that lay leaders in ELIJAH go through. During one evening session, before approximately sixty clergy members, Pete, an experienced white Catholic organizer in his late fifties who was on staff with ELIJAH, demonstrated a one-to-one with Reverend McCall, a forty-something Black pastor from another state whose congregation had recently affiliated with an FBCO federation there. Pete began the demonstration by asking Reverend McCall what it was like being a pastor in a poor Rust Belt city. Reverend McCall mentioned the neighborhood's struggles with drug abuse, homelessness, and mental health. But instead of linking these issues to larger questions of poverty and systemic racism, like one might expect in a social justice organization, Pete asked Reverend McCall whether he had seen any of those issues in his own childhood. As the conversation turned to family, Pete mentioned that his father had been a miner and died young as a result of exposure to harmful chemicals. Reverend McCall then noted that many families in his congregation were missing fathers, mostly because of addiction and mass incarceration but a couple because they had been murdered or committed suicide. Pete nodded along with the discussion but kept pushing Reverend McCall back to discussing his own history and family because he wanted the focus to be on Reverend McCall himself, not his congregants. Eventually, Reverend McCall mentioned that when he was a child, his father, often stressed from his hard work in a factory, had pushed him a little too hard in school and in football, straining their relationship. This was the opening Pete had been looking for: a *personal* connection between the reverend's life and the experiences of those in his congregation based on the way social conditions could disrupt fatherhood. Only after dwelling on Reverend McCall's childhood for a while did Pete eventually return to questions about the reverend's ambition to organize his congregation, asking him why he thought he had the power to help spur changes in the neighborhood and what kind of team he would need around him to do so.

During a debrief that followed this half-hour conversation, Pete asked the clergy members who had been watching what themes they had noticed. One woman said she was surprised how personal the questions had been. Pete immediately responded,

> You're exactly right, and let me tell you what, that's the whole point of what we're doing here. We have to get ourselves rooted in our past, in what really matters the most to us. For me, I grew up in a place where everyone's dad worked in the mines. And ever since I can remember, that's been a huge part of my life—my dad's work, which supported our family but also broke his back every day and eventually killed him. So any time I have a one-to-one with anybody I make sure that gets brought up. And look, it's not really to make the conversation about me. I just have to give them enough so I can level with them, like "Here's mine, now what's yours?" We have to be really direct, really personal about this, so that we can get people grounded in the experiences that are going to push them to think about the connections we need people to make.

As the clergy trainees moved on to having one-to-ones with people sitting near them, Pete encouraged them to follow his example and share deeply about their own lives so they could in turn ask questions about difficult issues and identify those issues' structural causes.

In teaching how to do one-to-ones, leaders explicitly encourage people to delve into others' stories of pain, anger, and trauma, in addition to stories of agency and power, as a means of identifying self-interest. At a different training session about a year later, part of a campaign against payday lending, roughly fifty people of various race and faith backgrounds were asked to pair up with people they did not already know and ask each other, "What makes you angry?" Trainees were told to listen attentively to the responses and then continue asking, "What makes you angry?" after each of their partner's responses for a full ten minutes, saying nothing else. Then the roles switched, and the people who had been answering the question asked the same question of their partners for another ten minutes. The idea was for everyone to practice talking about deep emotions for an extended period. Meeting organizers then moved on to explicit discussion of how predatory businesses in the payday lending industry cause feelings of anger, guilt, shame, and isolation in poor communities. This process helped attendees begin to see how their own anger was connected to the emotional trauma experienced by people stuck in cycles of debt. Notably, a majority of those at the meeting were white, while payday lending disproportionately harms communities of color. Self-interest rooted in emotions was key to generating this cross-racial empathy and commitment to action.

One-to-ones thus help people identify and articulate their motivations for being involved in social change work and discover how these motivations relate to those of people with different backgrounds and life experiences. After the mini one-to-ones about anger, Maddy, the staff organizer leading the training, told the group, "We have these conversations partly to hear from other people, why they're involved, why they're here, but also to figure out our own deep motivations, whether they're driven by our faith or by anything else. We need to go from being here because our pastor invited us to being able to stake out a Christian claim for confronting these injustices that are being done to people in our communities. And to do that we need to know our own stories and be able to tell them."

The cultural process that Maddy describes here situates a desired political action—working to confront payday lenders—within a larger cultural imperative: "a Christian claim" for fighting injustices more broadly. Yet this Christian claim is intentionally and explicitly vague. Maddy did not dictate any particular Christian claim to the trainees but invited them to develop their own, rooted not in external authority, like an invitation from a pastor or a commandment from a sacred text, but in their own stories, values, and identities—which may or may not have been intertwined with more external religious authority sources. External religious authority was a good starting point but on its own was not a strong religious motivation for sustained involvement and, ultimately, success. Maddy's point was that for faith to become a basis for moral citizenship, people must develop a personal religious stake, a moral vocation, by identifying their own self-interest and learning to share it with others.

As these examples show, one-to-ones serve a variety of important purposes in ELIJAH. First, painful experiences in life often spark emotions that can become motivations for involvement in social change work. Discussing pain, anger, and guilt can help people understand and articulate their deep motivations for being involved and thereby identify common ground for working together. Second, talking about pain and anger helps develop emotionally intimate relationships that expand people's understanding of who is a member of their community and thus comprise a strong basis for collective action.[16] Pete's issues are different from those Reverend McCall and his congregation face, but they have common roots: exploitative labor and the targeting of racial and ethnic minorities, including poor Black people and immigrants today as well as earlier generations of white-skinned ethnic minority immigrants like Pete's father, who toiled away in the mines and factories in decades past. When these connections are illuminated, each person's *individual* faith commitments, such as Pete's Catholicism and Reverend McCall's Black Protestant tradition, can run as parallel tracks supporting joint analysis of, and ultimately action against, the conditions that cause pain in different communities, while group dynamics attach religious significance to the connections themselves and the imperative to confront the systems that disrupt them.

## Self among Others

ELIJAH leaders strive to cultivate understandings of self-interest that are deeply personal, often rooted in experiences of injustice in one's life or memories about painful childhood events, but whose scope extends far beyond what any one person wants to achieve. Arguing that each person's self-interest depends on relationships and mutual commitment, ELIJAH leaders define self-interest as "self among others," emphasizing how social context and community influence personal life chances and outcomes. In an interview, Alissa described this approach:

> We teach self-interest to be . . . almost like call or purpose. It's like, where in you do you have a yearning for a larger thing? What's that about and how's it connected to your story? And how's your story connected to other people's stories? Sometimes self-interest can be taught very narrowly, like, I don't have a job and I want a job. Or . . . those kids hanging out on the corner make me feel unsafe; my self-interest is to get them off the corner. It can be very narrow. . . . The field of the human landscape is much larger than that. What motivates people is much larger than that. I mean people can be motivated by their faith, they can be motivated by values, they can be motivated by

their identity. . . . Like they're not just motivated by direct one-to-one correlations between this equals that.[17]

In mentioning different kinds of motivations, including faith, values, and identity, Alissa shows the degree to which ELIJAH's work depends on developing people's self-interest by expanding their understandings of who they are and what they want. It also reveals the power of organizing through relational practices that tap moral vocation as their underlying cultural strategy: some people are motivated by faith, others by values, and still others by identity.[18] Alissa argues that an undeveloped conception of self-interest, such as "I don't have a job and I want a job," fails to capitalize on the potential of deeply motivating cultural factors like faith, values, and identities for helping people connect their own stories to those of others. Thus, the self-interest taught in ELIJAH is embedded in society and community, an applied worldview wherein people situate themselves in a social context and articulate their goals for their own lives and the well-being of their families and communities. When discussed repeatedly over time, with different people in different settings, self-interest becomes an imperative to work in connection with others and a key element of one's broader moral vocation. Working for the common good becomes a key aspect of helping one's self, because each person's story is "connected to other people's stories."

The language of self-interest is not only apparent in intentional practices and training sessions but runs through the rhetoric leaders use to mobilize people and call for action. For example, an invitation to a 2017 leadership assembly read as follows:

On Saturday, September 23rd from 9 A.M.-3 P.M., ELIJAH is holding our launch of "Claiming Our Voices": Our Path to Transformation through 2018. We are gathering with 250 faith leaders across ELIJAH to reflect on our leadership, to *ground ourselves* in our current political reality and the power we must build to *protect our families and neighbors* and to *prepare ourselves to lead together* through 2018. Saturday will also serve as the training and launch of our plan to have more than 6,000 Faith leaders in congregational forums, house meetings and one-to-one conversations by January of 2018. In January, we will launch ELIJAH's Statewide Faith Agenda and we will prepare more than 4,000 leaders to caucus on our faith agenda across the state on February 6.

In order to build the relationships, leadership and political power we need to transform our state and to ensure that the next Governor is accountable to us and our faith agenda, we need to engage in a season for *spiritual and political formation* across ELIJAH. In these conversations throughout the fall, *we will deepen our relationships by creating space to share our pain and what's at stake for each of us*, and we will *ground ourselves in our values and our story* as we expand the base of leaders required to transform our society [emphases mine].[19]

The language in italics highlights the central role ascribed to processing stories, sharing pain, and developing an understanding of what each person has at stake. Another example is the invitation script that ELIJAH developed for a large public meeting it held in late 2015, a joint gathering with labor, neighborhood, climate justice, and other community groups. Organizers had set an ambitious goal of recruiting 1,500 people to the event, which meant pushing everyone in ELIJAH to work hard to get people from their congregations to turn out. An email Alissa sent to members of congregational core teams across the organization contained a suggested invitation:

HERE'S WHAT YOU CAN DO: take a few minutes and register TODAY and SHARE THIS WITH PEOPLE IN YOUR CHURCH!

Why join us? Well, *I am going because I want to see big changes happen in our state.* And as we continue to try to make those changes happen, *we continue to run into the same obstacles.* Corporate spending plays too big a role in shaping what's possible at the Capitol and even at local levels of government. AND elected officials from both major parties are not leading as boldly or powerfully as they should. We are at a turning point. And we have the chance to make history together.

*I can't do that by myself, but I am confident that you and I and 1500 people,* gathered together, can work together to reclaim our democracy, our economy, and our environment. We've already hit our goal of bringing 350 people of faith together with workers, neighborhood leaders, and economic justice champions.

BUT I *STILL NEED YOU WITH US* ON DECEMBER 12! All successful social movements have, at their center, people of faith. This is the start of a new people's movement in our state, and we must lead with an imagination of what can be made possible through God [emphases in italic mine].[20]

This script, especially the parts in italic, illustrates the central role the language of self-interest takes in supporting ELIJAH's emphasis on community empowerment. Rather than just inviting people, it encouraged the inviters to explain their own self-interest and hinted at how multiple communities' interests keep "run[ning] into the same obstacles."

These messages are examples of how the language of self-interest infuses ELIJAH's rhetoric. The aim is to create a culture in which people understand their own stories, view them as inextricably connected to others' struggles, and therefore work together to solve social issues. It also shows how ELIJAH's vision of self-interest is not a straightforward concern for one's own well-being but fuses people's diverse motivations and interests within a recognition of the interdependence of different political and economic issues. It connects deeply rooted cultural desires for personal dignity and family security with an imperative to work together in community.

Other scholars of organizing have argued that the language of self-interest is effective because it provides a cultural basis for connecting people with others who are different from them.[21] This is also true in ELIJAH, but I argue that ELIJAH's particular concept of self-interest is important for another reason as well. It provides individuals with a way to expand their understandings of what is needed for them to achieve their personal religious aims and desires, which are often put in flux by the depth of inequality in contemporary society. Suggesting that to live well is to be in community with one another encourages meaningful interactions across social difference and creates a public religious identity that connects individual moral vocation with pursuit of the public good.

Yet situating interests and commitments within this broader frame is a challenging process that demands considerable cultural work. As Alissa and Pete explained, the broad sense of self-interest that gives form to moral citizenship must be taught using techniques that encourage individuals to connect their own motivations with larger ideas about justice and community. To wrap up the chapter, I show how personal storytelling situates self-interest within broader frames, relying especially on the cultural appeal of concepts like family and personal dignity to make clear how structural conditions impede human care and connections and attach sacred value to those connections.

## Sacred Connections

In January 2015, ELIJAH held a legislative launch—a Saturday gathering where staff organizers, clergy, and lay leaders described the political work ELIJAH planned to undertake in the upcoming legislative session. Their intent was to motivate lay leaders to organize their congregations to call legislators, lobby at the state capitol, participate in public rallies, and otherwise engage in ELIJAH's work across different issue areas over the months to come. About 150 ELIJAH leaders were present, of whom roughly 80 were white, 40 Latinx, and 30 Black.

ELIJAH had identified four core legislative priorities for the year: making driver's licenses available to undocumented immigrants, restoring voting rights for formerly incarcerated people, increasing funding for mass transit in the region, and pushing for statewide mandatory paid sick time policies. Organizers had recruited lay leaders to tell personal stories about how each of these problems affected them and their families. Though focused on the storytellers' individual experiences, each story linked descriptions of personal troubles and the potential for resolving them to the imperative to act in community.

The first storyteller was Elena, an undocumented Latina immigrant in her late thirties. Elena has two children and a car but no driver's license. She spoke of the difficulty she has getting around: she avoids using the car for everyday tasks like taking her kids to school and doctor's appointments, but sometimes she feels she has no choice but to drive because she has no other way to transport her children given the poor mass transit in her region. This brings a great deal of fear into her life. Her family is dysfunctional, she said, because she cannot provide reliable transportation for her children, and each time she takes the risk of driving, her husband fears she'll be stopped by the police, arrested, and deported. This fear creates tension within their marriage, because her husband's concern about her potential arrest and deportation makes him question her decision to drive even when she sees no other choice.

Elena's use of the word "dysfunctional" is notable because it situates her challenges within the powerful frame of concern for family well-being. It indicates that for her, the lack of access to a driver's license has effects that are deeply personal, not simply political. To call one's own family dysfunctional is to make the painful admission that one is unable to meet the basic obligations of family life. This transcends the political question of whether undocumented immigrants should have driver's licenses and calls attention to the larger cultural question of what it means to have one's family life disrupted by the state. Elena's story located her self-interest in overcoming her family's dysfunction and assigned blame for it to the state's refusal to recognize undocumented people as capable drivers. This invited others in the room to think of ways that their own families were experiencing dysfunction or pain due to political or economic circumstances, and extended the ramifications of her experience outward from the driver's license issue toward the broader range of economic and political problems that disrupt family lives across different races, social classes, and faith traditions.

The second speaker was Charlotte, a Black woman in her fifties who has a bachelor's degree from a prestigious college. Earlier in life she held a good corporate job, but after one of her close family members died and another was imprisoned, she took to shopping, and then shoplifting, to fill the void in her life. She was caught, charged with a felony, and sentenced to a short prison term and ten years of parole. She cannot vote until her parole is up. Charlotte spoke movingly about the symbolic ramifications of not being able to vote, describing how the stigma of being a "political nobody" makes redemption seem out of reach. She regrets her past mistakes and wants to "do right by the world," but she feels that her disenfranchisement makes this impossible. She told the audience that she has to remind herself every day that God has forgiven her, because it does not seem like society has forgiven her yet. She said she had felt increased shame around a recent election because she'd had to tell her children why she couldn't vote.

Like Elena, Charlotte felt that the denial of full citizenship brought her basic dignity as a mother and family member into question. By revealing that being unable to vote makes her question her worth as a mother, she connected her interest in restoring the vote to formerly incarcerated people—a political issue campaign in which success would primarily benefit nonwhites—to a cultural interest in allowing families to flourish, a project with broad religious appeal. Her story endowed the political project of re-enfranchisement with a moral imperative to support families, central in nearly every religious tradition.

The last speaker was Wayne, a white man in his forties who said he was speaking on behalf of a woman from his church who could not be present because she was at work at a grocery store despite being sick. She received no paid time off and only three unpaid personal days per year, which she had used spending time with her dying father in the hospital. Since she had no more time off, she had to return to work immediately following his death. Later in the same year, her son took ill and also died. This time, she requested additional unpaid time off to spend her son's last days with him, but upon her return to work she was chastised by coworkers who were angry about having to cover for her. Wayne said that this was not a just or loving way for anybody to live and that God had a better way in mind for society.

Since Wayne was speaking on someone else's behalf, it was difficult for him to relate intense personal pain and suffering to the audience in the same way that Elena and Charlotte had. But his mention of the absent woman's chastisement by coworkers elicited anger from the audience, who responded with cries of outrage—"That ain't right" and "Lord have mercy"—that a person should be shamed or reprimanded for taking time off to care or grieve for a family member. This discussion of shame aligns with the talk about anger in one-to-ones mentioned earlier. Both examples point to the importance of affirming deep and painful personal emotions in order to illuminate connections between people's self-interests and make these connections the focus of the group's analysis.

Although the stories told at the legislative launch had been practiced in advance and told to an audience rather than come up with spontaneously in conversation with a single interlocutor, as relational practices they have a number of points in common with the one-to-ones described earlier. As in one-to-ones, each story involved relating a painful or embarrassing experience to a mostly unfamiliar audience. Further, each story connected personal pain brought on by social structure to the cultural imperative of being able to provide for one's family or to be recognized as a valuable human being. Together, the stories not only constituted a call to action against a social and political system that permits each of these injustices to exist but attached religious meaning to the imperative to combat them. The sequence of hearing one story after another created a compelling scene that connected the distinct storytelling performances and thus situated the issues raised by each within one overarching moral framework that positioned political action as the only logical means by which to confront the systems that impeded caring and connections among people.

The speeches delivered by ELIJAH leaders immediately following these stories cemented moral citizenship as a religious duty by explicitly pointing out connections between the issues that Elena, Charlotte, and Wayne had discussed. After Wayne's story, Kevin, a white man in his fifties who owns a construction business, said that the week before, a major national magazine had named ELIJAH's state the best place to live in the country. Then he asked, "Does it sound like the quality of life is all that great for the people whose stories we just heard? How can we in our state allow these kinds of injustices to go on while others of us enjoy such a great quality of life? And how can the people in power, the people who judge how good life is, ignore the struggles of so many?"

Kevin's message was followed by a brief speech from Alissa. She rallied the group by asking them to applaud the storytellers and then directed them to think about what society usually says about the issues the stories had addressed. She said, "Society is always telling us that we are in a zero-sum game against each other; that the narrative of our politics and culture is a zero-sum narrative. In schools, in communities, everywhere, we are told that there isn't enough money for things, that we must choose." She asked the audience to name places where they had heard this kind of talk—people mentioned the news, politicians, and their jobs. One person jokingly mentioned church budgets, eliciting laughs. Alissa continued, "This zero-sum narrative extends to issues of love and justice, too. The media and politicians tell us that if we have justice for Eric Garner or Tamir Rice, white communities will somehow lose some of their justice. That if we bring love to undocumented immigrants, somehow native-born Americans will lose some of their love. This is absurd! Absurd, absurd, absurd! [Alissa was shouting and beginning to cry by the fourth "absurd."] And it's not only absurd, but it's deeply internalized and deeply racialized. When communities of color ask for love, whites don't want to give it." With these remarks, Alissa cemented the connection between the issues discussed in the preceding stories and placed this connection at the center of a religious struggle: acting with others in pursuit of human dignity and justice.

The three summarized stories, along with Alissa's and Kevin's speeches, each link an individual's self-interest to a shared cultural struggle that involves supporting families' ability to thrive by countering the systems that prevent them from doing so. By exposing people to the pain, suffering, and embarrassment that structural inequities bring to others, ELIJAH links different kinds of self-interest within a shared struggle against systemic injustice, or what Alissa called the "zero-sum narrative" that pits communities against one another.

Discussion of the kind just described exemplifies ELIJAH's overarching cultural framework and demonstrates how self-interest, moral vocation, and moral citizenship are linked. ELIJAH's work is not only about connecting people across racial, religious, and class lines but also about exposing what the organization sees as pernicious cultural narratives that prevent people from advancing their real interests or pursuing their deepest motivations. These damaging narratives include the zero-sum narrative that Alissa described, along with a range of other cultural phenomena: fear of various types of others, stigma that often accompanies being poor or struggling to provide for one's family, and the shame some people feel when they are forced to ask others for help. Persistent affirmation of individuals' motivations, painful experiences, and faith commitments, produced and reinforced through the social performance of one-to-ones and narrative practices, seeks to bring individuals to confront these myths by engaging in collective action against the systems that support them. Moral citizenship becomes a religious duty when ELIJAH creates a cultural link between self-interest and the idea that a collective good is worth fighting for.

## Summing Up

This chapter has shown how relational practices make moral citizenship into a religious duty—an anchor for moral vocations—and highlighted the crucial role of self-interest in this process. We have seen how one-to-one conversations identify and expand people's motivations. Discussions of past life experiences and intense emotions like pain and anger illuminate ways that individuals' lives have been shaped by social structure, making the redress of structural problems a core element of people's moral vocations as self-interest develops from narrow personal concerns into broader cultural ambitions. Collective storytelling practices filter personal experiences through frames of dignity and family and thus embed discrete self-interests within a larger framework that exposes how the same structural problems impede many people's ability to live in community, support their families, and care for one another. Thus, structural problems like socioeconomic inequality and systemic racism become the targets of religious analysis as distinct moral vocations are tethered to the joint practice of moral citizenship.

The most notable thing about the process I've described is the way religion works at two discrete levels. At one level, it is a parallel set of individual motivators. Someone like Lydia, motivated by devout Protestantism, can work seamlessly with people of other religious backgrounds, and even nonreligious people like me, because the specific manifestations of religion at the group level are not about beliefs or doctrines. Rather, they are about helping people develop moral vocations based on the expanded sense of self-interest cultivated through one-to-ones and storytelling. These vocations are rooted in their own beliefs, culture, and traditions, making it possible for individuals to link their own religious commitments to the larger collective projects of the organization. This enables the group as a whole to use religion at a second level: as a setting and shared vocabulary for talking about goals and ideas, anchoring its critiques of racial and socio-economic injustice within a sacred frame that appeals across different belief systems. With each person grounded in a moral vocation, stories like those from Elena and Charlotte take on religious meaning, especially when they are framed effectively through shared cultural concerns like family security and personal dignity.

"Hello everybody. My name is Josiah Branson. I'm the father of three lovely girls and the husband of a beautiful wife. I was born in Liberia, but now I live nearby, about ten minutes away from here. And you know, I love this country, because this is the country of opportunity. At least that's how it's supposed to be."

A short, stocky Black man in his forties, Josiah stood holding a microphone behind a portable podium bathed in August sunlight. About 120 onlookers formed a semicircle in front of him, members of two Black churches and three white-dominated congregations whose ELIJAH teams had jointly planned today's action. A red and white ELIJAH sticker adorned each person's chest. Beyond the assembled listeners, cars sped loudly by on a divided highway. On the other side, Josiah was framed by a strip mall landscape dotted with signs. One of them advertised the used-car dealership Josiah was angry at, the target of today's protest. Two reporters and a photographer from local news outlets hovered.

As Josiah began his story, I was thinking about a meeting a few months prior, when I had first met Josiah and heard his account of predatory auto lending. That day, Samuel and Maddy had convened a training that brought about thirty people from ELIJAH's West Side congregations together in a small Black Baptist church to talk about what they called poverty profiteering: the extraction of profits from poor and nonwhite communities by predatory lenders and other businesses in the financial industry. I had been in a small group with Josiah. Along with everyone else at the meeting, we'd exchanged stories about how loans and credit had affected our lives and families. The meeting had been the kickoff for the political campaign the onlookers outside the car dealership were carrying out now—a campaign that had Josiah's compelling story about being tricked into a bad auto loan at its heart.

Between that meeting and today's protest, ELIJAH's West Side leaders had been organizing their congregations, using house meetings and one-to-ones to learn about the community's struggles with the financial industry as well as teach congregation members about the ways poverty profiteers took advantage of poor people and how the government let them do it. Now they were ready to put their hard work into public view. CarHop, the dealership that had tricked Josiah, had come up again and again in the house meetings and one-to-ones, so ELIJAH made the dealership its first protest target, calling it to account for its predatory business practices. The press coverage of the rally, I knew, would probably include a picture of the group and a headline like "Faith Group Protests at Local Dealership." Missing in the news stories would be the larger context of ELIJAH's work against predatory lending in all its forms along with the backstory I had seen—the story of the relational practices and commitments to moral citizenship that had made the protest possible.

This chapter explains how the background work we've seen play out in earlier chapters—using relational practices to stoke moral vocations and foster moral citizenship by expanding self-interest—infuses the more visible political work that most people associate with activist groups. In the analysis to come, we'll see how emphases on storytelling and relationships carry through into ELIJAH's political action, leading the group to focus on long-term leadership development over short-term political wins and fostering a commitment to broadly scoped action that transcends any one issue fight.

Listening to Josiah tell his story, it was easy to see why ELIJAH leaders thought it could humanize the financial practices they wanted to confront. "This country of opportunity, because of CarHop, it has not been true for me. About three years ago, I needed to buy a car so I could get to work. I went to all the banks for a loan, but I was turned down because I didn't have any credit history. By all of them, turned down. So I went to CarHop. They said they could give me a car, no problem. No money down, it even came with a warranty. The interest on the payment was very high, but they said the warranty would cover repairs. I had no choice but to accept this deal because I needed a vehicle so I could work and provide for my family. When I got this loan, I got behind on my monthly payment, but then I got caught up."

But caught up or not, getting behind came back to haunt Josiah. Buried deep in the fine print of his loan paperwork was a clause that voided his warranty if he missed a payment, even if he caught back up later. "A few months after that I had some issues with the vehicle and it needed some repairs. And that's when I found out the repairs wouldn't be covered because of this technicality they never told me about. I thought as long as I was current on my loan, the warranty would cover the repairs. That's what they told me, and that was a lie. So now because the interest is so high, I have paid more than fifteen thousand dollars for this three thousand dollar car, and the car is at home in my garage. It doesn't run, and I can't pay to get it fixed. I lost my job because I can't get to work."

As Josiah stepped away from the podium, cries of anger bubbled up from his listeners. "That ain't right!" one Black woman shouted. "It's dishonest!" others said. Josiah had been drawn into ELIJAH's work through a conversation at the same barbershop where Samuel had first opened up to Pastor Al. But this time, Samuel was recruiting instead of being recruited as he handled the clippers. Over a series of haircuts, he had learned Josiah's story and started working on involving him in ELIJAH's campaign against predatory lending in the region. Later, Samuel told me that helping Josiah develop into a leader who could tell his story publicly was one of his first big successes as a professional organizer. As Josiah spoke, Samuel looked on from a few feet away, beaming with pride despite his anger at the circumstances.

After Josiah had finished, Pastor Gregory, a white Lutheran in his forties, took the podium to add some religious context. "I'm a Lutheran pastor," he began. "I'm here to talk about what the Bible says and what this report says." He waved a copy of a report on predatory auto lending that a coalition of community groups, including ELIJAH, had just commissioned. "The Bible tells us, 'Beware of false prophets who come to you in sheep's clothing, for inwardly they are ravenous wolves. You will know them by their fruit.' And it goes on to say that bad trees will not bear good fruit, and good trees will not bear bad fruit." People urged Pastor Gregory on as he spoke, murmuring "Uh-huh" and "Yes, Lord." He continued: "Well, we have a building behind us, CarHop, where a bad tree is bearing bad fruit. CarHop is a nationwide predatory lending operation, run by a reclusive San Francisco private equity baron and a Texas-based pawn shop executive. It's no surprise that right next to CarHop is a pawn shop, another predatory business that makes money by extracting resources from poor communities and vulnerable low-income customers for high cost, high profit deals and loans."

Suffering from the heat in his black shirt and clerical collar, Pastor Gregory fanned himself with the report for a moment before moving on. "These businesses behind me are part of a larger industry of poverty profiteers that includes pawn shops, payday lenders, debt collectors, and car sellers that harass people. They have created a business model that takes advantage of low-income people in their most vulnerable moments. This is not right!" The crowd echoed him. "No, it's not! Amen!"

Pastor Gregory wound up toward his big finish. "This is greed! This is wickedness! And this is what we're up against! And Jesus warns us about it." More Amens and a loud wailing "Oh yes, he does, he does!" came from the listeners. Pastor Gregory went on. "Jesus says, 'You fools!' He actually calls them fools. They neglect justice and the love of God and the love of neighbors. So that is why we're here today. To end a chain of exploitation where CarHop preys on poor people to enrich the wealthy. These are people in the top one percent taking advantage of the poorest of the poor, and it's unconscionable! It's deplorable! There are big payoffs for the people who run the poverty profiteering industry. They have million-dollar homes. They have pools the size of people's houses. It's against the people. It's against our values. And it's against the word of God."

Samuel spoke for a few minutes to close the action. After thanking Josiah and Pastor Gregory and highlighting some of the report's findings about predatory lending, he began stating ELIJAH's demands. "The first thing we want from CarHop is we want some kind of reconciliation with our brother Josiah, who's making his last payment next month, and after that, he will have paid a total of fifteen thousand dollars for a car that's worth three thousand dollars at most."[1] People booed. "So we want compensation for our brother Josiah. But more than that, we want some transparency from Car-Hop and the way they do things. We want them to be open about their contracts." Motioning to the lot behind him, he said, "We even wanna see some prices on these cars![2] So we're gonna be launching a website so consumers can complain about them. This is just the beginning. We're gonna be here as long as it takes for us to dismantle this kind of systematic oppression. And right now, we've got a lot of powerful people assembled here today, and their CEO is gonna hear from us."

Samuel pulled out his phone and told everyone to get ready to make a call. "Right here I've got the phone number for the multi-millionaire from San Francisco who's living large off our brother Josiah's payments. Are y'all ready to let him know what you think about that?" Samuel was fired up, but even though people had been chiming in with vigorous Amens throughout the previous speeches, only a few tepid cheers answered him. People looked around uneasily as they considered the prospect of confrontationally calling someone they didn't know. Samuel pushed on. "Don't worry, it's his office, not his house; we're not interrupting anybody's breakfast. Tell me again, are you ready to let this man know how you feel about what he's doing to Josiah? Okay, let's go then. Here's the number." He read ten digits aloud and repeated them twice. "Everybody got that in your phones? Okay, don't be nervous now; it's Saturday, he's not there. Nobody's gonna answer that line; all you gotta do is leave a voice mail. Just wait for that tone, then tell him your name, tell him you're with ELIJAH and you want to talk about Josiah Branson, and you want to hear from him whenever he's ready. Okay, let's get to it."

## ELIJAH's Political Work

Most of the action in chapters 1 to 4 has taken place in background settings—church basements and other spaces where ELIJAH participants interact mostly with one another, building their collective commitments to moral citizenship but not directly confronting politicians or corporate leaders. These settings need our attention because they are where relational practices stir moral vocations and expand self-interest. Yet public-facing political action has been a constant subtext to this point. After all, the goal of organizing is to pursue change together, not just talk about it. How is the intimate, emotional, relational work we've seen so far connected to the more directly political and strategic action that most people associate with activist groups—action like the scene at CarHop?

This chapter analyzes ELIJAH's public-facing political action. In what follows, we'll see how ELIJAH's culture of relational organizing supports political action that is broad in scope, flexible across issues, and rhetorically incisive. Extended descriptions of events within campaigns to enact a paid sick time law and make driver's licenses available to undocumented immigrants will illustrate how a long-term focus on leadership development and relationship building animates campaigns that on the surface look more like short-term policy work. With these examples in view, we'll be able to see how a sweeping, strategically astute, and morally powerful political worldview emerges from the background work explained in chapters 1–4. What makes ELIJAH into a powerful political organization is not persuasive rhetoric, massive numbers, or financial resources but the strength and character of the commitments to moral citizenship generated in relational practices.

## The Central Tension: Strategy versus Solidarity

So far, we've seen people in ELIJAH working together to develop moral vocations and channel them together in a collective commitment to moral citizenship. But it is not always easy for organizations to turn commitments to an idea into practical strategic action to advance that idea. For religious groups in particular, it can be difficult to move from a world of moral reasoning into one of strategic maneuvering and political calculation.[3] There are practical challenges regarding logistics, coordination, expertise, and, of course, financial resources. But the cultural challenges can be even more significant. Many religious people perceive that entering the political arena means abandoning the moral high ground, debasing sacred claims by getting them dirty in political fights.[4] Others feel it's just not something that's appropriate for religious groups to do.[5] Lisa, the white Lutheran leader who recruited Marco into ELIJAH as explained in the introduction, described the tension aptly: "It's hard because . . . that whole conundrum of separating church and state, which our church still struggles with. I think all churches struggle with that. And trying to really just bring it back to what are we told to—I mean, how are we told to live? So if you live the way we're told, it's inevitably going to spill out into politics, because that's where things are decided. But we have to work really hard to convince people that's okay for us." When I asked her to elaborate, she mentioned the poverty profiteering campaign. "Let's just take payday lending again, how does that change? We can't wish our way out of it; we can't educate our way out of it; we have to change the rules of the game. We have to make sure there are interest rate caps. There's no other way to do it. And to do that you have to go the political route. I mean you have to get the legislators to do something about this. We can't as individuals change those laws, and so doing what we're called to do means we have to be involved with politicians." For Lisa, getting her fellow congregants to see that political work is part of a religious calling, and not a separate world, was a big challenge.

Sociologist Paul Lichterman explains that this kind of messiness, in which a group's habits, bonds, and routines are an imprecise fit for the strategic action needed to achieve its goals, is common in civic life.[6] Every group has a style, a set of shared ideas about who they are and what activities are appropriate for them to do together.[7] Group styles develop over time through interaction, as members build connections; determine their boundaries; and develop routines for how to speak, act, and think together. They provide a road map for what "a group like us" can and should do.[8]

Group styles can be powerful. As we've seen, ELIJAH's dominant style beckons people to share about their lives and vulnerabilities more deeply than they otherwise might and offers an expanded understanding of what concepts like self, faith, and community mean. Emphasizing togetherness through emotions and personal sharing, ELIJAH's group style teaches people about social structure by pushing them to analyze their own experiences and empathize with those of others. This gives it the potential to be politically powerful. Illuminating commonalities is the first step to coalition building.[9]

Yet group styles sometimes constrain action as well as support it. Lichterman points out that groups typically run into trouble when they take up action plans that don't match well with their prevailing styles. The housing advocacy groups he studied faced tough decisions about how to position themselves vis-à-vis decision makers. Should they act as confrontational outsiders holding power holders' feet to the fire? Or should they instead act like insiders—strategic allies working with officials to illuminate new ideas? Of course, each strategy might make political sense at different times. The problem arises when a group that has fired up its membership with confrontational language and an outsider identity tries to pivot to an insider strategy (or vice versa). This is usually ineffective in practical terms, and worse, it can dampen members' enthusiasm for the group and sometimes even the cause itself.[10]

Of course, the most effective groups are aware of such dynamics. They know their energy is best spent on projects that align with the group styles they have developed over the long haul, and they are often choosy, forgoing action plans that are a poor fit for those styles even when they might be strategically sensible. For groups like this, political work isn't only, or even usually, about winning in the short term. It's also about keeping a group together by making sure that when participants take public political action, they have an experience that validates and extends the bonds and commitments that drew them in to begin with. Social movement scholars long thought of social change groups as rational actors that do whatever they think will help them win the struggle at hand. In reality, Lichterman argues, "previous research has tended to overestimate how much claims making is about appealing strategically to others and underestimate how much it is about maintaining the solidarity of the claimants."[11]

ELIJAH leaders work hard to align their political action with the prevailing group style they develop in background settings—a style focused on moral vocation, storytelling, and relationship building. But while sacrificing strategy for solidarity is occasionally necessary, it turns out that many aspects of ELIJAH's group style are quite politically advantageous. Relational practices create a sense of community that's broad, inclusive, and flexible, based on a willingness to be vulnerable, hear others' stories, and share one's own. We'll see in the examples that follow how the internal *cultural* focus on leadership development and relationship building—that is, ELIJAH's group style—supports a long-term *political* framework that embeds issue campaigns within a broad moral imperative, making it easier to switch gears when needed, respond resiliently to defeats, and keep pushing after victories. Moreover, the emphases on family and community that develop in relational practices can prop up personal stories that make clear populist distinctions between morally worthy families and greedy corporate elites.

## A Campaign for Earned Sick and Safe Time

In early 2016, progressive organizations in ELIJAH's city were on the verge of a big victory. A grassroots coalition called People for a Fair Economy (PFE) was pushing the city council to mandate earned sick and safe time (ESST) for all workers.[12] Besides ELIJAH, coalition members included mostly neighborhood-based organizations and labor groups. A few months prior, in summer 2015, the mayor had championed a legislation package known as the Working Families Agenda (WFA). The WFA had included ESST among a range of other policies designed to help low-wage workers, including a fair scheduling ordinance and a reinforced anti–wage theft policy. After the mayor came out in support of the WFA, it earned unanimous approval from the city council in a nonbinding procedural vote. However, a group of business interests led by the chamber of commerce quickly and effectively organized in opposition. Taken aback by the number of small business leaders who spoke out vehemently against the WFA, the mayor and the council decided to put it on hold.

After the WFA was tabled, the PFE coalition decided to break the agenda into a collection of smaller pieces and pursue them one at a time, choosing ESST as its first target. There were plenty of signs that it was a winnable issue. It was polling well in opinion surveys nationwide, and the mayor had campaigned on paid sick time before the WFA had been proposed. But the previous fall had shown how strongly organized the business groups were. ELIJAH and other members of the PFE coalition wanted to make sure they were well-organized enough themselves to head off any setbacks. Thus began a short but intense campaign to lobby the city council to approve a strong ESST policy.

While eager to deliver a big win for workers in the city, ELIJAH leaders also wanted to use the campaign as an opportunity for expanding their organizing base. At a tenser than usual weeknight meeting in January 2016 that lasted considerably longer than its planned two hours, ten people—three staff organizers, six experienced volunteer leaders, and me—gathered to talk strategy for the upcoming campaign. Wendy, who we met in chapter 2, set the tone early on: "I'm an organizer and I want to win, but this is bigger, about building power in the long term, tying what we're talking about in this room to what's going to happen five years from now. That has to be part of the focus of every meeting that we have, or I don't want to go. There is no point in going through the mechanics of organizing if it isn't coupled with a laser focus on building a bigger, broader base for the power agenda that we want."

Wendy's remarks reflect the same goals that animate the relational practices described in other chapters: leadership development and relationship building. She felt it was important to carry out the ESST campaign in a way that affirmed and extended these cultural commitments even though for other coalition partners, winning was all that mattered. Wendy wasn't alone in taking a longer-term view. Shannon, a staff organizer, had been disappointed that paid family leave had recently fizzled out at the state level, and she was thinking ahead to the next time the state might take that up. She wanted to make sure that the campaign for a municipal ESST policy also laid the groundwork for a more effective state-level push later. She echoed Wendy: "All of this is designed to have us expand who's engaged and develop some new leaders who can share powerful stories, especially in the areas where we're weak right now. So that's the internal goal. The external goal, obviously, is winning ESST." It was imperative to these leaders that ELIJAH not switch styles by pivoting from long-term relationship building and leadership development to short-term political strategy.

Although Wendy, Shannon, and the rest of ELIJAH's top leadership envision every issue campaign as a relationship-building opportunity, the political context of the ESST campaign made it especially promising in this regard. At the planning meeting, the group agreed that influencing the city council as a whole depended on influencing the powerful council president, a white woman in her sixties who for two decades had represented District 6, a mostly Black area where ELIJAH had little presence. Shannon explained, "The mayor technically has more power, but the council president essentially controls seven votes out of the thirteen on the council . . . so we are going to be trying to build a new outpost in her ward, contacting churches there." Since there were no ELIJAH-affiliated churches in the council president's district, demonstrating that her direct constituents cared about this issue would require a massive organizing push in a part of the city where

ELIJAH had relatively few connections. It meant asking ELIJAH leaders to find a place in District 6 where they could hold the meeting, identify contacts in the District 6 community who could supply them with calling lists, then make hundreds of phone calls into unfamiliar turf. But it was also a chance to engage new people in ELIJAH's faith-based organizing project and win something big at the same time. Despite the daunting logistics, it was a golden opportunity to use a meaningful policy campaign to extend ELIJAH's relational culture into new territory.

Besides the council president, ELIJAH decided to target three other council members, all of them swing votes representing districts where ELIJAH had a strong presence. All three had originally supported the WFA but withdrawn their support in response to the well-organized business opposition. The planning team decided that the best strategy was to ask three of the best-organized ELIJAH churches in the city to lead the organizing effort. These included two mainline Protestant congregations and one Catholic parish, St. Martin's, where I was embedded in the core team, which Wendy co-chaired.[13] These three churches were located in prosperous neighborhoods and composed primarily of well-educated, middle- to upper-class white people. ELIJAH leaders believed that because they had strong core teams and several powerhouse organizers like Wendy among their ranks, these churches could turn out large numbers to public meetings where council members would hear stories from direct constituents about how the lack of paid time off affected them and their families.

As the other two churches organized meetings with the three on-the-fence council members (both churches had many members living in those council members' districts), the St. Martin's core team debated how to carry out the enormous high-stakes task it had been assigned with the council president in District 6. St. Martin's is a large, politically active congregation, and over the years its ELIJAH core team had collected the phone numbers and email addresses of hundreds of parishioners who had shown up to various ELIJAH events. The parish priests were also ELIJAH supporters. With a word from Joanne—the parish's social justice ministry coordinator and a member of the ELIJAH core team—either of the two priests would have eagerly announced the upcoming meeting at Sunday Mass and encouraged people to go. Combined with a few phone calls and emails, along with a note in the church bulletin, this would likely have gotten a good number of St. Martin's parishioners to show up, even though District 6 was on the other side of town.

Some of the St. Martin's core team members advocated this approach. They argued that time was short and the stakes were high, and since the council president served the whole city, not just her district, it would be appropriate to find a community space in District 6 and fill the meeting with St. Martin's parishioners, or even host the meeting at St. Martin's. Besides, some people said, this issue was too important to take the risk of a poor show of support. It was regrettable that the team didn't have many contacts in District 6, but ultimately it was more important to show strong citywide support for the ESST ordinance.

Wendy, following the plan developed in the earlier meeting with Shannon and others, took a different view. She explained to the team that ELIJAH had a "dead zone" in District 6, and it had been bothering her for years. She was dismayed that one of the city's poorest areas wasn't well represented in ELIJAH. She lamented that this majority-Black district was represented at city hall by "an old white woman who only wins because she's been there forever and people know her name and nobody's willing to challenge her." She saw the ESST meeting as a chance to start rectifying the problem.

The chance to develop relationships in District 6 meant that instead of leaning on the St. Martin's network, Wendy and a few others on the team favored pushing hard to identify District 6 residents who would attend the meeting, tell stories, and hold their council member accountable. Wendy insisted that this plan was feasible, though daunting. With help from ELIJAH-affiliated clergy, she had identified a white Lutheran pastor, Reverend English, who led a non-ELIJAH-affiliated church in District 6 and wanted to get her small congregation more involved in citywide social justice work. This was the perfect opportunity, Wendy said. She would tell Shannon to lean on another ELIJAH-affiliated Lutheran pastor to call Reverend English and ask her to host the meeting with the council president at Glory Lutheran, her church. St. Martin's core team members would have one-to-ones with congregants at Reverend English's church, then work with a PFE-affiliated neighborhood organization in District 6 to recruit district residents to show up. "We need to make it so she walks into the room and sees five people she knows but that she didn't know all knew each other, and now they're all sitting together, waiting to talk to her about this. That's what changes the power dynamic. That's how we win this." Wendy argued that building new relationships and demonstrating them publicly was the key to strategic success.

After a lengthy discussion that took up almost an entire two-hour core team meeting, Wendy carried the day—mostly. The team agreed that it would be a good idea to enlist Reverend English and her congregation, but they also decided to do some limited outreach at St. Martin's to establish a backbone for the meeting. That way, if things didn't work out with the District 6 turnout, it would still be possible to put a not-damagingly-small crowd in the room with the council president.

Over the next few days, Wendy and a few others put the plan in motion. It wasn't long before Wendy sent the core team an email eagerly proclaiming that Reverend English was on board and a date was set. A couple of days later, she sent another email:

Subject: District 6 Meeting—March 3 with Council President: IMPORTANT

Dear Friends,

The exciting and wonderful news is that the City Council President is confirmed to attend our in-district meeting in the 6th district on Thursday, March 3. The news that means that we need to take our work in the 6th very seriously in the next less than 3 weeks is that the City Council President is confirmed to attend our ELIJAH meeting.

We have set up a couple of check-in points:

St. Martin's ELIJAH core team planning meeting: 7 P.M. this Wednesday, February 17 at St. Martin's

6th District Planning Meeting: Thursday, Feb 25 at 7 P.M. at hopefully Glory Lutheran

Please join us at any meeting you are able to attend. This is an all called event but really this is an all called to support the ELIJAH 6th District organizing effort. We are in it to have a meaningful meeting with the Council President on March 3 but we are also in it to develop a leadership team in the 6th District that goes beyond any particular issue and into the intersectionality of all of our issues and allows for a faith voice to be heard above the political rhetorical discourse that sometimes passes for democracy these days.[14]

Wendy was excited, but now the work had to begin. Labeling this an "all called event"—one that all core team members were expected to prioritize, even those working mostly on other issues like education equity or criminal justice reform—she pointed out that the purpose of the all called was not just to win ESST but to support the organizing push in District 6. She made clear that the issue campaign was just an element of the broader ambition: developing a leadership team, illuminating how different issues intersected, and raising a faith voice to shine through the messiness of city politics. Though this was strategic issue-focused political work, Wendy was taking great care to ensure that it advanced ELIJAH's emphasis on developing leaders and building relationships.

Immediately after sending the email, Wendy texted me and three others: Would we agree to spend the coming Saturday afternoon at the offices of a neighborhood-based organization in District 6, using its contact lists and dialing software to call area residents to ask them to attend the upcoming meeting? Yes, we would. The goal was to pack the church; anything less, Wendy warned, would signal tepid community support for the paid sick leave proposal. Wendy asked Mallory, who had experience working as a corporate manager and had seen how a lack of sick time had made things hard for her employees, to write a call script. Mallory's script made clear that the idea was not just to tell people about the meeting but also to ask whether they had what they needed to care for their families, had ever had to work while they were sick because they couldn't get time off, or had a personal story to tell about how a lack of paid time off had affected them or their families. If anyone said they had such a story, a note was made to follow up with them later. Wendy and Mallory didn't just want the church to be full of District 6 residents—they also wanted to identify people living in the area who could tell their stories publicly, like Josiah had learned to do as he got to know Samuel. This was a turnout operation, but more importantly it was a chance to engage in relational work with a new group of community members.

Making stories central was not just a way to identify potential storytellers; it was also key to keeping the hard, often thankless task of phone banking rooted in ELIJAH's underlying group style and hence appealing to the core team members that Wendy was asking to carry it out. The script Mallory wrote made the phone banking into a religiously meaningful task rather than a political drudge. Asking callers to "speak from the heart" and give their own reasons about why they supported ESST, Mallory's script gave people the opportunity to infuse this political operation with whatever religious language or ideas were most meaningful to them. Calls became opportunities to act out moral vocations and even engage in miniature versions of relational practices with people on the phone.

*District 6 Calling Guide*

Remember:

Speak from your heart about why paid sick & safe time matters
to you.

*Listen respectfully—this is not an argument. This can be difficult
sometimes. Probe for a deeper understanding by lightly using phrases
like: "Oh, can you tell me more about that?" or "Okay. Can you tell me
why you feel that way?"*

Engage a conversation—we are "fishing" here, and you never know
what treasures we might uncover in the process.

Take notes (on conversations and incorrect information) and get them
to Wendy. Make sure Wendy knows who you did *not* reach as well.

SUGGESTED SCRIPT

Hello, is _____ there? Hi _____, my name is _____ and I'm a
volunteer with ELIJAH* (or St. Martin's Catholic Church). We are /
I am working to pass earned sick and safe time, because we /
I believe that *(pick one or give your own):*

— People should not have to choose between taking care of themselves
or their family and keeping their job.
— Families matter, and we should all be able to take care of our
families when they need us.
— Employees deserve to be treated fairly and with dignity.
— It helps keep all our families and communities healthy and productive.
— Not having paid sick time leads to public health issues when
employees come to work sick because they can't afford to take time
off without pay.

Have you heard about this issue?

— *If yes:* What do you think about the idea of all workers in the city
having access to paid time off to care for themselves or their loved
ones? *(Listen especially for their experiences and values. Explore
respectfully. Note if they have a story re ESST.)*
— *If no:* You might be as surprised as I was to learn that 42% of workers
in our city don't have access to paid time off to care for themselves or
their loved ones—that's 80,000 workers, many of them women and
workers of color. This lack of access has far-reaching consequences for
family health, workplace safety, economic stability and racial equity.

We are organizing a meeting with your City Council representative to talk with her about the need for all workers to have access to earned sick and safe time. It will happen on Thursday March 3 at 7 P.M. at Glory Lutheran Church.

Do you think you could join us that evening? We are looking to put as many supporters in the room as possible that evening to show your council representative just how important this issue is to the people in her District. *(Assure them that just being in the room is being supportive.)* *Record answer.*

We are also looking for other people who live in, or who employ people in, your District who care about this issue.

— Do you know anyone in your neighborhood who has needed paid time off to take care of themselves or their family members? *Try to get contact info or find a way to connect.*
— Can you think of any employers in your District who treat their employees fairly who we might talk with? *Note any ideas we can follow up on.*
— Do you know of any places of worship that might be interested in learning more about Earned Sick and Safe Time? *If so, try to get a name of someone there to connect with.*

Can I get your email address so I can send you information about the meeting? (Or to send you more information about this issue . . .) Thank you!
* If asked, say ELIJAH is an organization of churches working together for racial, economic and social justice.[15]

Phone-banking efforts continued for a couple of weeks, with members of the core team rotating through shifts at the District 6 neighborhood group's offices. But as the meeting date approached, the team started to worry. Most calls into District 6 went unanswered, and few of the residents who picked up said they could attend. Many expressed interest but said they had to take care of their kids or work, or that the time didn't work for them. Shannon and Wendy had set a goal of getting 150 people to the meeting and identifying five District 6 residents who could tell stories about why their families needed paid sick time. Although the team had made hundreds of phone calls, a week before the meeting there were fewer than eighty commitments to attend from District 6 residents, and everyone knew that fewer than half of those who'd pledged to attend would actually show up. A forty-person crowd, which would have been damagingly small, began to look like a real possibility.

At this point, the team decided to set the backup plan in motion, and a few phone calls and emails to St. Martin's parishioners eased some of the concern about a too-small crowd. But this outreach, done mostly at Mass the Sunday before the Tuesday meeting, was too late to have a big effect. Fortunately, working their connections to the neighborhood group that had hosted the phone banks, Wendy and Shannon had at least been able to find a couple of District 6 residents, both people of color, to tell stories at the meeting. Wendy and Mallory met with each of them during the week before the meeting to give them a crash course in powerful public storytelling and a chance to practice and hone their messages.

When March 3 came, about eighty people showed up to the public meeting at Glory Lutheran—barely half the original goal but large enough to show community support. Nearly half the faces were brown or Black, a smaller proportion than that of District 6 overall but enough to signal that this wasn't purely an outsourced crowd. The District 6 storytellers spoke passionately about why ESST would help them and their families; two other storytellers not from District 6, both recruited and trained by other members of the ELIJAH core team, did, too. The council president listened politely to the stories and said she was supportive of the idea in general but also concerned about the effects on small businesses.

Thanks in large part to ELIJAH's pressure, it had become evident by this time that the council would pass an ESST policy in some form. Two of the three swing votes that had been targeted by the other ELIJAH churches had come out in support after attending ELIJAH-organized public meetings where large numbers of their constituents had shown up. But the devil was in the details. Would businesses with fewer than ten employees, or twenty, or fifty, be exempted? The PFE coalition wanted no exemptions; the chamber of commerce and the council president favored some exemption threshold. How would violations be reported? Could employees report them anonymously to the city, with no threat of retaliation from their bosses? PFE wanted this; the council president (and, again, the chamber of commerce) said it might be too hard to set up. The council president was noncommittal on these details but seemed to get the message of strong support from the community for a robust paid leave policy. She even stayed for the whole meeting, even after the part engaging her directly had ended, something elected officials often don't do.

In the debrief afterward, Wendy expressed satisfaction. True, the meeting had fallen far short of its turnout goal, and that might have been a problem if other council members hadn't already committed to supporting the ESST proposal. But the storytellers had been engaging and made a clear moral case for how a lack of ESST hurt their families. Besides, in organizing the meeting, ELIJAH had gotten a new congregation involved, established some contacts in District 6, and set up a foundation for future organizing there. This was what Wendy and Shannon had wanted. It meant that regardless of what happened on ESST, the meeting was a success for the organizing team. They could take pride in how they had worked hard to engage a new constituency and establish new relationships, recruited powerful storytellers and trained them to be effective, and exerted a faith voice in an important policy debate. Even if the council had gone on to reject ESST, this meeting would have been an organizing win that the core team could be proud of.

Ultimately, the city council passed a strong ESST policy. Exemptions were carved out, but only for businesses with five or fewer employees. The anonymous reporting system was not set up; employees had to file complaints through a public records system that could not protect their anonymity. Largely thanks to ELIJAH's citywide organizing, the March 3 meeting with the council president turned out to be mostly anticlimactic, since it had become evident by then that an ESST policy would pass. But this had not been clear a month earlier, when momentum had seemed on business groups' side. Faced with the choice between ensuring a room full of St. Martin's people, who would take little effort to recruit, and taking the chance on District 6 residents, who would take much more effort to contact, the team chose the latter. It was riskier and much more work-intensive, but it laid the groundwork for long-term leadership development and relationship building in District 6 in a way that no other method could have done. It did this by making what seemed like a technical and strategic issue fight into an organizing project that extended ELIJAH's relational culture into its political action.

The St. Martin's team navigated the ESST campaign by prioritizing leadership development, relationships, storytelling, and community bonds. In a situation in which it would have looked to any outsider like the team had switched styles and pivoted to a concern for short-term issue work, the team had actually stayed engaged in their long-established highly relational style throughout the campaign and found success by doing so. They held one-to-ones, told and listened to stories, and worked to develop new leaders. They were driven not just to win ESST but to "raise a faith voice," in Wendy's words, and to "provide a moral narrative," in Shannon's, in expanding protections for working families in the city.

Legislative Visits

The ESST campaign exemplified how issue campaigns can present civic groups with a choice: stick with the style that had made people devoted to its work, or switch into a win-now mode, potentially abandoning certain core principles or practices. ELIJAH faced another such choice during a campaign to win driver's licenses for undocumented immigrants, and I observed the tension involved when I accompanied a group of four Latinx high school students, all with undocumented parents, and Luke, a young white Catholic priest just out of seminary and interning as an organizer with ELIJAH, to visit state legislators in early 2015.

Each winter, as a new legislative session begins, ELIJAH organizes visit days, on which people gather at the state capitol to meet with members of the state House and Senate. Typically, each visit day is focused on one issue or theme. In 2015, I tagged along on all five visit days ELIJAH held: racial justice, voting rights for the formerly incarcerated, driver's licenses for undocumented immigrants (the one I'll discuss in detail here), mass transit, and paid family leave. The number of participants varied: only about thirty people showed up for the driver's license day, while the paid family leave day attracted about a hundred and the restore the vote day—co-organized with several other local groups—pulled in more than five hundred.

Each visit day began early in the morning on a weekday at a church near the capitol. There, after opening prayers, a brief session of relational practices like storytelling and mini one-to-ones helped get people warmed up and ready to tell their stories to legislators—and reminded them that whatever might happen at the capitol that day, they were making progress in their larger goals of building relationships and developing a long-term power agenda. Following this, staff organizers gave an overview of the political terrain surrounding the day's issue, typically including a brief general education in the legislative process (explaining how bills become laws and which committees they pass through on the way) as well as specific dynamics about the issue at hand. For instance, on the mass transit visit day, attendees learned how the state's political geography incentivizes Republicans to demonize urban areas and oppose projects perceived to benefit them, such as commuter rail.[16]

Following each visit day's grounding session and political education, staff organizers sorted participants into groups of roughly six to eight who would visit legislators together. Then, with the groups formed, everyone walked together about a quarter mile from the church to the capitol building, singing religious songs (such as "We Are Marching in the Light of God") along the way. On each issue, staff organizers had identified specific legislators to target—swing votes, party leaders, members of key committees—and tried to make sure they each received visits from direct constituents. Often, either no constituents of key legislators were present, or the legislators were unavailable. In these cases, groups were encouraged to meet with whichever legislators would agree to see them. A great deal of planning went into matching visitors with their own representatives. Leaders explained that legislators didn't really listen to people they didn't represent directly unless they were lobbyists. On the driver's license visit day, my group met with five legislators: three Democrats and two Republicans. Two of these legislators, one from each party, had constituents in our group, but the other three did not.

During my first couple of legislative visit days, still early in my fieldwork, I assumed the main goal of this work was to influence legislative outcomes. I'd seen some of ELIJAH's relational work by this point but didn't yet fully understand how it infused the political activism that had drawn my research interest to begin with. Now that people were heading to the capitol, strategy would surely take center stage, I thought. Each issue struggle was described as high stakes—the morning grounding and political education sessions made it clear that people's livelihoods and families were on the line when legislators made decisions. I expected that now was when ELIJAH would pivot to a more direct-action style.

But it turned out that as in the ESST campaign, the real goals of the driver's license campaign were rooted in a bigger picture; it was more important to keep developing leaders than to sway votes. In a closely divided legislature, votes typically fell along party lines, and no amount of public engagement would get Republicans to support anything perceived to be pro-immigrant or antibusiness. Visits by ELIJAH, or any other group of everyday people, were unlikely to alter a bill's fate. One day at the capitol, as we chatted briefly while waiting for an elevator, Alissa explained to me that there was another, more important goal. More than changing outcomes, these visits were intended to build and sustain a culture of engagement and political participation:

The real idea is never passing a particular bill, even if it's a bill we strongly support. We're trying to dig into the political debate and use it to develop people into leaders, to recognize themselves as participants in democracy instead of spectators. It's kind of a dirty little secret, but we have to face up to the reality that talking to legislators doesn't usually move votes unless you're a lobbyist. With Republicans in the majority, most of the bills we support will be killed in committee. But that doesn't mean it's not a powerful experience for people. When we give people those experiences, especially a series of them that are connected, they start realizing they have more power than they ever knew.[17]

Alissa made it clear that the style of the conversations—people telling their own stories and raising moral voices—mattered more than the strategic context. An observer looking at ELIJAH's legislative visits from the outside would likely have assumed that policy change was the only goal. As Alissa explained, this was incorrect. This work was more about the visitors and their ongoing development as moral citizens than what the legislature would do.

Alissa's points came into clearer focus when I accompanied Luke and the four students at the driver's license visit day. The students' home parish was in a former farming town that had gradually transformed into an exurb. It had been mostly white until the 2010s but was quickly becoming majority immigrant. An Amazon warehouse had recently opened there, providing plentiful but low-paying, backbreaking, and insecure jobs. The warehouse combined with a sizable amount of newly built, relatively affordable housing to attract large numbers of Latin American, Southeast Asian, and African immigrant families. Shannon, the Southwest Suburban organizer, was eager to capitalize on the opportunity to make the area parish, which was drawing many of these newly arrived families, into an organizing hub. Partly at Shannon's urging, the parish's priest had agreed to make getting involved in ELIJAH a way to advance toward confirmation. Hence, these four students had all been working on developing personal stories about the importance of driver's licenses to their families. The idea was that each of them would share their story with legislators, emphasizing how their parents' inability to drive had impeded their progress in school and participation in extracurricular activities. As in the case of the ESST campaign, the apparent goal was enacting a policy change, but the deeper aim was developing leadership among new communities. Shifting votes would be a desirable secondary outcome, but it was unlikely and wasn't needed for the organizing process to be considered a success.

Walking around the capitol and visiting reception desks, the group arranged five meetings with legislators that day. The students did almost all the talking in each meeting, introducing themselves to the legislative staffers and asking when they could meet with the representatives. Four of the meetings went according to plan. The students told their stories and the legislators listened politely, asked a question or two, and then sent us on our way. But during the last visit, in the office of the Republican who represented the students' home district, things took an unexpected turn. The visit began with Danny, an athletic kid wearing a Barcelona soccer jersey, telling his story first. He was the most confident speaker in the group, and he frankly recounted growing up in a neighborhood with a lot of gang violence. He said his parents had always wanted to move but couldn't, because it was the only place in town close enough to walk to both an affordable grocery store and the local schools. With driver's licenses, they could have moved to a safer neighborhood and gotten better jobs. Then Danny spoke about his social life and extracurricular activities. He didn't join many teams or clubs until after he got his own license because his parents couldn't take him to and from practices and concerts. When he did join teams, his parents usually couldn't get to his games. He would carpool with friends to soccer games straight from school, but he "didn't get to experience the joy of seeing my parents in the bleachers after I scored a goal."

As Danny spoke, the legislator, a bearded white man in his fifties, nodded along silently. Then he said something surprising. He was an insurance agent, and he knew that having unlicensed, and therefore uninsured, drivers on the road made insurance costlier for everyone. Without reference to the story he'd just heard, he explained that he'd consider supporting the driver's license bill if he saw data suggesting it might lower insurance premiums for the average driver. He added that hospitals might also be supportive, because uninsured drivers often left them unreimbursed after emergency room treatment resulting from accidents. Luke's jaw dropped. He had not foreseen the conversation going in this direction. He quickly asked whether other Republicans were thinking similarly. "Not that I know of, but maybe I can bring a few around," was the reply. Even though the other three students had not told their stories yet, Luke quickly thanked the legislator, ended the conversation, and hurried the group out of the office.

In a debrief later, as the group sat on the floor in a busy capitol hallway with staffers, lobbyists, and legislators hurrying past, Luke congratulated the students and asked them how they thought the day had gone. Then he told them about some upcoming public meetings ELIJAH was organizing, where, as in the ESST campaign, elected officials would be invited to churches in their districts to talk about the driver's license bill. He pushed them to attend these meetings and speak at them, saying, "Politics is never a one-shot deal. We made a lot of difference today but we have to keep the pressure on, keep showing up, know what I'm saying?" Only at the end of the debrief did he discuss the insurance agent: "That one where we talked about insurance, that was a really amazing meeting. He leaked information to us that we didn't know before, and now we can take advantage of that." Looking at the three students who hadn't been able to speak before he ended the meeting, Luke said, "It would not have been helpful for us to keep telling him our stories, because the people he needs to win over, they only want to hear about the economy, health care, effects on taxpayers, that type of thing. See how that's different from what we've been talking about?" Thinking strategically, Luke wanted to allocate energy where it would be effective and avoid irritating potential allies with rhetoric they weren't sympathetic to. He even thought it might impede other Republicans' support if word got around that the representative had been moved by stories about immigrant families instead of discussions of insurance rates. He hoped that approaching the bill through a purely economic frame, rather than the moral one ELIJAH leaders had been developing among Danny and his friends, might help get Republicans on board. After the debrief, I saw Luke chase down ELIJAH's political director on the walk back to the church. Presumably, he was in a hurry to tell him about this new strategic angle.

A few days later, I met with Alissa in a coffee shop for a check-in about how my nascent research project was going. I told her about Danny's story, the visit with the insurance agent–legislator, Luke's decision to end the meeting early, and the debrief that followed. To my surprise, Alissa told me that ideally, that wasn't quite how things should have gone. She was also a little worried that Danny—and I—might have gotten the wrong impression of what happened in the meeting. Luke was new to the ELIJAH staff, she explained, and new to organizing in general. He was learning on the fly. He'd done a lot of work in immigrant communities in seminary, though, and he was passionate about supporting them. "Luke, you know, he *really* wants to win driver's licenses. It's a passion issue for him because of his experience working in those communities." But her tone suggested that Luke might have lost sight of the bigger picture. As I recounted how he had grown excited about the legislator's economic framing of the driver's license issue, Alissa responded,

See, that's Luke still getting used to the way we try to develop leaders. You need to understand, I really want to stress this, the most important thing that happened in that room was not whatever the legislator said. He's a Republican. He's not going to vote for the bill, no matter what he told you. He's going to say he will, but then he's going to change his mind, or actually what'll really happen is the bill will die in committee before he ever gets a chance to vote either way. And he knows that. So what happened is he got to look good to you, to those kids, without having to put anything on the line. He won, see? He won that meeting because he got you out of his office without having to listen to his constituents' stories about how our society's cruel policies are disrupting their lives. He told you all what you wanted to hear and you left smiling. Am I right?

I nodded. Alissa continued: "So what really happened there is three kids got denied a chance to tell their stories, and the one kid, Danny, did you say? Yeah, Danny got told that his story, his voice really, wasn't as important as some crap about insurance rates. That's not really what we're trying to do. I don't blame Luke because I wasn't there and it sounds like it was a judgment call, but that's a shame. That's really not how we want things to go."

Alissa then asked me what had happened after the meetings. When I told her Luke had led a debrief during which the students reflected on what it had been like to tell their stories and talked about upcoming opportunities to tell them again at other meetings, her face brightened. "Okay, see, now I'm a little relieved. Whatever happened with the legislators, it's important that the kids got to reflect on their experiences as developing leaders and understand this as an experience of developing power." Alissa advised me to keep focused on leadership development and avoid getting sidetracked by the progress of different bills through the legislature. "Luke is eager, and talented, and he deserves a lot of credit for getting those kids into a place where they could go and tell their stories like they did. But just don't lose sight of the big picture here, how we have to keep focused on story building and storytelling, the development of our capacity as leaders, and making sure our moral voice is heard." Her words were addressed to me and my research focus, but it was clear they also described ELIJAH's approach to political work, which, I was learning, was more about developing leaders and building relationships than winning policy fights.

Danny's story, together with Luke's eagerness to accept the representative's pivot away from it and Alissa's reflection afterward, reveals much about the kind of political work that ELIJAH's relational culture supports. Thanks to its efforts organizing in a diversifying suburban church, four young people with undocumented parents entered the political process, telling powerful stories that used the language of family and dignity, so often conservative-coded themes, for a progressive cause instead.[18] While immediate success on the driver's license campaign would have been welcome, it was also unlikely—something ELIJAH's longtime staff and most experienced leaders, though maybe not Luke or the kids he recruited, knew very well. Still, Danny and the other students learned how to connect their religious faith with issues in their lives, understand the structural dimensions of those issues, develop and publicly proclaim powerful stories, and confront power holders to demand what their families needed. This was what mattered most to Alissa.

## Political Action as Religious Action

In the ESST and driver's license campaigns, ELIJAH participants faced decisions about how to balance short-term political strategy with relationship building and leadership development. As some members of the St. Martin's core team expressed, prioritizing the latter can be cumbersome, work-intensive, and politically risky. The team collectively invested more than a hundred person-hours into its District 6 plan, but this work yielded only about forty District 6 residents to its public meeting. The meeting fell short of its turnout goals, and this might have been a problem if not for ELIJAH's success in other districts. Yet in the process, the team formed a relationship with a new church in the city and developed a couple of new storytellers in District 6. Shortly after the meeting, the council passed a strong ESST ordinance, with the council president's support. Buoyed by their experience, the St. Martin's team then turned to working on poverty profiteering. In fact, many of the people who showed up to the CarHop action, which took place about six months later, had been first contacted by ELIJAH during its District 6 meeting-turnout work.

For Luke, Danny, and the other students, the driver's license campaign ended in disappointment. As Alissa had foreseen, the bill died in committee and never received a floor vote. But through their work with Luke leading up to the visit day, the students learned that they had the power to confront their representatives and pursue justice for their families. Elements of Catholic social teaching, in the form of religious precepts they'd been absorbing in their confirmation classes, were given practical, political meaning as they were trained to demand what their families needed from the state. The transactional approach to politics that Danny's representative employed was out of keeping with this cultural project, which is why Alissa opposed engaging with it.

Steps like these ensure that ELIJAH's issue work affirms and extends its group style: the relational culture built in training sessions and leadership assemblies. Taking a long-term view of politics and subordinating issue wins to leadership development, ELIJAH leaders make the political world into a site for faith-based action that advances the religious visions of equity and community they develop together. While this approach occasionally requires sacrificing short-term expediency on issue campaigns, on the whole it supports a program of political action that is religiously meaningful to participants and effective for setting a long-term agenda targeted at racial justice and economic fairness. In practical terms, the critiques of CarHop leveled by Josiah, Pastor Gregory, and Samuel didn't result in much. The CarHop CEO never returned the calls he got that morning, and the company's practices have not changed in response to public pressure. But in cultural and religious terms, the CarHop action was important. It laid out a religiously infused populist agenda with clear moral lines between everyday working families and wealthy corporate leaders. In stark, personal, and approachable language, it showed how corporate excess impedes working families and harms communities. It linked the kind of personal story that ELIJAH participants are used to hearing—and strive to develop and refine themselves—with a clear action plan for how to improve living conditions in poor communities. Most important, it demonstrated how people can come together to raise a moral voice in response to problems in the world. It was a political action whose consequences would be felt not in an immediate response from its targets but in the ongoing leadership development of those who participated. Its success was evident the following winter, when hundreds of people who had been organized through the poverty profiteering campaign showed up to the Prophetic Resistance rally and became leaders in ELIJAH's opposition to the Trump administration.

These examples demonstrate how ELIJAH's political work unfolds as an extension of the faith commitments its participants develop together through relational practices. Especially important is the connection between moral vocation and personal stories. Though the three political actions discussed in this chapter addressed different issues with different tactics in different settings, storytelling was central in each of them. The narratives put forward by Josiah, the District 6 speakers, and Danny and his friends were strong anchors for their respective political actions because they illuminated the personal consequences of structural problems and inequalities. They captured the populist sentiment that animates broader progressive movements, with its focus on the dehumanizing consequences of racial injustice and corporate excess, and filtered it through a powerful but nonsectarian religious lens that highlights human dignity and family flourishing as core concerns. Stories like these do not develop by happenstance. They are the products of intensive conversations and training that stoke moral vocations and intertwine them with expanded understandings of self and community. Many progressive movements try to center powerful stories in this way.[19] ELIJAH is particularly successful in doing so because, as chapters 3 and 4 showed, its relational culture makes developing strong stories into an element of religious commitment. As people learn about the concepts of self-interest and community that ELIJAH teaches, their stories become part of their religious identities. In turn, as people develop their own stories, they become more attuned to the political and religious meanings of others' struggles. Thus, religious commitment and political consciousness develop in tandem, each reinforcing the other.

Besides centering personal stories, each of these campaigns featured a rhetorical emphasis on families. Although "family values" became code for religious conservativism in the 1980s and '90s, conservatives and liberals both try to marshal the language of family to garner support for their ideas.[20] For the most part, conservatives have been more successful in this in recent decades. Sociologist Rebekah Peeples Massengill argues that this is because conservatives' and progressives' use of family metaphors is rooted in different cultural foundations.[21] Conservatives' family rhetoric usually emphasizes thrift, self-sufficiency, and consumer choice, while progressives typically appeal to institutional benevolence and fairness, asking businesses and governments to do the right thing for its own sake. Both sides try to appropriate family language for their own goals, but conservatives tend to win because their rhetoric appeals to a sense of empowering people to make good choices, while progressives' claims ask institutions to exert more control over daily life—a dubious proposition for many in the individualist culture of the United States.

ELIJAH's work is a counterexample to the trends Massengill identifies. Family rhetoric like that observed in the stories in this chapter indeed calls on institutions to treat people fairly, but it does so by highlighting families' self-sufficiency and freedom to make good choices as the reasons why reform is necessary. Danny explained that his family's choice of where to live was restricted by limited transportation options. Josiah recounted how he had no choice but to borrow from CarHop, since no bank would lend him money and he needed a car to work and support his family. Mallory's call script probed for ways families' choices and freedom are impinged by a lack of paid leave. These claims emphasize how individuals' and families' choices are restricted by contemporary resource and power distributions—the same logic that, according to Massengill, conservatives tend to use effectively.

Danny, Josiah, and other ELIJAH storytellers don't come up with these ideas completely on their own. Their stories are honed through one-to-ones, intensive training, and the analysis and ritual that take place at leadership assemblies, like the "Wade in the Water" exercise described in chapter 3. Thus, ELIJAH's family rhetoric develops through the religious culture the group is always building in less publicly visible settings. From mainstream political figures like Elizabeth Warren, whose 2020 presidential primary campaign rhetoric alluded frequently to families and dignity for working people, to the Black Lives Matter movement's call for "family villages" of support rooted in extended families and community bonds, there seems to be a resurgence of family language coming from the progressive sphere. Such language has promise, but as we've seen here, that promise may work best when it extends background cultural processes of relationship building and leadership development that many groups forgo.

Finally, it is important to highlight how in both rhetorical and practical terms, ELIJAH's political action does not address each issue on its own but as part of a broader pattern of conflict and deprivation in U.S. society. In her email, Wendy reminded the St. Martin's core team that more than ESST was at stake in organizing District 6 and called attention to "the intersectionality of all of our issues." Mallory's call script used similar language. At CarHop, Samuel and Pastor Gregory elaborated on how predatory auto lending fit into a larger frame of poverty profiteering, which in turn was an example of how corporations prey on poor families and communities. Such language is effective because it builds on the relational work we saw in settings like the legislative launch discussed in chapter 4, where people hear how multiple issues combine to impede dignity and economic security for poor and working families. As noted earlier, ELIJAH held not one visit day at the capitol but five of them, each targeting a different issue. At least a dozen dedicated people showed up to all five. This kind of commitment across issues is possible because of the background work that illuminates how different issues not only intersect in people's lives but share root causes: white supremacy, corporate power, and the lack of political voice that working people and communities of color possess in a system in which lobbyists and wealthy campaign contributors reign supreme. With some exceptions, ELIJAH participants generally don't identify as criminal justice activists, voting rights activists, or workers' rights activists. Instead, they see themselves as moral citizens pushing back against the underlying structure that props these issues up. Their religious identities are bound together with the fight to restore balance to society. This means they can be easily convinced to quickly mobilize in nearly any issue fight.

As the discussion in this chapter has shown, ELIJAH's political action is driven by a consistent focus on preserving and extending the group style it develops in background settings—a style focused on stories, relationships, and faith rather than on bills, ordinances, or specific issue campaigns. Knowing this helps us see how the specific brand of religious commitment developed through relational practices supports a robust political action program that cuts across multiple issues, addresses long-term power-building goals, and reclaims the language of family and choice for progressive causes. To an outside observer, ELIJAH's political work might not look much different from what other progressive groups do, including secular organizations. Like other groups, ELIJAH holds protests, organizes public meetings with elected officials, and lobbies legislators. What's not visible from the outside is the degree to which this work is enriched by the religious culture participants develop together in the background. It is not only religious groups that can do politics this way, but having a firm but flexible set of shared moral commitments is imperative for developing the kind of political action observed here.

## 6 Challenges of Moral Citizenship

In previous chapters, we've seen how ELIJAH uses relational practices to channel experiences and stories across a wide range of race, class, and religious backgrounds to expand people's collective power on issues that affect their lives. Pushing people to identify their self-interest, share their stories, build relationships, and claim their public voices, ELIJAH constructs moral citizenship: a worldview that cuts across belief systems, social locations, and issue areas to bring thousands of people's faith commitments to bear on civic life and the political process.

This approach to social change work has considerable advantages. Foregrounding stories and centering emotions, relational practices minimize the social distance between constituencies that often plagues progressive movements. Moreover, framing collective social change work as a moral vocation aligns it with the individualist undercurrents of American religious culture. Yet ELIJAH's work is no silver bullet for solving the serious problems plaguing U.S. society, nor for bringing about the large-scale infusion of religion into social justice movements that many religious leaders, scholars, and advocates have long hoped for.[1] In this chapter, I explain a few key challenges that confront ELIJAH and peer organizations in the faith-based community organization (FBCO) field. Some of these challenges are beyond FBCO federations' control. For instance, ELIJAH has no influence over the declining rates of religious belonging and behavior in the United States and can do nothing about them on its own, yet the decreasing proportion of Americans who gather weekly in churches raises serious questions about the long-term viability of congregation-based organizing strategies. Other challenges are internal, stemming from specific choices ELIJAH has made in how it goes about its work. While my research leads me to believe that on the whole, ELIJAH's project holds real promise for empowering people to stem the tide of deepening inequalities and perhaps eventually begin clawing them back, it is essential to understand the limitations of this model as well as its benefits.

The challenges I discuss in this chapter fall into two broad categories. The first involves challenges related to religious identity and culture. The fit between faith principles and progressive political action is often messy. I saw this regularly in my fieldwork, in several variations that I will discuss in the following pages. The second set of challenges relates to race and class. More than just inviting members of marginalized communities to meetings, ELIJAH makes sure to staff organizers of color and make sure people of color are overrepresented on its board of directors; offer Spanish translations at many of its meetings; address political and civic issues that matter to non-white, poor, and working-class communities; and explicitly confront systemic racism and white supremacy, rather than shying away from such topics. But despite all this good work, certain aspects of ELIJAH's culture continue to limit access and appeal among members of marginalized constituencies. We'll see that some participants find the timing, location, pace, and style of meetings off-putting. And ELIJAH's relational culture itself can be problematic in one key way. Though storytelling can foster empathy among people with different life experiences, it also involves risk. When organizers invite people from different backgrounds to share stories together, they risk falsely equating the real-but-manageable struggles of privileged people with the much more serious challenges that marginalized people deal with. While organizers strive to avoid this false equivalency, it's not always possible to do so, and the consequences can be serious.

Of course, this chapter only scratches the surface of the many challenges ELIJAH and peer organizations encounter. Entire books could be—and have been—written on the difficulties social movement organizations face, especially as they work to build coalitions across race, class, and religious difference.[2] My aim here is not to survey the full range of obstacles that contemporary progressive social change groups deal with but to identify challenges particular to ELIJAH and the broader FBCO field: the things engendered by these groups' specific organizing style, goals, and position in the civic and religious landscape.

## Religious Identity and Culture

Why has the Religious Right been stronger, or at least louder, than religious progressives over the last fifty years or so? Without denying the numerous achievements of progressive religious movements, it is difficult to refute that religious conservatives have been more effective in consistently building and exercising power since the 1970s.[3] While public attention tends to focus on national political dynamics, religious conservatives have been particularly impactful at the state and local levels, where they have gained power by intensively lobbying—and often filling seats on—school boards, town councils, planning boards, and other mundane yet influential governance bodies, as well as the boards of directors and charitable arms of civil society institutions like arts foundations, universities, museums, and nonprofits.[4]

When I ask students to posit explanations for the relative influence of religious conservatives and progressives, often their first guess is that most religious people are conservative. But the available data do not bear this out. The Pew Forum's 2014 Religious Landscape Study queried a nationally representative sample of more than 35,000 religious Americans.[5] Of these, 36 percent said they were conservatives, 33 percent were moderates, and 24 percent were liberals, suggesting a significant demographic advantage for conservatives. But considering party affiliation complicates the picture: only 37 percent of the Pew respondents were or leaned Republican, while 45 percent were or leaned Democrat. These numbers indicate that there are more than enough Left-leaning religious people in the United States to fuel a strong movement. The challenges facing progressive religious organizations are not just about numbers.

Researchers now mostly agree that culture, rather than demographics, is most responsible for religious progressives' relative lack of influence on the political process.[6] Simply put, in the contemporary United States, connecting religion with progressive politics involves a host of cultural challenges that religious conservatives do not have to deal with, at least not in such a serious way. As I've written elsewhere, much of ELIJAH's work is targeted specifically at overcoming these challenges and making social justice work into a culturally appealing project for religious progressives.[7] Yet even to the degree that this work is successful, it diverts time and resources from other priorities. In the next sections, I sketch the most significant of these cultural challenges.

## Fractured Religious-Political Identities

In 2015, I traveled with ELIJAH leaders to a training seminar attended by about eighty Christian, Jewish, and Islamic clergy members from several FBCO federations from around the country. At the end of the first day, which had focused on identifying and confronting challenges that clergy encounter in leading their congregations in social justice work, Pastor Anthony, a Baptist who leads a large ELIJAH-affiliated Black church in a poor neighborhood, addressed the gathered trainees. Pastor Anthony explained that his church had been an ELIJAH member congregation for several years, but he still heard negative remarks about ELIJAH from congregants. Some told him the work was "too political." Others complained it "wasn't Baptist enough" or "was not the kind of work the church should be doing." Pastor Anthony rejects these critiques, but he said they hamper ELIJAH's activities in his congregation anyway. Echoing themes raised throughout the three days, he described these complaints as symptoms of a view of the church as a "comfortable club for comfortable people." Addressing the assembled clergy, he said,

> Why am I here? I'm here to exercise the power God has given me. I have to admit that this work has been a challenge for me and for my church. But I also know that every time we say, "I can't," we slander God. I have the power to do whatever he has called me to do, and I've come to see over the last few years that this is it. So I must ask myself every day, every time I preach, every time I pray, and especially every time I have to make a decision about what my church's priorities are, "Do I really believe what God says, or am I just playing church?"

Despite Pastor Anthony's enthusiasm for ELIJAH's work, many in his congregation were skeptical, and he received consistent pushback from members who thought the church should focus on less political, less controversial ministries. In each decision he made as pastor, he was tempted to let ELIJAH work slide and take the easier route, sticking to the charitable activities that most of his membership was more comfortable with. But he viewed this as an inauthentic way to lead his congregation: not real commitment but "just playing church."

Earlier, clergy had broken into small groups to discuss the biggest obstacles to organizing in their churches. Reverend Jill, a white Lutheran in her thirties who is associate pastor at a suburban Lutheran church, observed a similar dynamic to that of Pastor Anthony: her congregants often didn't see social justice organizing as appropriate for a church setting. During the group discussion, she told the others at her table that "feeding people and giving them clothes is in the comfort zone. Charity, people are comfortable with that. But charity's not justice. People give money or food and feel like they've done their good deed. It's easy. Asking why people are hungry, that's outside the comfort zone."

Pastor Anthony is head pastor at a large Black Baptist church. Reverend Jill is an associate pastor, with much less decision-making power, at a much smaller suburban church with a mostly white congregation—a very different kind of environment. Yet both found that many of their congregants don't feel that social change work is "in the comfort zone" of what people at church should be doing. It's not necessarily that congregants don't think the issues ELIJAH works on are worth addressing; rather, many of those who support social justice causes in the abstract think church isn't an appropriate venue for doing that work.

The challenge these pastors encountered tracks with sociological research about the uneasy fit between congregational cultures and social justice work. In short, even when clergy members are heavily invested in social justice organizing, it can be hard for them to bring their congregations around to the same view. In her study of Chicago-area congregations, Penny Edgell Becker found that only a small minority of churches built sustained commitments to societal-level socioeconomic or racial justice activism.[8] Becker observed that to do community organizing work, congregations had to be willing to risk inviting internal conflict among their members and angering denominational authorities—risks that most clergy members and denominational leaders prefer to avoid, especially in an era of declining church membership. Congregations willing to take these risks are far outnumbered by those that prefer to avoid conflict, which can be achieved by prioritizing charity and locating both the need for change and the potential for transformation within individuals rather than at the level of social systems and structures. Data from the National Congregations Study likewise show that while nearly all congregations engage in charitable work, fewer than 20 percent of religious service attenders in the United States had been invited by their churches to participate in a political rally or demonstration, and most of these were about abortion, gay marriage, and similar issues, not socioeconomic problems.[9]

The experiences of ELIJAH pastors align with these broader data sources to paint a picture of congregations—including many ELIJAH affiliates—that have no shortage of people who identify as progressive among their members but still struggle to connect faith precepts with social justice goals. Part of the problem, according to sociologists Paul Lichterman and Rhys Williams, is that religious people who are also political liberals often compartmentalize their identities in a way that most conservatives don't. Religious conservatives in the United States tend to build an all-inclusive identity that fuses the religious and political worlds, whereas religious liberals are more prone to separating their religious identities from their political commitments.[10] They may respond positively to ideas about social and racial justice, but they don't always hear these claims *as religious people,* understand them through a faith lens, or, most importantly, connect their faith values to political action. Similar to Margaret from chapter 3, who was religious and political but not *religiously political* before her ELIJAH epiphany, many vote Democrat and even get involved in political organizations, but this activity usually stops short of deep engagement in systemic-level organizing and often remains separate from their church lives.

This dynamic means that some people whose political preferences align with ELIJAH's issue platform in the abstract are uneasy about making social justice part of congregational life. Lisa, a veteran ELIJAH leader who leads the core team at a mainline Protestant church she has attended since childhood, saw this pattern in action as she worked with Steve, a staff organizer, to bring her congregation into ELIJAH membership in the mid-2000s. Lisa's church sits in an inner-ring suburb that has undergone significant demographic change, shifting from mostly white before the 1980s to largely immigrant today. When Lisa was growing up in the 1970s, her church was wealthy and white: a "fur coats and gossip kind of place—you know, not really into the social justice world at all." By the 2000s, the neighborhood and congregation had changed, and an elementary school down the street was full of kids from immigrant families, many of whom lacked necessities like clothes and backpacks. In response, the congregation, still composed mostly of older white people who had moved away from the neighborhood but commuted back for church, organized aid drives to provide supplies to the school. But when Lisa tried to use the school program as a springboard for social justice organizing, she hit headwinds.

> The people who had been on board with everything, you know with the school . . . suddenly when we tried to expand, and get at the issues why the families in the school are struggling in the first place, suddenly a lot of them got cold feet. They were thinking, "Uh-oh, you're leading us down a path we're not sure we wanna be affiliated with; next thing you're going to have us rioting in the streets and things like that." So there's kind of a holdover of that kind of thinking, you know, to be very cautious in terms of what people commit themselves to.

Lisa's co-congregants were eager to provide charitable assistance to the school's struggling families but much less interested in probing the structural causes of those families' situations. Dynamics like these are impediments, but not necessarily crippling ones for ELIJAH's work. In many congregations, small teams flourish even as most of the membership ignores ELIJAH and some even view it with suspicion. In fact, at most ELIJAH-affiliated congregations, only a small proportion of the membership is even sporadically engaged in ELIJAH's work. At St. Martin's—one of ELIJAH's most powerful affiliated churches—only about 150 of its nearly 2,000 parishioners showed up for the Prophetic Resistance rally discussed in the introduction, and recruiting that many people required hours of effort from core team members, who routinely make hundreds of calls to turn out just a few dozen people to any given ELIJAH event. The ELIJAH core team at Lisa's church has only four members. While these small numbers do not preclude effective organizing, when looking at the big picture, they not only put a ceiling on how large faith-based social justice movements can get but also force the teams that do exist to spend a great deal of their time on turnout and recruitment—time that might otherwise be spent on other organizing tasks, like developing relationships with people from other backgrounds and communities. ELIJAH's rhetoric frequently emphasizes the importance of scaling up the group's efforts and expanding the number of people involved—a clear sign that while those involved in its work are effective, they need a larger movement to achieve their ambitious goals. For the time being, anyway, widespread hesitancy among rank-and-file congregants to connect their faith values with structural thinking is a serious impediment to building that larger movement.

The Inclusivity Dilemma

A second cultural challenge for FBCOs arises from a key organizational goal for ELIJAH and nearly all FBCO federations: inclusivity. In *A Shared Future*, Wood and Fulton point out that FBCOs' focus on inclusivity is rooted in two core commitments. "First and most crucially . . . [the FBCO field's] constituent base reflects the fact that income—and even more so wealth—in the United States are skewed on racial and ethnic lines. . . . Second . . . among their coalitions' best strategic assets is their ability to speak credibly for a variety of sectors."[11] Thus, both ethical and strategic imperatives push FBCO federations toward racial, religious, and socioeconomic inclusivity.

However, inclusivity is not just an organizational goal but a key part of the identity that FBCO federations cultivate, as sociologist Ruth Braunstein found in her study of a Northeastern group. Like ELIJAH, the federation Braunstein studied made inclusivity a focal point in its practices and messaging and saw it as worth pursuing for its own sake, not just as a means to an end. Father O'Donnell, a Catholic priest Braunstein interviewed, captured this sentiment with a memorable image: "Twice a year, we have a blood drive in partnership with a local synagogue. And when you hold up a bag of blood, you can't tell whether it's Christian blood or Jewish blood . . . black blood or white blood, rich blood or poor blood. It's blood that's saving a life."[12] He elaborated, "The meetings we have when we have Muslims, Catholics, Protestants, Jews, everybody together . . . what are we there for? Human dignity. And that rises above all these creedal things."[13] Father O'Donnell made sure to explain that the strict cultural boundaries so important in white evangelical culture do not apply in his religious world.[14]

I heard language like this constantly in ELIJAH, too. A good example is an email invitation to a leadership assembly hastily scheduled in late 2016, after Trump's victory. It read:

> Over the past several months, as we reflect on all of the efforts we've undertaken, we see a stark reality and a deep urgency.
>
> The stark reality is this: our efforts to build a radically inclusive democracy, a racially equitable society, an economy that puts people over profits, and an environmentally sustainable planet, are all being disrupted by well-organized, well-funded corporations, who spend millions to advance their agendas in halls of power at the local, state, and federal level.
>
> The deep urgency is that this disruption is hurting our families. Our values are being violated every single day. We cannot stop the crises that have been created in our communities without each other. With that in mind, please join us.[15]

This message called for a "radically inclusive democracy" and appealed to "our values"—values purportedly shared by people in the many communities receiving this invitation but that were really being built together in and through ELIJAH's ongoing work. It acknowledged that different communities face different crises and argued that the communities need one another to abate the crises. In response to the shock of Trump's election, ELIJAH appealed to inclusivity as not just an organizational goal but a core identity. Being inclusive was part of what made people in ELIJAH different from the "well-organized, well-funded corporations" whose agenda they opposed.

Yet the context of this message—emphasizing inclusivity in response to Trump's exclusionary politics and the political maneuverings of corporate actors—evinces a key irony. As sociologist Laura Krull explains, inclusivity in contemporary progressive religious spaces doesn't just mean welcoming all comers. More than that, it means opposition to the narrow cultural vision expounded by the Religious Right and the broader conservative movement.[16] This is not to say that religious progressives don't value inclusivity for its own sake, but goals and identities don't exist in a vacuum. Rather, the ways people enact any value—including inclusivity—are shaped by the surrounding social context. In contemporary America, practicing inclusivity means pushing back against those who are less inclusive, including—and for religious progressives, especially—the Religious Right. Sociologists Joseph Baker and Gerardo Martí point out that a key part of what many religious progressives are trying to do is distinguish themselves from their conservative counterparts.[17] Being inclusive and proclaiming that inclusivity loudly is a key way they go about this. Consequently, the particular ways they construct and practice inclusivity are shaped by the Religious Right and the cultural attention it receives.[18]

This is a dilemma for religious progressives, because over the last thirty years, many left-leaning and moderate Americans have responded to the Religious Right's specific exclusionary vision by condemning the infusion of religion and politics entirely.[19] The logic goes like this: The loudest religious voices in American politics recently have been those of conservative white Christians, and those voices articulate a narrow vision of national identity that excludes LGBTQ Americans from full membership in the social community; restricts women's choices, roles, and opportunities; blames the poor for their own problems; and denies resources and equity to immigrants and people of color. Religious progressives observe that despite their pushback against this vision, it has come to dominate many Americans' perceptions of what religion *in general* is about, such that the average observer tends to associate any religious involvement in politics with the Religious Right exclusionary platform.

A key consequence of all this is that progressive religious communities often come to believe that to appear inclusive, they must avoid politics altogether. They fear that the moment they enter the political fray, others will infer that they are like the Religious Right and therefore exclusionary. Moreover, staking too strong a set of progressive claims would make religious conservatives feel uncomfortable and uninvited and thus compromise inclusivity by excluding them, as Krull observed in the liberal Protestant congregation she studied.[20] Through these cultural dynamics, the impulse to be inclusive can become a barrier to political action.

Lisa told me she experienced something like this in 2014, when ELIJAH launched a voter turnout operation called the Prophetic Voters Campaign. As the November election approached, teams of ELIJAH leaders fanned out across the region to knock on doors and encourage residents to vote according to "their faith values," which in ELIJAH's telling called for sheltering immigrants, providing dignity and security for all people, and ensuring economic fairness. This was not the deep canvassing mentioned in chapter 3 but a more traditional voter turnout program that did not include much storytelling or follow-up.

Partly because it seemed so standardly political, Lisa found that the Prophetic Voters Campaign was counterproductive for recruitment into ELIJAH: "We lost a lot of people in that door knocking. . . . We'd had some success building up our discussion of the school and why the kids were in need, and we built up our team gradually, but that was our first foray into election-related stuff and people kind of felt it was too political." The problem was that the church's collective identity is based on inclusive cooperation across political lines. "Our church, we don't know for sure but we think it's probably about sixty/forty people who lean Democrat versus Republican. And that's a really tight balance and we're really proud of how we keep people coming together through faith across that difference when in the world around us, it's getting harder and harder to do that." The Prophetic Voters Campaign, though officially nonpartisan, was clearly targeted at increasing voter turnout in Democratic areas, and even though its message and literature never mentioned candidates, it was not subtle in its support for progressive ideas. Lisa explained that this political slant violated her congregation's norm of inclusivity and nonpartisanship and turned people—even political progressives—away from ELIJAH.

After the jolty door-knocking campaign resulted in a loss of ELIJAH participants in the congregation, Lisa was able to rekindle interest by turning the focus away from elections and back toward direct engagement with social justice issues:

We reconnected with all of these people to say, "Do you still have interest in these social justice problems? And how can we make it so that you'd be willing to give it another whirl?" . . . So then I got them out to the protest at the CarHop, and for our church that was big . . . and then there was another contingent that we got out to US Bank to protest their involvement in payday lending. So you never really know what's going to strike people's interest, but . . . at least they're game to think about it and to go out there and do something. Which is a huge, huge shift in thinking for our church.[21]

Election work was off-putting to members of Lisa's congregation, but direct issue work wasn't, especially when it addressed economic fairness using populist rather than partisan language. Since it targeted corporations, centered around personal stories like Josiah's (chapter 5), and wasn't connected to an election, it didn't violate the norm of inclusivity that Lisa's congregation proudly fosters.

Largely because of experiences like this, FBCO federations have typically prioritized issue-based community work, like the poverty profiteering campaign, over electoral politics. Yet while avoiding electoral work is a way to mitigate cultural challenges within congregations, recent years have revealed this strategy's broader limitations. Republicans, despite losing ground in the national presidential popular vote and the generic ballots for congressional and many state legislative contests, have consolidated their majorities in many statehouses across the country thanks to a combination of gerrymandering and the deepening geographic polarization of the electorate, as Democratic voters grow more concentrated in urban areas.[22] These patterns apply in ELIJAH's state, and they mean that no matter how well ELIJAH or any other FBCO federation organizes locally, Republican-controlled legislatures often step in to quash municipal-level progressive bills such as minimum wage increases, mandatory sick leave policies, and renewable energy commitments, which are often quite popular statewide and appear nonpartisan until they become the targets of Republican ire. For instance, each year during my fieldwork and continuing to this day, legislative Republicans in ELIJAH's state pushed a policy called local preemption, which would prevent cities and counties from making their own policies on numerous issues, for example, strengthening worker protections or pursuing climate solutions. If enacted, local preemption would roll back most of the victories that ELIJAH and other organizations have secured in cities and counties, so strong pushback is required. But the opposition to preemption that must be organized each and every year requires a huge proportion of ELIJAH's resources. During each legislative session, leaders organize multiple phone banks, rallies, and even disruptive actions to make sure Democratic leaders aren't tempted to join Republican support for preemption and, when the governor's office is held by a Democrat, to gain a commitment to veto any potential preemption bill the Republican-controlled legislature might pass. Thus, while preemption has not yet been enacted in

ELIJAH's state, the need to fight it every year is a major drain on ELIJAH's other work, and other FBCOs have similar experiences.

Partly because of this persistent pattern, by the time I left the field, ELIJAH was developing ways to get more involved in electoral politics, so that rather than beating back preemption and other damaging policy proposals every year, they could elect legislators who would never put such ideas forward at all. Therefore, like numerous other FBCOs across the country, ELIJAH formed a spin-off organization that uses a 501(c)4 tax status, rather than the 501(c)3 status typical of nonprofits, since 501(c)3 organizations, which include nearly every FBCO federation, are forbidden from activity supporting or opposing any candidate for office. In contrast, 501(c)4s like ELIJAH's new spin-off can engage in limited electoral work as long as the bulk of their activities are not related to elections. Thus, by creating a 501(c)4 arm, ELIJAH empowered itself to do election-related work and support candidates explicitly.

Under the auspices of this new spin-off organization, leaders worked hard identifying Republicans who had supported preemption and targeting them with voter turnout drives and phone banks. These efforts helped bring Democrats within one seat of a bicameral legislative majority in 2018 and also heavily influenced the Democratic gubernatorial primary. A moderate ultimately won the primary, but thanks in large part to ELIJAH and the campaign its 501(c)4 spin-off ran during the primary campaign to elevate progressive candidates, the eventual winner committed to key progressive ideas he likely would have rejected otherwise. Across the country, more and more FBCOs are taking similar steps, spinning off new 501(c)4 organizations as they realize that influencing policy in any context other than large cities, and sometimes even there, requires becoming more active in electoral politics and working to elect representatives who support causes aligned with their own. Yet as Lisa's experience suggests, this entry into electoral work comes at a cultural cost, even if it brings political gains.

## Race and Class

Bringing all participants to develop and articulate a personal account of what they have on the line in social justice work is a key element of ELIJAH's organizing model. We've seen throughout this book how storytelling helps achieve this. By developing personal stories and learning to tell them in public, people develop their own accounts of why social change matters to them, articulate their self-interest to others, and empathize with people whose lives are different from their own. Yet there is no denying that social change work has different meanings and different stakes for members of marginalized communities than it does for privileged people. A few times during my fieldwork, I saw evidence that ELIJAH's culture, including its relational practices, can sometimes amplify, rather than minimize, these differences.

Victor is a thirty-year-old immigrant from Mexico who is married to Kristin, from chapter 3. When the two met, Victor began accompanying Kristin to All People's Church, and before long, he became a member, too. Before meeting Kristin and joining All People's, Victor had a negative assessment of religion, typical of secular progressives his age who leave organized religion after childhood.[23] Victor had grown up Catholic in Mexico, but he said, "It had never been my experience that pastors would speak about social justice, and white supremacy, and systems of oppression; I didn't think religious people could talk like that, that there was even space for that kind of dialogue."

Attending All People's as a young adult, Victor developed a new sense of how faith could support critiques of inequality and oppression:

The first three sermons I heard there, it felt like I was meant to be there. They felt pretty empowering, and healing, and they spoke to me personally. Particularly because Pastor Park, being a Korean, it was the first time I had seen a pastor who wasn't white in a while. . . . It was just kind of like this kind of brand-new thing of, I have a nonwhite pastor who is speaking about the Gospel in a way that makes sense to me. Not only that, but it was the first time in my life where I had heard a pastor talk about white supremacy from the pulpit, or talk about the sins that this country has committed: genocide, and stealing land, and all these things. And not in a way to rile people up to like, let's overthrow the U.S., but what does our faith say about that. I think those experiences combined, and also the people, the warmth, and the openness, it was kind of like a culture shock in a good way. I got a sense that I was going to be sticking around for a while.

Yet even as Victor found a satisfying religious home at All People's through its discussions of race, white supremacy, and colonialism, his relationship with ELIJAH has not always been smooth. If ELIJAH is to realize its broader goals and grow its movement, Victor—a passionate, highly committed young Christian of color with experience organizing in secular progressive spaces—is the kind of person it has to be able to recruit. But early in Victor's membership at All People's, he did not find ELIJAH's culture appealing:

> The relationship between me and ELIJAH, it hasn't been the best all the time. It's been filled with tension, just because as an undocumented person who's carried many different identities, marginalized and oppressed identities, I think I'm pretty, what's the word? When you don't trust. Distrusting? . . . I would say there are, I guess, some strong criticisms between ELIJAH to All People's and All People's to ELIJAH. ELIJAH has said that we're pretty insular and small minded, and my wife will tell you ELIJAH has been pretty white, particularly in the past. The pace at which we speak at meetings, which I have brought up consistently, and the language that we use, and setting up a culture and language. Yeah, the relationship between All People's and ELIJAH, and my personal relationship with ELIJAH through our church, has been filled with tension.

Without questioning ELIJAH's intentions or sincerity, Victor identified cultural challenges that encumber his and his congregation's engagement. Some of his criticisms, such as the pace of speech and the culture and language he encounters in ELIJAH meetings, are commonly levied by people of color working in mostly white organizations, and others in ELIJAH made similar observations.[24] Janelle, a low-income Black Catholic and a single mother, told me she has been bothered by "the obvious things, like okay, you have your meeting on a weekday evening? Well lots of us are at work, and if we're not at work we're taking care of our kids. So yeah, offer childcare. But ELIJAH doesn't do that and they should." Janelle also mentioned the location of meetings as a factor:

> It's about when are you having these meetings, and where. I was able to serve on the sexual violence task force for a while because I'm disabled and don't work, but these meetings were happening at 3 in the afternoon in the most isolated, western area of town. . . . It takes two hours to take a bus to it. Talk about stupid. So yeah, I was the only person of color there that wasn't on staff. They just don't think about, like they never ask themselves, "What are we offering in terms of transportation needs, in terms of childcare?" What about weekends or the opportunity to call in?

In Victor's and Janelle's views, ELIJAH's good intentions on inclusivity have yet to be matched by changes in how meetings are run and scheduled and how attendees are supported with childcare, food, and other things working people need once there. Such lingering problems indicate that while ELIJAH prioritizes inclusivity and diversity across all its issues and campaigns, many meetings and actions are still planned and run mostly by middle- or professional-class white people, without sufficient input from people of other backgrounds.

Logistics like scheduling and support for attendees aren't the whole problem, either. Victor and Janelle also told me about ways ELIJAH's emphasis on storytelling and other relational practices can impede substantive inclusion. No one denies that relational practices often open paths for cooperation and empathy, but at the same time, developing a personal story and learning to tell it in public, as ELIJAH asks all participants to do, is a learned skill associated with particular cultural traits. Social movements scholar Betsy Leondar-Wright explains that putting oneself at the center of social change analysis requires thinking about institutions as flexible, malleable, and open to change rather than external authority sources.[25] Research shows that this disposition is more common among middle- to upper-class people than among those with working-class backgrounds. In a study of nearly two dozen social movement organizations, Leondar-Wright saw how this made groups that prioritized self-stories inhospitable to people from poor and working-class backgrounds. On these grounds, she criticizes groups' tendency to insist that attendees have identity-based reasons, rooted in personal stories, for being involved. When groups hold that people must see the work as essential to their own identities, they make shorter-term, less intellectual incentives, like a desire for social connection or even a free meal, seem like unworthy motivations for getting involved. By consistently neglecting these concerns, organizations implicitly cater to those whose motivations align with the more intellectual, self-as-project ethic—namely, middle- to upper-class people.[26]

Janelle observed this dynamic operating along racial lines in ELIJAH, too, calling it "still a totally white organization" despite recruiting a growing number of people of color and having a Black president. She points out that in public settings, the people who speak most frequently are white and middle class, and people of color must work harder than white people to figure out what is going on and then gain meaning out of their participation: "[I remember a] wonderful moment where I don't know how many faith leaders took over the rotunda in city hall, and it was a kaleidoscope of colors, and you know male and female leaders, gay and straight, but those who had the microphone, well I heard mostly white people. And there were nonwhite people there to talk, but I just wonder if they have to . . . [make a] more concerted [effort] about giving the mike to people of color."

Knowing that Janelle had recently been spending more time working with a secular community organization called Action and less time in ELIJAH, partly because of dynamics like this, I asked her whether Action also struggled in elevating people of color's leadership:

> *Janelle*: Yeah. However, they were able to build a really strong woman of color table, where we were definitely supporting the great coalition initiatives, like Fight for 15 . . . and they hired a bunch of really powerful Latinas at Action, so the table is now primarily Latina, but still a force. So they're trying.
>
> *JD*: And do you think ELIJAH does that?
>
> *Janelle*: No. . . . [long pause] But, well, it's hard, you know, unless you have the leadership, women and people of color, you gotta take the mike away from the white leadership. And just let that be the standard in which you want yourself heard in the community. So when you have an action, or you join an action, the people that are going to speak on your behalf are going to be women and people of color.

In Janelle's view, Action does a good job of giving women and people of color their own dedicated spaces and putting them in leadership positions. ELIJAH, in contrast, focuses on using relational practices to put people in shared spaces where they can learn to empathize across racial lines but fails to explicitly "take the mike away from the white leadership." Natosha, a thirty-one-year-old Black woman who had recently moved back to the Midwest from Washington, D.C., concurred. When I asked her what challenges she thinks ELIJAH faces, she replied:

> It's about allowing the people you're trying to support to speak for themselves. Handing them the microphone and letting them, using your privilege to make sure that they have the microphone or a seat at the table. And I think that's what people have to do as allies. I think people also have to understand their different levels of privilege. 'Cause there's a privilege each person has, in a way, right? So I would be foolish to say that I don't have any privilege. I do. Because I'm a straight Christian woman. . . . Yes, there are targets on

my back because I'm a Black woman. There's, everyone has a target, but then everyone has a privilege. I can use my privilege to give the microphone to someone who is being targeted in a different way that I am not. But I don't always see the white leadership in ELIJAH being quite as mindful of that.

Natosha did feel, however, that ELIJAH was making progress, especially compared to what she had seen five years earlier, before she left the area. She explained that like all social change organizations, ELIJAH needs to work on helping white people understand that when their privilege is questioned, it's not necessarily a personal attack.

It's something that I see that they're intentionally speaking about and intentionally wanting to do. And I think that's important. It can be scary to have your privilege called out. It's uncomfortable. Especially if you feel like you're not directly doing something. Like, am I directly harming transgender people? No. But a lot of people who look like me are, right? So being okay with collectively being called out and understanding that even if you're not doing that thing, because you are of that group, you have an obligation and ability to change the perspective of people around you.

Natosha's and Janelle's remarks about white people's tendency to dominate ELIJAH's public speech and actions echo research arguing that privileged people are often more skilled in and confident about the kind of performative personal testimony ELIJAH encourages because they are accustomed to using institutions and organizations as venues for self-cultivation and self-expression.[27] This phenomenon is well documented in sociological literature, but no white ELIJAH leaders mentioned to me that they were aware of the potential for their organizing model to reinforce social structure along these lines. Yet I observed numerous instances in which this seemed to happen.

One of them involved a public storytelling session that prompted a strong negative reaction from Victor. At a leadership assembly, Deontae, a Black staff organizer in his early thirties, led an exercise intended to foster trust and connections between ELIJAH participants who did not know one another. He introduced the session this way:

We as people of faith know that when the enemy is winning, it's because of division. It's because we've been separated into all these different categories, and we don't know how to connect with each other anymore. So today we're going to do an exercise in being vulnerable with each other. We're going to break up into pairs with a person you have never had a conversation with before, and person A is going to tell their story. And person B is going to listen, do nothing but listen. And then person B is going to name where they heard anger and suffering and woe in that story. And then we'll switch roles.

To demonstrate, Deontae invited Hannah, a twenty-seven-year-old white woman, to share her personal story before the audience. The idea, Hannah told me later, was to get white people thinking about their own pain and struggles so they could move beyond altruism and see social justice work as their own project. Thus, the exercise aligned with ELIJAH's broader cultural goals, but in this setting, it fell flat.

For about ten minutes, Hannah described how for as long as she could remember, her parents' relationship had been polluted by conflict about gender roles. Her mother was a feminist, but her father preferred a more traditional division of household labor, and frequent spats ensued. Although her parents stayed together, Hannah said that her relationship with her mother had suffered because of how patriarchy had divided her parents. They had both tried to get her to take their side in the ongoing quarrel, and Hannah now felt that she had not been the powerful ally her mother needed in the face of her father's unfair expectations. Her self-interest derived from this experience. The pain of knowing how patriarchy had harmed her family motivated her to work with others in ELIJAH:

> I don't want to cast my family in a negative light, because they have done so much for me, but also I can't shake the feeling that I didn't do enough for my mother to be her ally in her relationship with my dad and in other parts of her life. But knowing these dynamics, and my privilege, makes me want to work for a level playing field for everybody. So how can I be a strong woman by myself, and how can God steer me toward that, because of but also in spite of what I grew up with?

Hannah acknowledged her own privilege while talking about how gender roles and patriarchy hampered her mother's life and her parents' marriage. Guilt about her mother's pain became an emotional basis for her own engagement in collective action to create a "level playing field for everybody," giving her a stake in ELIJAH's work that goes beyond simply helping others. In line with Natosha's call for white people to acknowledge their pain as well as their privilege, Hannah's testimony used her guilt about not having recognized or acted on her mother's troubles with patriarchy to generate solidarity with people who are suffering from problems caused by other damaging social hierarchies.

Though Hannah's story was tearful and courageous, people in the audience had mixed reactions. Everyone applauded, but I could hear people around me murmuring reactions that were not all enthusiastic. Here was a paradox: Hannah had bravely shared the intimate personal details that honed her self-interest in organizing and sincerely acknowledged her privilege. By using her story to demonstrate the exercise, Deontae had signaled that acknowledging vulnerability is not only a task for poor people or people of color—that privileged people also have a responsibility to probe their experiences for emotions and experiences that can be the basis of activism. Yet by making a story like Hannah's—rooted in concerns about identity, not material struggles—the focus of attention, Deontae gave voice and a platform to a privileged person whose struggles were clearly less urgent than those of many of the other people present.

This did not please Victor. He told me later,

> I mean, I understood what they were trying to do, but as a person who was undocumented for over ten years, I just didn't need to hear about that [Hannah's experience]. It was good for her to work through that, and I'm glad she has done that, but I know my own pain. I live with it every day, when people second guess me because I'm not white or because I didn't have papers. And that day I didn't need to be part of talking about white people's pain. I was ready to talk about action! I was angry, I was fired up, I was ready to talk about how we were going to get to work and what we were going to do. And here we were listening to this white woman talk about her mother, and that just seemed like such an affront to me at the time. So I texted Steve [the staff organizer Victor had worked with most closely] and said, "This is bullshit, Steve. This is not cool. I'm leaving."

Victor felt that hearing a privileged person process her troubles in this setting was an inappropriate use of his time and that of other people of color in ELIJAH. He does not dispute that Hannah's story is essential for her own activism, but he was frustrated that ELIJAH organizers had chosen to spend precious time at a leadership assembly elevating privileged people's stories and helping them learn how to talk about emotions that marginalized people already understood.

For Victor, hearing privileged people tell emotion-laden personal stories that probe their own painful experiences is a double-edged sword. On the one hand, he welcomes it, because he knows that connecting personal experience with systemic forces is a way to bring privileged people into activism and to help them see that they have something at stake. His wife Kristin, for instance, has come to recognize the harm that systems of oppression bring to all people by thinking about her own family history and the linked roles of race, masculinity, and corporate power in shaping her relationship with her father. But on the other hand, privileged people's stories about emotional pain do not reflect the same degree of marginalization as those told by people who have grown up poor, undocumented, or racially stigmatized and systematically oppressed. Moreover, while talking about pain is a necessary first step to developing the kind of self-interest ELIJAH strives for, such discussions can obscure larger questions about action and anger. Victor told me that in his experience, it often takes a lot of time, thought, and emotional energy for privileged people to learn how to talk about pain. While they are trying to process their own stories, the marginalized people in the room are silently clamoring to talk about anger and how it can be pointed toward action.

The impediments to inclusivity discussed in this section—the pace, timing, and location of meetings; white people's continued tendency to dominate the microphone at actions and meetings; and the false equivalency between different experiences that storytelling practices can create—speak to the tremendous scale of the challenge that organizations like ELIJAH face in their efforts to transform themselves into racial justice organizations. Notably, each of these problems arose because privileged leaders in ELIJAH failed to pick up on ways that their standard operating procedures excluded others, especially those of poor or nonwhite backgrounds. Yet as Natosha pointed out, calling people to account for the invisible-to-them ways their practices exclude other people is risky, because many people, and especially many white people, tend to take such critiques personally, rather than "being okay with collectively being called out and understanding that even if you're not doing that thing, because you are of that group, you have an obligation and ability to change the perspective of people around you." This "white fragility," as Robin DiAngelo calls it, continues to stand between racially diverse faith-based organizations like ELIJAH and the racial and social justice goals they espouse.[28]

## Potential amid Challenges

This chapter has described some of the challenges that confront faith-based organizations working across race and class lines. FBCO federations like ELIJAH have developed powerful ways to recruit, train, and empower leaders, and they have made serious strides toward meaningful diversity. Still, their activities play out within a broader social context where people hesitate to link faith with progressive politics, and where race and class differences impede lasting, substantive cooperation. For all the advantages moral citizenship offers as an organizing model, its prospects for driving the change its adherents envision remain tied to its ability to surmount these contextual obstacles.

Reflecting on these challenges offers an opportunity to zoom out from ELIJAH's highly successful day-to-day practice and consider the significant barriers that impede such movements on a broader scale in the contemporary United States. As we have seen, race and class in organizing spaces are not just markers of individual identities and community experiences but also rubrics that shape the kinds of stories people tell and the ways they interpret the stories that others tell. It is unlikely a marginalized person would have told a story like Hannah's; it is equally unlikely a privileged person would have reacted like Victor did. The hierarchies of U.S. society thus divide people even in spaces specifically designed to bridge gaps—not through discriminatory individual attitudes but by conferring on people different degrees of privilege, deprivation, and stigma and their associated cultural traits, which individuals in turn carry with them into organizing settings.

Lisa found that refocusing her practically all-white congregation on economic fairness—notably a race-neutral, seemingly nonpolitical frame— was a good way to recover after the choppy Prophetic Voters Campaign had stalled ELIJAH's momentum in her church, and similar moves may hold promise for overcoming the lingering challenges that race presents in organizing spaces. While ELIJAH has adopted a racial justice frame that cuts across all its issues of the last ten and especially five years, this frame draws on the theory of change adopted by the Black Lives Matter movement, which calls for restoring racial justice by assuring economic fairness for all members of society. In the wake of the murder of George Floyd and the ensuing protest wave, *New York Times* columnist Jamelle Bouie reminded readers of how race struggles overlap with economic inequality: "In our society . . . the fight for equal personhood can't help but also be a struggle for economic justice. And what we see, past and present, is how that fight against the privileges and distinctions of race can also lay the foundations for a broader assault on the privileges and distinctions of class."[29] Echoing W. E. B. Du Bois, Bouie argues that economic insecurity continues to drive wedges between white people and people of color and suggests that ending that insecurity can go a long way toward mitigating racial animus, if not destroying white supremacy entirely. In this context, ELIJAH's poverty profiteering and economic fairness campaigns seem like promising ways to get white people on board with critical racial analysis.

# Conclusion

......................................................

"There is a reason that over two thousand people registered for this event. Including the folks at New Kingdom, and they're every bit a part of this building. Our conscience is calling us. Whether or not we protect our families and preserve our republic depends on the choice we make today. This can be a meeting that you went to, or you can recognize this day as an invitation to one hundred days of prophetic action and a lifetime of moral citizenship. Thank you."

With these words, Alissa closed her speech at the Prophetic Resistance rally. As she indicated, the overflow crowd, so large it had to be split across two venues, with a livestream at New Kingdom accommodating latecomers who'd been shut out of packed-to-bursting Broadway, signaled enormous enthusiasm for using religious faith to counter the recently inaugurated Trump administration, the forces that had brought it to power, and the persistent inequalities that it seemed poised to deepen further. But in ending her speech by naming a choice between remembering the day as just another meeting people had gone to or making it the launchpad for a lifetime of moral citizenship, Alissa also suggested that too many religious people—including many of those assembled before her—have made what she saw as the wrong choice: to passively lament other people's problems rather than coming to see them as their own. To view racism as a regrettable reality that people of color must resolve or endure. Poverty as a problem for poor people. Deplorable working conditions and paltry wages as an unfortunate fact of life for those without the training or credentials to secure better work. Police violence as a problem for overpoliced communities. And so on. For too long, Alissa implied, too many religious people have gone to meetings where they talk about how sad and terrible these things are, maybe dropped a donation on their way out the door or signed up for a volunteer shift, and then gone on with their lives, occasionally remembering the downtrodden with a prayer but never joining them in action to improve social conditions for all.

How can people move from passively lamenting other people's struggles to seeing those struggles as their own and working together to confront them? This book has used the case of ELIJAH to show how faith-based community organizing (FBCO) federations are powerfully inviting religious people to think differently about their relationships to other people, social problems, and democracy. Leaders in these organizations realize that congregations, even liberal ones, typically approach inequality in a manner insufficient for sparking the kind of sustained, broad-based collective action that real change depends on.[1] Instead of merely pointing out ways that social conditions transgress faith values and perhaps asking congregants to vote, volunteer, or donate to or pray for key causes, FBCO leaders build relationships through relational practices that illuminate how problems that seem distant at first often bear on people's own lives in unexpected ways, and make resolving these problems the target of people's moral vocations. For them, using religious faith as the basis for unraveling socioeconomic inequality and systemic racism requires more than explaining why conditions are unjust and voting and praying for better. It means making moral citizens—and doing all the demanding relational work that entails.

## Expanding Self and Community

Lots of stories I heard in ELIJAH stick with me. So do the pangs of anxiety I felt early in my fieldwork, when, under intense questioning from ELIJAH leaders, I couldn't yet articulate my own self-interest in social justice work, or even understand why I needed to. Like many middle-class white Americans, I was taught from a young age to draw clear lines between my own life circumstances and those of people we called "less fortunate"—as if poverty and racism were matters of chance and not the products of social structures that humans have designed and perpetuated. Even as a sociologist, it took time, thinking, and listening for me to recognize how my life is tied to those of people who are harmed in more obvious, direct ways by racism and socioeconomic inequality. As I sat through training sessions, planning meetings, one-to-ones, and leadership assemblies, I gradually came to see how my ability to procure things that I and my family need, such as reliable and affordable health care, good public schools, security against unexpected job loss, and time off to care for ailing loved ones, is hampered by the same systems that unjustly imprison and kill people of color; ensnare poor people in cycles of predatory debt; and depress wages and benefits for retail, restaurant, and service workers. As I spent time in ELIJAH and engaged in its relational practices, the lines that I had previously subconsciously drawn between my life and those of people around me began to blur.

In showing how leaders in ELIJAH use relational practices to erase these lines and bring people to recognize how their struggles are connected across lines of race, class, and religion, this book has sought to broaden the focus in which we view progressive religious activists and their social change projects. The people driving many of today's most influential social justice movements are not just acting out religious worldviews, pursuing policy changes that align with certain beliefs and doctrines. More than this, they are creating meaning and moral community in a society divided by inequality and racism by creatively appealing to people's personal religious callings. They are not simply responding to threats and demands imposed on their own families and neighborhoods by politics and the economy but using political activity to create a "common life," as political theologian Luke Bretherton puts it.[2] Bretherton argues that religious communities are among the very few institutions in contemporary societies capable of fostering the meaningful, sustained interactions a common life can emerge from. My analysis has shown that this happens when leaders tap religion in a particular way, bringing people to work collectively across difference to identify their moral vocations, link them in a framework of shared struggle, and fuse them into a broader vision of and call to moral citizenship.

Understanding this kind of organizing, I have argued, requires adapting the way we think about religion and its role in social movements. Throughout the book, I have tried to show that understanding moral citizenship requires moving our focus from the political implications of religious beliefs to the relational practices that can transform individuals' identities and support collective moral visioning. The diverse arrays of beliefs, traditions, and values that people of different backgrounds bring into ELIJAH do not inherently support any one political platform or set of civic demands. But they do support the idea that each person, whatever their race, age, immigration status, faith, or anything else, has a moral vocation—a unique personal story and a compelling moral mission. The enormously diverse religious traditions in the United States have different histories and focal points, distinct political theologies and languages of the common good.[3] But across these differences, they mostly share the cultural assumption that individuals are called to make choices and that the choices they make matter. Moral vocation is the sense of feeling called to a specific purpose and choosing to answer that call, and moral citizenship is the daily practice of acting out a moral vocation focused on disrupting systemic inequalities and restoring power to everyday people. In ELIJAH, relational practices teach people that while their moral vocations are motivated by different traditions and emerge from different contexts, they are all ultimately oriented toward the same end goal of building the collective power needed to make it possible for all people to live secure, dignified lives.

When we recognize these relational practices as the hinges that connect religious beliefs and identities with civic engagement and political action, we can see the relationship between religion and progressive political action in a new light. In the context of ongoing religious disaffiliation and deepening racial and socioeconomic inequalities, participants in FBCOs set out to make their faith into a source of connection and a springboard for solving society's biggest problems. This requires not only confidence in one's own convictions but also the patience and humility to listen to others' stories and the willingness to be interrogated about one's own goals and values, as we saw in chapter 3. People may come into ELIJAH with a set of beliefs that they think will motivate action, but inevitably these beliefs are given new meaning through the sharing and listening that relational practices entail. Faith-based community organizing is thus not a matter of acting out beliefs but creating meaning together through the intentional construction and ongoing maintenance of relationships across various kinds of difference.

This investigation of the daily practices of faith-based community organizing sharpens our understanding of how everyday religious people bring widely shared faith precepts to life and make them the basis of civic action. As chapter 4 showed, when they gather to share stories and forge relationships, ELIJAH leaders spend surprisingly little time talking about beliefs, doctrines, and sacred texts. Instead, they devote the bulk of their energy to identifying each person's self-interest and moral vocation and pushing them to see how realizing these depends on ensuring a more just society for all. In showing how these complex processes played out in this case, I have paid particular attention to how individual vocations and collective commitments intersect and shape each other. When people come to see how their own life projects are intertwined with the common good, their religious commitments become imperatives to disrupt inequalities and build collective power.

## Religious and Secular Organizing

The 2020 election produced a victory for Joe Biden but also serious Democratic losses in the House of Representatives, smaller than expected gains in the Senate, and an uptick in Trump support among people of color, especially men. Writing afterward in the *New Left Review*, social theorist Mike Davis described Biden's victory as pyrrhic and lamented the state of today's progressive sphere: "Despite the huge popularity of our ideas and the dynamic example of BLM [Black Lives Matter] we remain clueless and disorganized as a national force. We need to stop looking for electoral silver linings and get ourselves together. Renew our commitment to BLM and work like hell to build a multi-issue national coalition for life and justice."[4]

Perhaps we should not expect a figure like Davis, a staunch leftist whose career took flight in the 1980s just as the Religious Right was ascending, to look for progressive organizing in religious settings. But were he to spend some time among ELIJAH and its peers in the FBCO field, Davis might see some inklings of hope. In these organizations, people are building lasting relationships, committing to BLM and its racial justice platform, and developing precisely the kind of multi-issue coalition Davis and other left theorists have been calling for.[5]

This kind of long-term power-building work is less glitzy than electoral campaigns. Problematically, it is also much less well funded.[6] But if the nation's top leftist intellectuals see broad-based coalition-focused organizing as foundational to equity and democracy, why do they seem unaware that it is precisely what nearly 200 FBCO federations are doing—and have been for decades? Despite the publication of numerous books on faith-based organizing and FBCO federations' contributions to important political wins, many analysts and thought leaders on the left seem unaware of the FBCO field's existence, let alone its promise.[7] Why, amid all the calls to multi-issue, multiracial organizing that emerged in the late 2010s, especially following Trump's election, do commentators fail to see that this very work is happening, perhaps not in the places they most expect but in church basements and sanctuaries across the country?

One possibility is that faith-based organizing escapes many progressives' notice precisely because it is faith based. Even though religious voices have been at the center of many of U.S. society's most successful progressive movements, the Religious Right's ascendance, on the one hand, and the decline of nearly every other form of organized religion, on the other, have cast long shadows across a generation's worth of progressive political thought. For observers of American politics from roughly 1980 to 2008, the possibility that religion could contribute to movements for anything besides ending abortion and preventing gay marriage understandably seemed remote.

Today, though religion's broader decline has not abated, faith-based organizing continues to flourish and even grow. Proportionally to the population, fewer people are religious than in the past, but as we've seen in this book, many hunger for something more than the passive charity-focused approach to social problems that has long prevailed among many American congregations. Participants in faith-based organizing are not satisfied with being seen on Sunday morning and living a life of private devotion. As the world's inequalities, and those of the United States in particular, become harder and harder to ignore, they feel called to turn their faith outward—not only into electoral politics but, more importantly, into relationships with people who aren't like them.

Of course, there is no denying that the changing demographics of American religion are flashing red warning lights for FBCOs. Fewer people in congregations obviously means fewer people that can be reached through the congregation-based organizing methods that FBCOs employ. Of potentially deeper concern, it is not clear that religious spaces are being replaced with other venues where people can build the trust and empathy needed for relational practices to succeed. Studies in the 2000s found that membership-based organizations conducive to lasting relationships were being supplanted by donation-based advocacy and nonprofit organizations with little relationship-building potential.[8] These days, people can interact with hundreds or thousands of others online at any time. But how many of those digital interactions run deep enough to support the story sharing and authentic lasting relationships that strong organizing thrives on? How many physical spaces can bring people together with anything like the degree of emotional intimacy that religious congregations have historically done? Zero is not the answer to either question, but there is serious concern among scholars and practitioners of community organizing that today's venues of public interaction are less conducive to building and maintaining the relationships needed to support social change than those they have replaced.[9]

These are warning signs, not death knells, however. Religious communities provide fertile ground for stirring moral vocations and making moral citizens, but organized religion is not the only venue where relational practices can flourish. This book has shown how FBCOs' work requires attaching sacred value to caring and connections—and how beliefs and doctrines are background motivators, not central foci. Religious spaces are a natural fit for organizing, but notably, early community organizers, from Saul Alinsky in Chicago to Ernesto Cortés in San Antonio to Cesar Chavez and

Dolores Huerta in California, chose to organize in congregations not because of the beliefs their members held but because they were centers of community where people knew, trusted, and cared about one another.[10] The key for transferring the model they developed into secular spaces is finding other venues where the potential for such intimacy, trust, and care exists.

Toward this end, since my fieldwork ended, ELIJAH has been expanding its organizing beyond congregations. In 2018, it began its Black Barber and Beauty Shop Cooperative, targeting venues where members of the Black community have historically gathered and shared stories. Its web page reads:

> For years, barbershops have been staples of community as they provide both individual and collective empowerment, esteem, and morale. These are spaces where people come for physical and communal transformation. At the core, barber and beauty shops foster intentional relationships with community members while also providing a service. Several shops in our region have chosen to use their collective voice and people power to create the community they know is possible. By operating in the political arena, they are ensuring that the issues that matter most to them are a priority and the communities they serve have the same opportunities to thrive as anyone else.[11]

Drawing on Samuel's experience running the barbershop where he met Pastor Al and recruited Josiah, ELIJAH is now working to reach Black people who may not attend church or whose churches are not linked to ELIJAH in a space where they build community and establish trusting relationships with one another. The fact that barber and beauty shops are small businesses and thus carry a degree of esteem in debates about workplace issues is an added benefit.

Childcare centers are another place where parents and providers build trust and community together.[12] ELIJAH's Kids Count on Us initiative involves "community and political organizing towards a fully funded childcare system that centers the voices of childcare providers and their families. Full funding includes living wages for teachers, resources for centers, and access to care for all families, no matter where they live or what's in their wallets."[13] This campaign, together with coalition partners, has procured additional state funding for early childhood care and successfully countered a Republican-led effort to require the collection of biometric data from families receiving state childcare assistance.

Since the Black Barber and Beauty Shop Cooperative and the Kids Count on Us initiative began after my fieldwork ended, I did not get the chance to observe how the cultural dynamics of faith-based organizing translates into these secular and commercial spaces. But the staff involved in these new efforts are the same people who support the long-standing congregation-based work, and the barbershop and childcare-based leaders attend the same leadership assemblies as the faith-based leaders do. It seems reasonable to hypothesize that their methods are similar even though the settings are different. It is essential for future research to investigate how community organizing methods developed in faith settings can be adapted for use in these alternative venues. But at the very least, the fact that ELIJAH has campaigns flourishing outside its favored congregational terrain is a sign that moral vocations can be stoked and moral citizenship can flourish outside congregations.

ELIJAH's new projects are a sign that FBCOs' organizing hinges less on religious belief than often assumed, and this makes it tempting to ask what other kinds of secular spaces might be most capable of supporting this kind of organizing. Could neighborhood associations be fertile ground? Parent-teacher associations? College campuses? All of these seem plausible. But I think focusing on particular types of organizations and spaces involves asking the wrong question. When considering what about religious communities makes them good organizing terrain, it is important to remember that (a) religious relationships and practices are, at their core, *social* relationships and practices that humans enact together, and (b) social relationships and practices can draw on religious phenomena without being explicitly or exclusively religious. As sociologist Nancy Ammerman explains, thinking of "religious" life as inherently different and separate from other parts of life imposes occidentalist, modernist, and often white and middle-class assumptions.[14] We should not assume, for example, that organizing works in religious spaces because there is something uniquely empowering about religion. Rather, we should investigate what it is about the social relationships and practices religious people do together that makes them fertile ground for organizing.

As explained throughout the book, I believe religion works for organizing because it provides a sense of personal mission that can be transformed by skilled leaders into a morally situated sense of self whose actualization depends on being in accountable relationships with others. In FBCO settings, people are brought together through strong social networks (congregations), build relationships through intimate practices that tap their deepest abiding senses of self (their moral vocations), and, through these relationships, come to see how their lives and fortunes are intertwined through social structure. The reason faith is such good fuel for this process is not that it has some unequaled ability to generate networks, practices, and relationships. Religion generates these well, but in principle so could neighborhoods, school-based groups, workplace groups, and more. The problem is that most of the other settings capable of supporting strong, durable social relationships have been systematically decimated since the mid-twentieth century, as plenty of sociological research shows.[15] State and market forces have combined to smash labor unions; underfund, privatize, and segregate schools; and hollow out poor neighborhoods, depriving them of stable housing and employment and hampering community-based relationships among underprivileged populations. The pattern across these sectors is the replacement of community-based, bottom-up democratic governance with public-private partnerships and business-oriented, top-down development that makes people, especially poor people, into clients of the state rather than constituents of it.

To make moral citizens beyond religious settings, then, does not mean finding alternatives to religious belief as the linchpin for people's commitments to equity, justice, and democracy. Rather, it requires developing public sphere institutions where people can relate to one another authentically, accountably, and over a long enough period for their self-stories to develop as their interactions reveal common interests and shared aspirations. There are thousands of skilled organizers, both professional and nonprofessional, who have the moral vision and leadership skills needed to make moral citizens in secular spaces, but there are currently few settings that offer both the social networks and community-rooted relationship-building potential these organizers need to flourish. As we have seen, nothing about moral vocations need be religious, and studies have found a similar pattern of personal growth and moral transformation being kindled among participants in immigrant rights movements, climate justice movements, and others.[16] What's lacking, I believe, is a robust public sphere where people can encounter one another with the sincerity and accountability that relational practices depend on. Organizers do not create relationships out of whole cloth; they patch them together from threads built of social connections rooted in public sphere institutions.

The bad news for people who find ELIJAH's work promising is that the public sphere institutions capable of supporting these relationships have been declining for quite some time. The good news is that they are not completely gone, and that in at least some places, creative leaders are building community out of the social wreckage wrought by state and market forces. Besides ELIJAH's forays into small businesses, one example is documented in Edward Flores's research on community organizing among the formerly incarcerated, where organizations bring returning citizens into spaces where they can develop a moral imperative together. This work points to how a common experience—in this case, being incarcerated—can provide the basis for trust and vulnerability that relational organizing depends on.[17] In other research, Jennifer Cossyleon suggests that motherhood-focused community organizing in poor neighborhoods can also help strong leadership and common cause emerge from shared precarity.[18] Labor settings, too, can be organizing venues, declines in unionization notwithstanding. Research by Jennifer Chun, George Lipsitz, and Young Shin explains how a multiethnic group of Asian women have established a strong lasting coalition on the basis of their shared status as vulnerable immigrant workers. These women have developed a community organizing strategy "designed to enable participants to recognize, analyze, and address the overlapping layers of marginality and discrimination in their lives" through which they "envision their transformation from a subordinated state of voicelessness and devaluation into an empowered state of self-representation and self-activity."[19] The key theme in all this research is that shared vulnerability—incarceration, precarious labor—brings people together into settings where, with the help of organizers skilled in relational practices, they can transform from atomized, isolated selves into empowered members of a collective that can build power.

Faith-based organizers in ELIJAH and elsewhere have developed an organizing process that can be—and is being—used to build power in settings outside institutional religion. What is preventing this process from fueling a larger-scale rejuvenation of democratic participation and collective power is *not* that it is an inherently religious process in an increasingly secular world. Rather, the issue is that religious communities provide some of the vanishingly few stable public institutions where the relationships that the organizing process depends on can be built. The degree to which moral citizenship can take root elsewhere will be determined not by whether it can be "made secular" but by whether society can reinvigorate the public sphere institutions it depends on or develop alternatives.

### Organizing and Religious Change

For many people in FBCO federations, reclaiming or rekindling religion's vitality as a source of ethical commitments to democratic life is a central goal.[20] When Alissa named the "great American moral geniuses" of eras past in her speech at the Prophetic Resistance rally, she named religious figures. Beyond the famous example of Martin Luther King Jr., these included people like Christian abolitionists Frederick Douglass and William Lloyd Garrison; Dorothy Day, the radical founder of the Catholic Worker movement; Jane Addams, whose activism, reform, and urban social analysis were inspired by the Protestant social gospel tradition; and Sitting Bull, the Lakota holy leader at the center of a decades-long resistance to land seizure and forced resettlement of Native Americans. Alissa saw these leaders and others like them as representatives of a sacred tradition of connecting faith values with principles of ethical democratic governance that makes all people co-participants in decisions about their political and economic lives.

Rank-and-file ELIJAH leaders likewise aspire to make religious communities into incubators of ideas about democracy and movements to advance those ideas. In chapter 3, we heard people declare that they needed to disrupt systems of power so they could restore the tradition of Catholic social teaching or live up to the Black Church's civil rights movement legacy. Implicit in these remarks is a sense of leadership lost or even duty abdicated—a view of religion having lost its way, dependent on the moral visioning of today's moral citizens to restore its proper function. And this book is far from the only research to suggest that claiming, or reclaiming, a prophetic role for religious voices is a key motivation for people involved in faith-based social justice movements. As sociologist Grace Yukich explains, contemporary progressive religious activism often targets social change and religious change at the same time.[21]

In ELIJAH, people often talk about that religious change as if they envision a return to a time of former glory, when religion did more to advance social justice causes than hinder them. This is not surprising, because the stories people collectively conjure about who they are, are most convincing when rooted in a sense of heritage and history that casts current actors as descendants of some sacred tradition from times past.[22] Yet it might be more useful to think of today's efforts to forge shared moral projects across various forms of social difference as carving out new terrain more than returning to past glory. The religious and political contexts of the United States have changed dramatically even since my fieldwork concluded, let alone since before the Religious Right emerged. These changes undeniably include not only a reduced number of people active in religious organizations and a steep and persistent rise in inequality but also an increasing field of competitors to religious authority.

These competitors include science, consumerism, and nationalism but also, crucially, an emerging consensus, hastened by movements like Occupy and Black Lives Matter and particularly salient among younger Americans, about the importance of intersectional, social justice–oriented thinking and practice. Some conservatives decry this as antithetical to religious—and particularly Christian—epistemology and freedom. Rod Dreher, a formerly Catholic, now conservative evangelical thought leader and author of *Live Not by Lies: A Manual for Christian Dissidents*, describes social justice and "wokeness" as a kind of "soft totalitarianism," imposed on everyday Americans from above by cultural and political elites rather than brought forward from below by grassroots movements of previously marginalized voices.[23] Sociologist Alexander Riley makes a similar argument.[24] But despite such objections, the intersectional thought that now dominates millions of Americans' worldviews, focused on social and racial justice, can be a complement to religious commitment and practice rather than a hostile suppressor of it. With this upswell of secular moral commitment, developing a common cause and a common moral language may be a promising path forward for religious actors interested in injecting their ethical commitments more deeply into civic life.

One reason to consider this possibility—though of course it is far from assured—is that secular social justice spaces constitute moral communities as much as political movements. One of the most salient insights from the last thirty years of social movement research is that effective movements draw their strength from roots in communities where people make meaning together.[25] In ELIJAH's case, this means congregations. But it is not only congregations that can fill such a role. Workplaces, community spaces, schools, and, as ELIJAH is hoping to show with its forays into barbershops and childcare centers, small businesses can, too. Alexis de Tocqueville famously argued that small-scale civil society institutions of this sort were the beating heart of American democracy.[26] Tocqueville perceived that when people came together in small civic groups to discuss issues that affected their lives, they learned to recognize how their fortunes were intertwined. Of course, Tocqueville was speaking of a highly restricted social stratum: white male property owners. But more recently, sociologist Kenneth Tucker has explained how, in Black Lives Matter groups, campus protests, and other spaces where young Americans gather to discuss their lives, the languages of *visibility* and *authenticity* have largely replaced the more instrumental, rational, policy-oriented language that characterized previous social movements.[27] In these and other venues, including climate justice movements and immigrant and LGBTQ rights forums, intersectionality is not just an academic theory but a mode of daily practice.[28] And as scholars of intersectionality have long argued, this demands that storytelling and other practices that reflect and elevate lived experience replace strict policy analysis and end-means thinking in civic spaces. Thus, the most important meaning-making spaces for a high proportion of young secular Americans today elevate the same kinds of practices that have produced success in the FBCO field.

In this book I have tried to show that the relational practices that leaders in ELIJAH and other FBCO federations have developed hold a great deal of promise for engaging people in deep, meaningful, and highly reflexive thought about who they are, what they value, who else values those things, and how they can achieve them together. Making moral citizens means transforming moral community—religious or otherwise—into morally inspired action. Wherever moral community can be found, or built, moral citizens can be made. Whether such community is widespread enough or can be built on a sufficient scale to stem the tide of inequalities by making enough moral citizens to build collective power remains to be seen.

# Appendix

## Research Methods

This appendix explains the methodological choices I made in conducting the research for this book. I collected the data through participant observation and semistructured interviews from November 2014 to May 2017. During this time, I conducted approximately 450 hours of participant observation and thirty-one in-depth interviews. These efforts produced over 1,100 pages of written field notes and interview transcriptions. I also had access to more than 900 email messages and over 200 other documents distributed by ELIJAH at meetings or electronically, which I analyzed selectively to support key themes and help me recall certain details, such as dates and meeting attendees. Together, the field notes, transcripts, and documents constitute the sources for the analysis and arguments.

### Case Selection

As I began this project, I wanted to study three broad phenomena. First, I wanted to learn how religious progressives were responding to being overshadowed in public culture and the media by the Religious Right. Prior research had highlighted progressive religious organizations' successes in securing gains for marginalized constituencies through local politics, but I wanted to know what kinds of strategies such organizations were using and how effective they could be. Second, since it was obvious that building power to advance progressive causes would require marshaling a diverse coalition, I wanted to investigate how religious progressives were dealing with the challenges of racial and ethnic diversity among their many constituencies. What tactics were they using to reveal common interests among distinct communities? Were material interests the basis of their organizing, or were cultural factors like identity and narrative more important? Was it possible for people from different denominational, racial, and ethnic groups to rally around religious faith as a cultural basis for civic cooperation? Third, while I knew that my project would likely be limited to one case, I wanted to choose an organization whose practices and strategies were likely shared to some degree by others across the country. I wanted to illuminate dynamics and processes that emerged from the structural and cultural contexts of faith-based organizing that would be conceptually significant even if they were not generalizable in the strictest sense.

These criteria directed me toward the field of faith-based community organizing and to ELIJAH in particular. Faith-based community organizations (FBCOs) are unique among progressive religious groups in combining a focus on building long-term cultural power with explicit attention to racial, religious, and class diversity and a nationally federated organizational structure. Within the FBCO field,

ELIJAH is a particularly suitable case organization because it is among the oldest and largest regional federations, and it has been a part of two different national organizing networks over the course of its history. Its long track record of success in its region has meant that several of its top staff organizers have gone on to found and direct new FBCOs in other parts of the country, and others among its top leaders consult with its national network in developing training strategies and materials to distribute to other coalitions nationwide. ELIJAH's stature within the FBCO field provides confidence that the processes and strategies I observed in ELIJAH are likely in effect in other FBCOs as well. The things that happen in ELIJAH are not idiosyncratic but structured by the political and cultural fields in which the organization and its participants are embedded. Hence, my observations of ELIJAH are likely to illuminate significant dynamics that can increase knowledge of other activist organizations, including both faith-based and secular groups.

## Gaining Access

After determining that I wanted to study ELIJAH, I approached Maddy, one of its staff organizers at the time, in October 2014. She was listed on ELIJAH's web page as its "economic justice organizer," and this job title seemed the best match to my nascent research questions. I had no existing relationship with anyone in ELIJAH at the time. Maddy agreed to meet with me at a coffee shop, where I told her about the scope and ambitions of the project I was proposing, and she expressed tentative support. Maddy had two main concerns about my conducting research within ELIJAH. First, since ELIJAH is large, complex, and diverse, she pushed me to design a research plan that would give me as complete a picture as possible of the organization as a whole, rather than focusing on just one issue campaign or region. Second, she told me that if I wanted to study ELIJAH, I would need to do so as a participant, not just as an observer. She believed that in order to understand what was happening in ELIJAH, I would need to experience its leadership development process in much the same way as its regular participants do, not simply by sitting around with a notebook. She was right.

Once Maddy was satisfied that I could complete my intended research while conforming to her two guidelines, she asked me to design a research plan that she could pass on to Alissa, the executive director, and Pastor Al, then the president of the board of directors. I prepared a rough timeline and a preliminary fieldwork strategy. Alissa and Pastor Al approved this plan (they seemed to take Maddy's word for my good intentions, as they did not insist on meeting with me before approving the project), and from that point on, I had access to nearly any ELIJAH event I wanted to attend, with the exception of the staff organizers' internal weekly meetings. Alissa told me that I could attend these "when I and the staff were ready," but I was soon collecting as much data as I could handle anyway, and I ended up never asking for an invitation. My lack of access to organizer-only spaces in fact turned out to be a good thing, because studying the staff organizers would have been a tempting but ultimately unhelpful shortcut toward making sense of the organizing process itself. Without direct guidance from ELIJAH staff, I was forced to make my own connections. This allowed me to approach ELIJAH with a more open mind and fewer preconceived ideas about what was happening there than would have been the case if I had been guided directly by the staff organizers.

## Positionality and Trust

Qualitative research, especially participant observation, requires attention to how the relationships between the researcher, the research participants, and the social positions of both shape the research process. I chose to use a "reflexive model of science . . . that embraces not detachment but engagement as the road to knowledge."[1] Following feminist theorist Patricia Hill Collins, I believe that complete objectivity is impossible when a researcher embeds in a social context and builds relationships with informants.[2] Instead of pursuing the unattainable goal of objectivity, I carefully scrutinized how my position relative to ELIJAH affected my observations throughout the project while also acknowledging that my findings cannot be separated from my status as a white male academic who is politically liberal but not religious.

Because of this status, I occupied both insider and outsider roles at various times during my fieldwork. I support many of the political causes that ELIJAH works on. On the one hand, this created an imperative to constantly question my observations in order to avoid taking the appeal of ELIJAH's messages and strategies for granted. On the other hand, being a supporter of ELIJAH's projects allowed me to wholeheartedly participate in, rather than merely observe, much of ELIJAH's political activity. Through this participation, I not only established credibility and trust among my research participants but also experienced how the cognitive and bodily aspects of participation colored my informants' experiences. I could fully participate in prayers and songs because I believe that most of the projects ELIJAH pursues would result in a more just world if they were successful. This participation not only enhanced the trust that other participants placed in me but also helped me to better understand the emotional and cognitive dimensions of their action.

While my political views were a boon to ELIJAH participants' willingness to trust me, my lack of religious commitment was not. Because I visibly participated in religious rituals like prayers and songs, this most often became an issue when people asked me which church I was affiliated with, and I replied that I was not part of any church. At many ELIJAH meetings, participants wear name tags that also list their home churches. People tend to cluster with others from their own congregations even when attending regional or organization-wide events, and this made me an outsider at times. My lack of a congregational affiliation stuck out, and I gradually realized that in addition to inviting skepticism of me, it meant that I was missing a crucial part of what happens in ELIJAH: the congregational component.

After a few months of fieldwork, I decided that in the interest of gaining trust and developing a complete picture of ELIJAH, it was not enough to attend meetings where people from many congregations gathered. I needed to also become part of a congregation's ELIJAH team. This presented a dilemma, because I'm not religious and didn't want to pretend to be. In my early fieldwork, I had met a number of ELIJAH participants from St. Martin's, a West Side Catholic parish, and I had learned that their congregation prides itself on being open to all comers, whether they are formally Catholic or not. Since I was a Catholic until I started college, I knew I could feel comfortable and conversant in a parish setting, and I arranged a meeting with Joanna, the social justice coordinator at St. Martin's, to tell her about my research and ask her whether I could join the ELIJAH core team at the parish.

The people at St. Martin's welcomed me into their work. They did not mind that I was not Catholic—there were plenty of people in the church who had never been baptized or confirmed but who attended Mass weekly nonetheless. What they cared about was that I take them and their commitments seriously and that I participate in all the activities at meetings I attended, including prayers and other religious rituals. To them, this was part of demonstrating a sincere desire to understand what they were doing and why. When Joanna introduced me to the cochairs of the core team, they asked me detailed questions about my goals and approach, and they expressed concern that, despite my good intentions, I would not be able to develop a full understanding of their work. While they were assured by my Catholic background and my knowledge of Catholic social teaching, they worried that I would merely attend a few meetings and then be on my way. In response to this concern, I said I would commit to full participation in the St. Martin's core team for two years, including attending as many meetings as I could, participating in issue campaigns, helping to conduct outreach within the parish, and occasionally attending Mass and other events at St. Martin's that were not related to ELIJAH. I never indicated that I was considering reconverting to Catholicism, but I showed that I was interested in learning how ELIJAH participants' political activity extended from their faith commitments. The team found this satisfactory, and I began participating in the St. Martin's core team in May 2015. This meant that for the next two years, I could identify myself as affiliated with St. Martin's when I attended larger ELIJAH events, which in turn made me more trustworthy in the eyes of other ELIJAH leaders, including organizing staff.

My position as a white male academic also influenced my perspectives on ELIJAH and community organizing in general. Community organizers draw heavily on social science concepts and theories to contextualize their issue campaigns within larger questions of power, identity, and culture. As a sociologist, I was often able to marshal prior knowledge to demonstrate that I understood the kinds of structural issues that organizers wanted to address. Moreover, as a professional-class white male, I was often implicitly trusted and recognized as an expert. Organizers and lay leaders recognized that I understood many of the issues that they were working on and occasionally enlisted me to help explain these issues at meetings. At times they introduced me as "a person from the university who is researching ELIJAH and faith organizing," but more often they did not, and I was known to most non–St. Martin's participants as simply a member of the St. Martin's ELIJAH core team. At the same time, my enthusiasm for social analysis occasionally led me to do more talking than I should have during meetings or to focus more on the goals of the organizing itself than my academic observations of them.

The astuteness and complexity of ELIJAH's social critique at first seemed a barrier to my success as a researcher. Community organizers are uncredentialed but highly skilled applied sociologists, akin in some ways to theorist Antonio Gramsci's conception of organic intellectuals.[3] Their understandings of politics, culture, and power are sophisticated while also reflecting the needs and contexts of their communities, and the one-to-ones and house meetings they conduct share some features with qualitative research. Early on, it often seemed like I was studying a group of lay sociologists who had already figured out everything sociologically interesting about the fields they worked in. While this was a source of frustration at times, it ultimately became a benefit because it forced me to probe more deeply than I otherwise might have into the cultural complexities of the organizing process rather than just its outcomes. During the frequent occasions when I found myself growing too interested in the politics of what was happening rather than my own social scientific observations, the nuanced social analysis offered by people like Alissa, Steve, and Janelle reminded me that I needed to focus on the process rather than the outcomes and pay more attention to the people in ELIJAH than to the issues they were working on.

## Significance of the Case

My goal in this project was to identify and theorize processes rather than explain outcomes, and I did not intend for my findings to be strictly generalizable to other settings. Rather, my goal was for my findings to reach what sociologist Mario Luis Small calls "societal significance"—that is, useful for explaining other cases if they were appropriately contextualized within those cases' structural and cultural surroundings.[4] By immersing myself in a rich setting of local practice that was shaped by larger structural features that also influence other organizations, I sought to understand and theorize some of the mechanisms and processes by which collective action against inequalities by racially and religiously diverse groups becomes possible. It is my hope that the things I observed in ELIJAH might help to shed light on the dynamics of other organizations, even if they cannot be expected to apply exactly as they did here.

I developed this project using an interpretative paradigm and logical hypotheses rather than a positivist paradigm and causal hypotheses.[5] Logical hypotheses take the form "when X occurs, whether Y will follow depends on W," where W is a set of theoretical propositions that can be logically justified by the observations the researcher conducts in particular settings.[6] For my purposes, X was the ongoing effort by organizational leaders to engage religious constituencies in political activism. Y in this case comprised the many variables I discussed in the empirical chapters: whether a strong collective identity emerges where none existed before, whether that identity can give rise to a compelling narrative that facilitates social movement participation, whether the emerging collective narrative is strong enough to subsume previously existing narratives, and whether conflict among previously existing narratives manifests as a hindrance to engagement. In this research, I have sought to identify the mechanisms that condition the relationship between X and the various Ys. Hence, while no other organization can be expected to function exactly like ELIJAH does, I believe that my discussion of the unique benefits and drawbacks of organizing in this fashion can shed light on happenings in other diverse social movement organizations.

## Data Collection and Analysis

### Participant Observation

As I explained in chapter 2, ELIJAH is a sprawling organization in which many things are happening at any one time. This meant that one of my first challenges was determining which ELIJAH events to attend. On many weeknights there were events on multiple issue campaigns and in different regions, and on Sundays I could choose from dozens of ELIJAH-affiliated churches to attend to try to make connections. After an initial period of attending nearly every event I heard about and visiting various ELIJAH churches on Sunday mornings in early 2015, I realized that answering my research questions required a more careful selection. If I wanted to learn how people in ELIJAH thought about power, I needed to follow its legislative work and particularly the long-term planning thereof; if I wanted to learn how they thought about race, I needed to find settings where new relationships among distinct constituencies were being formed; and if I wanted to verify that the processes I was observing in ELIJAH were also at work in other organizations, I needed to find a way to observe other FBCOs, at least for a short time. In addition, in order to fulfill my commitment to the people at St. Martin's who had welcomed me into their work, I needed to accomplish these goals while also contributing fully to their team.

I chose events to attend and issue campaigns to follow in ELIJAH based on these criteria. Since the legislature was in session early in my fieldwork period, I spent most of my first few months in the field following legislative activities, including planning sessions, strategy meetings, visits to legislators, and protest and rallies at the state capitol. In addition, since a large chunk of ELIJAH's legislative work during this period was focused on immigration issues, this fieldwork allowed me to make connections among some of ELIJAH's Latinx participants. After the 2015 legislative session ended, West Side leaders began planning the longer-term poverty profiteering campaign discussed in chapter 5. Maddy and other leaders wanted to join the rich veins of social and political capital that ran through affluent, mostly white West Side churches with the energy around payday lending that was bubbling out of Black churches. This gave me the opportunity to observe ELIJAH's efforts to organize in an explicitly multiracial fashion. To observe other FBCOs, I obtained authorization from Alissa to attend two national FBCO conventions to which ELIJAH sent delegations in 2015. I paid for my travel to these conferences using a grant I had obtained from Wheaton College's Institute for the Study of American Evangelicals.

Since I attended all events as a participant rather than just an observer, I quickly became involved in numerous elements of ELIJAH's work—not only the note taking that qualitative researchers often volunteer for but various elements of the organizing itself. I called and visited legislators and city council people alongside ELIJAH leaders, helped plan public meetings, conducted one-to-ones, and drew on my sociological training and classroom teaching experience to help conduct power analyses and create presentations and other materials for use in ELIJAH's work. Through this participation, I became heavily involved in the West Side and South Suburban regions as my fieldwork progressed. As a full participant in ELIJAH's organizing, I learned a great deal about how ELIJAH's work comes together across regions and issue campaigns, how staff organizers allocate resources among competing demands, and especially the complexities of coordinating a campaign across multiple cultural contexts.

At each participant-observation session, I had to determine how best to record my observations. At approximately 80 percent of these sessions, I used an audio recorder to capture all or part of the proceedings. When I used my recorder, I usually did so overtly, placing it on the table in front of me so that all present could see I was using it. For my first few months in the field, I always asked permission to record meetings, but as my presence became familiar and the fieldwork continued, this grew unnecessary. The recorder's visible presence sometimes invited questions about what I was doing. This gave me the chance to explain my work and further enhance trust. On the rare (a half dozen or fewer) occasions that a person expressed discomfort about my recorder, I turned it off and recorded as much as I could in a notebook. Only a few times did I covertly record events, keeping my recorder hidden in a pocket. I typically did this in the presence of politicians, who may have been concerned at seeing a recorder present, fearing opposition research or other stealth. In these cases, I was interested in what ELIJAH people, and not the politicians, were saying, and so I kept my recorder hidden to avoid a situation in which politicians might alter their words because they thought that the things they said might appear in later campaign advertisements or social media posts. At approximately 20 percent of observation sessions, I felt that using the recorder was not appropriate for various reasons, most often because I felt that people in the room were emotionally distressed and would not have wanted their remarks captured verbatim.

Whether or not I used my recorder, I nearly always made jottings in a notebook while in the field, and expanded my jottings into full field notes within twenty-four hours afterward. In writing field notes, I typically composed a first draft that was as descriptive as possible, recounting merely what happened without imposing my own thoughts. Once I had produced a detailed account of the proceedings, I elaborated on the account with theory and analysis, typically using italics to distinguish my analytic impressions from my descriptions. I kept my field notes in a set of folders stored on an encrypted drive on my computer, with a separate document for each observation session labeled by date and a short description of the event in the file name. This strategy allowed me to organize my notes effectively so that I could easily return to older documents to update the analysis or copy relevant themes forward into new documents.

## Interviews

I conducted semistructured interviews with thirty-one ELIJAH leaders to contextualize my observations and elaborate on themes I had observed in the field. These interviews took place from late 2015 through mid-2017. I chose interview participants based on several criteria. First, I wanted to speak mostly with people from outside the West Side and South Suburban regions, where I was conducting the bulk of my observation. Second, I wanted to talk with people who had been in ELIJAH for different periods of time, from new participants to seasoned veterans and people who had left the organization. Third, I wanted to speak with as many people of color as I could, since St. Martin's, where I had done more observation than anywhere else, was a mostly white congregation.

I recruited interview participants through in-person, email, and text-message invitations. Mostly, I recruited people with whom I had spoken briefly at meetings but had not interacted with for more than a few minutes. In some cases, I reached out to people I had seen or heard about but not actually met. In order to avoid making potential participants feel obligated to speak with me, I always contacted them myself, even when working through a mutual contact might have been more effective. Of the thirty-one interviewees, nineteen were women and twelve were men; eleven were people of color (six Black and five Latinx) and twenty were white. Among the group, experience in ELIJAH ranged from one month to seventeen years, and four informants were no longer part of ELIJAH at the time I spoke with them. Two interviewees were on staff with ELIJAH, and three were members of the clergy (all white Protestant pastors). The interviews ranged in length from one hour to two and a half hours, and took the form of semistructured open-ended questions. I paid interviewees forty dollars each for their participation using grant funds from the Society for the Scientific Study of Religion (SSSR).

My interview sample was generally effective, but I had a harder time than I expected recruiting interview participants of color. I cannot be certain about the reasons for this. It is likely that as a white male, I was understandably seen by a few potential participants as unlikely to be willing or able to empathize with people of color's concerns. My interviews with Latinx participants were also limited by my inability to speak Spanish. But more important than these factors was the fact that the strategies I used for recruiting participants—typically email or text messages sent after I had met the potential informant earlier—were biased toward white people. I would likely have had more success in recruiting participants of color if I had asked religious leaders in their communities to put them in contact with me, but again, this would have introduced the problem of participants feeling obligated to talk with me, which I was trying to avoid. In all, my interview panel was whiter than I had hoped it would be, and this likely limited my ability to understand how nonwhite people understand ELIJAH's work.

Interviews were audio-recorded and transcribed by me and an undergraduate research assistant who was also paid from the SSSR grant. I coded the transcripts for emergent themes using the NVivo software program. In a second round of coding, I searched the interviews for discussions that explicitly elaborated on key events I had observed in the field (such as Victor's discussion of Hannah's story in chapter 6).

## My Decision to Mask Real Names

Given the amount of detail this book provides on ELIJAH, some readers may wonder why I chose to mask its real name. To make ELIJAH completely unidentifiable, I would have had to change so many details as to render meaningful analysis impossible. This means that people familiar with the FBCO field or the political landscape of ELIJAH's region will be able to determine its real identity. Those who know ELIJAH well may even be able to ascertain the real names of some of ELIJAH's most prevalent individual leaders based on my descriptions of them. Certain features of ELIJAH's history, culture, and organizational structure are distinct enough that academics and practitioners familiar with the FBCO field will know immediately which organization I studied, even if they have not been part of ELIJAH or studied it themselves.

For some social scientists, this would constitute a reason to dispense entirely with masking.[7] By using real names, sociologists Colin Jerolmack and Alexandra Murphy argue, researchers can avoid overgeneralizing from unique cases and be more forthcoming about important nuances that maintaining confidentiality might have required altering or withholding. When authors can determine unilaterally which details to omit or change, the line between real people and events and selective or amalgamated representations can become blurrier than it should be. Besides these drawbacks of masking, another is that in this case, numerous leaders in ELIJAH would have preferred that I identify the organization by name. Press reports on ELIJAH's activity tend to highlight its work on issue campaigns rather than its long-term power-building project, and some people expressed an interest in my publishing research that could have provided a fuller picture of its work. While no one in ELIJAH ever sought to influence my findings or the way I reported them, there were occasionally implicit, well-intentioned suggestions that my research reports would provide a more complete view of ELIJAH's work than typically circulates in the news.

Yet even with these considerations in mind, I decided that the benefits of masking outweighed the costs in this case. The reason pertains to my own intellectual honesty. Early in my fieldwork, before I knew what my findings would be or what publications or reports might ensue from this research, I realized that I would have both positive and critical things to say about ELIJAH, and I wanted to follow methodological practices that would allow me to be as candid as possible about its affairs. As I thought about the potential written outputs of this project, the possibility of my writing appearing in search results for ELIJAH's real name concerned me. Debate continues within many of ELIJAH's member churches about whether dues are an effective use of limited funds and whether ELIJAH's work is appropriate for religious communities. As I thought about these debates, it occurred to me that if I used ELIJAH's real name in my research, it was conceivable that my writing could become ammunition for one side or the other in these debates. This, in turn, made me worry that using its real name in my writing might have caused me to implicitly prioritize portraying ELIJAH in a positive light. While the critiques I make of ELIJAH are mostly mild, I believe it is better that people not be able to find them simply by googling its real name. By masking the organization, I cannot prevent enterprising readers from learning its real identity, but I can prevent my writing from being discovered and potentially (mis)used by interlocutors in internal debates about whether participation in ELIJAH makes sense for a given congregation.

# Notes

## Introduction

1. The names of people and organizations appearing in this book are pseudonyms, including ELIJAH. See the appendix for a discussion of why I chose to do this.

2. Doussard and Fulton, "Organizing Together."

3. Wood and Fulton, *Shared Future.*

4. Dennis DeSlippe, "As in a Civics Text Come to Life."

5. Braunstein, Fuist, and Williams, *Religion and Progressive Activism*; Morris, *Origins of the Civil Rights Movement*; Zald and McCarthy, "Religious Groups as Crucibles of Social Movements."

6. Oyakawa, "'Turning Private Pain into Public Action'"; Braunstein, Fulton, and Wood, "Bridging Cultural Practices"; Wood and Fulton, *Shared Future.*

7. Madsen, "Archipelago of Faith"; O'Brien, "Individualism as a Discursive Strategy of Action."

8. Leondar-Wright, *Missing Class*; Hart, *Cultural Dilemmas of Progressive Politics*; Lichterman, *Elusive Togetherness.*

9. Delehanty and Oyakawa, "Building a Collective Moral Imaginary."

10. R. M. Smith, "Beyond Tocqueville, Myrdal, and Hartz"; Braunstein, "A (More) Perfect Union?"

11. Readers familiar with previous literature on civic organizing will note the parallels between my concept of moral citizenship and similar ideas developed in work by other scholars, including Ruth Braunstein and Paul Lichterman, both of whom use the term "active citizenship." What distinguishes moral citizenship from these other ideas is its explicit roots in, and flexibility across, individuals' different ethical commitments. *Active* citizenship is a useful concept because it illuminates how, across the political spectrum, the idea of being engaged, or active, can be mobilized as a boundary marker to delineate those who are willing to stand up and take action from those who are not. But *moral* citizenship captures something different: the specific appeal that leaders in grassroots organizations make to engaged individuals in order to extend their deepest moral commitments into public action. My concept of moral citizenship thus draws attention to the deeply personal, identity-driven nature of civic commitment and the practices that engender it in ways that previous concepts, including active citizenship, do not.

12. Oyakawa, "'Turning Private Pain into Public Action.'"

13. Braunstein, Fulton, and Wood, "Bridging Cultural Practices"; Giorgi, Bartunek, and King, "Saul Alinsky Primer for the 21st Century"; Han, *How Organizations Develop Activists.*

14. Braunstein, Fulton, and Wood, "Bridging Cultural Practices."

15. Lichterman, *Elusive Togetherness*; Hart, *Cultural Dilemmas of Progressive Politics*.

16. Wilde, "Complex Religion"; Edgell, "Agenda for Research on American Religion in Light of the 2016 Election."

17. Lichterman, "Beyond the Seesaw Model."

18. Goffman, *Interaction Ritual*.

19. Madsen, "Archipelago of Faith," 1281.

20. C. Smith, *Souls in Transition*.

21. O'Brien, "Individualism as a Discursive Strategy of Action," 175.

22. Billingsley, *Mighty Like a River*; Morris, *Origins of the Civil Rights Movement*; Nepstad, *Convictions of the Soul*; Ewick and Steinberg, *Beyond Betrayal*; Yukich, *One Family under God*.

23. R. M. Smith, *Stories of Peoplehood*.

24. Barber and Wilson-Hartgrove, *Third Reconstruction*; Gorski, *American Covenant*.

25. Braunstein, "(More) Perfect Union?"

26. A full account of the methodological choices I made in conducting this research is provided in the appendix.

27. More details on ELIJAH's structure, including a discussion of what core teams are and their importance, appear in chapter 2.

## Chapter 1

1. See, among others, Swarts, *Organizing Urban America*; Warren, *Dry Bones Rattling*; Wood, *Faith in Action*; Stout, *Blessed Are the Organized*.

2. At the time, FIA was known as the PICO (People Improving Communities through Organizing) National Network. The name change occurred in 2018. Throughout the book I refer to the organization by its current name, but there are occasional instances in which research participants are quoted talking about PICO. In these cases, I leave the name as they said it.

3. Besides these national networks, a number of regional FBCO networks exist, including the Ohio Organizing Project and the InterValley Project in New England.

4. Wood and Fulton, *Shared Future*.

5. Wood and Fulton, *Shared Future*, 28, 40.

6. Doussard and Fulton, "Organizing Together."

7. Wood and Fulton, *Shared Future*, chap. 3.

8. Warren, *Dry Bones Rattling*; Wood, *Faith in Action*; Swarts, *Organizing Urban America*; Braunstein, Fulton, and Wood, "Bridging Cultural Practices"; Giorgi, Bartunek, and King, "Saul Alinsky Primer for the 21st Century."

9. Edgell, "A Cultural Sociology of Religion"; Ammerman, "Rethinking Religion"; O'Brien, *Keeping It Halal*; Lichterman, *Elusive Togetherness*; Polletta, *It Was Like a Fever*; Leondar-Wright, *Missing Class*.

10. Piketty and Saez, "Inequality in the Long Run."

11. National Low Income Housing Coalition, "Out of Reach 2019."

12. Krippner, "Democracy of Credit."

13. Oliver and Shapiro, *Black Wealth/White Wealth*.

14. Seamster and Charron-Chénier, "Predatory Inclusion and Education Debt."

15. Du Bois, *Black Reconstruction in America*; Itzigsohn and Brown, *Sociology of W. E. B. Du Bois*; Roediger, *Wages of Whiteness*.

16. Hurwitz, "Gender and Race in the Occupy Movement"; Warren, *Fire in the Heart*.

17. Hoffman, "Politcal Economy of TARP."

18. Brooks and Manza, "Broken Public?"

19. Massengill, *Wal-Mart Wars*.

20. Massengill; Lakoff, *Moral Politics*; D. E. Smith, "Standard North American Family SNAF as an Ideological Code."

21. Hacker, *Great Risk Shift*.

22. Saez and Zucman, "Wealth Inequality in the United States since 1913."

23. Braunstein, "Theory of Political Backlash."

24. Hout and Fischer, "Why More Americans Have No Religious Preference"; Kettell, "Faithless."

25. Yukich, *One Family under God*.

26. Pew Research Center, "In U.S., Decline of Christianity Continues at Rapid Pace."

27. Pew Research Center.

28. Wong, *Immigrants, Evangelicals, and Politics*.

29. Pew Research Center, "In U.S., Decline of Christianity Continues at Rapid Pace."

30. Edwards and Oyakawa, *Smart Suits, Tattered Boots*.

31. Jenkins, *American Prophets*, chap. 5.

32. Barnes, "Black Church Culture and Community Action"; Bracey, "Black Movements Need Black Theorizing."

33. McRoberts, "Civil Religion and Black Church Political Mobilization."

34. See Hunter, *Culture Wars*; Jones, *End of White Christian America*; Layman, *Great Divide*; C. Smith, *American Evangelicalism*; O'Brien and Abdelhadi, "Re-Examining Restructuring."

35. Herberg, *Protestant, Catholic, Jew*.

36. Wuthnow, *Restructuring of American Religion*, 73.

37. Wilde and Danielsen, "Fewer and Better Children."

38. Today, the former Northern Baptist Convention is known as American Baptist Churches USA. The Southern Baptist Convention retains its nineteenth-century name.

39. Wuthnow, *Restructuring of American Religion*.

40. McAdam and Kloos, *Deeply Divided*.

41. Jones, *End of White Christian America*.

42. Wuthnow, *Red State Religion*; Wuthnow, *Small-Town America*; Wuthnow, *Rough Country*.

43. Martí, *American Blindspot*.

44. McRoberts, *Streets of Glory*; Barnes, "Black Church Culture and Community Action."

45. Stout, *Blessed Are the Organized*; Wood, *Faith in Action*.

46. Stark and Finke, *Acts of Faith*; Becker, *Congregations in Conflict*.

47. Ellingson, *Megachurch and the Mainline*.

48. Jones, *End of White Christian America*, 65.

49. Wood and Fulton, *Shared Future*, chap. 3.

50. Geraty, "Challenges and Opportunities of Community Organizing in Suburban Congregations."

51. Wuthnow, *Restructuring of American Religion*, 133.

52. Since McBride is a well-known public figure who was making a public speech, I use his real name rather than a pseudonym.

53. For an extended discussion of Pastor McBride's work in these areas, see Wood's interview with McBride in Wood and Fulton, *Shared Future*, chap. 6.

54. Each of the cities Pastor Mike named has an FIA affiliate federation that was represented at the Philadelphia summit.


## Chapter 2

1. Because congregations' membership status in ELIJAH is not always clear, these numbers are approximate. The best indicator of congregational membership is the payment of dues from the congregation to ELIJAH, yet individuals from congregations that lapse on their dues often continue participation, while newly joined congregations can participate without paying dues for a time.

2. ELIJAH spent its first fifteen years as an almost exclusively urban and suburban organization, but after I left the field, and partly in response to the urban-rural divide that Trump's election revealed, ELIJAH aimed more of its organizing efforts into the state's small cities and rural areas. Much of ELIJAH's growth in the last few years has been in these areas.

3. Wood and Fulton, *Shared Future*.

4. For a helpful explanation of house meetings in community organizing, see Stout, *Blessed Are the Organized*, chap. 12.

5. Wood and Fulton, *Shared Future*.

6. Alexander, *New Jim Crow*.

7. Skocpol, *Diminished Democracy*; A. Smith, *Revolution Will Not Be Funded*.

8. Language from the ELIJAH web page as of May 4, 2020.

9. Becker, *Congregations in Conflict*; Delehanty, "Prophets of Resistance."

10. Speer and Hughey, "Community Organizing"; Warren, *Dry Bones Rattling*.

11. Fuist, "'Not Left-Wing, Just Human.'"

12. Armstrong and Bernstein, "Culture, Power, and Institutions"; Yukich, *One Family under God*.

13. Alexander and Smith, "Discourse of American Civil Society."

14. Alinsky, *Rules for Radicals*.

15. Gecan, *Going Public*.

16. Braunstein, Fulton, and Wood, "Bridging Cultural Practices"; Giorgi, Bartunek, and King, "Saul Alinsky Primer for the 21st Century."

17. Eliasoph and Lichterman, "Culture in Interaction"; Lichterman and Eliasoph, "Civic Action."

18. Eliasoph and Lichterman, "Culture in Interaction"; Lichterman, "Beyond the Seesaw Model"; Enriquez and Saguy, "Coming Out of the Shadows."

## Chapter 3

1. McAlevey, *No Shortcuts*; Han, *How Organizations Develop Activists*.

2. Becker, *Congregations in Conflict*; Krull, "Liberal Churches and Social Justice Movements"; Lichterman and Williams, "Cultural Challenges for Mainline Protestant Political Progressives."

3. McAdam, "Recruitment to High-Risk Activism"; Wiltfang and McAdam, "Costs and Risks of Social Activism."

4. Oyakawa, McKenna, and Han, "Habits of Courage," 2.

5. Taylor and Whittier, "Collective Identity in Social Movement Communities."

6. Oyakawa, McKenna, and Han, "Habits of Courage," 2.

7. Oyakawa, "'Turning Private Pain into Public Action.'"

8. Bean, *Politics of Evangelical Identity*; Lichterman, "Religion in Public Action."

9. Oyakawa, McKenna, and Han, "Habits of Courage."

10. Snow and McAdam, "Identity Work Processes in the Context of Social Movements"; Gamson, "Must Identity Movements Self-Destruct?"

11. C. Smith, *Souls in Transition*; Bellah et al., *Habits of the Heart*; O'Brien, *Keeping It Halal*.

12. Dreher, *Benedict Option*.

13. Ewick and Steinberg, *Beyond Betrayal*.

14. By confessing, Kristin simply meant declaring one's troubles to others, not the formal act of confessing sins to a religious leader. People in ELIJAH often use the term this way.

15. Mills, *The Sociological Imagination*.

16. Emerson and Smith, *Divided by Faith*.

17. C. Smith, *Souls in Transition*.

18. Ward, "White Normativity."

19. Warren, *Fire in the Heart*.

20. Oyakawa, "'Turning Private Pain into Public Action.'"

21. Phipps, "Whose Personal Is More Political?"; Oyakawa, "'Turning Private Pain into Public Action.'"

## Chapter 4

1. Mills, *The Sociological Imagination*.

2. Bender et al., *Religion on the Edge*.

3. Lichterman, "Beyond the Beliefs-Driven Actor."

4. Edgell, "Cultural Sociology of Religion."

5. Wilde, "Complex Religion."

6. Braunstein, *Prophets and Patriots.*

7. Olson, *Logic of Collective Action.*

8. Oyakawa, "'Turning Private Pain into Public Action.'"

9. Weber, *Economy and Society*; Delehanty, "Emotional Management of Progressive Religious Mobilization."

10. Hart, *Cultural Dilemmas of Progressive Politics*; Eliasoph, *Making Volunteers.*

11. Polletta, "How Participatory Democracy Became White"; Fulton, Oyakawa, and Wood, "Critical Standpoint"; Leondar-Wright, *Missing Class.*

12. Delehanty, "Becoming 'People of Faith.'"

13. C. Smith, *Souls in Transition.*

14. Ganz, "Resources and Resourcefulness"; Warren, *Dry Bones Rattling.*

15. Gecan, *Going Public*; Han, *How Organizations Develop Activists.*

16. Warren, *Dry Bones Rattling*; Wood, *Faith in Action.*

17. This interview with Alissa was conduct by Michelle Oyakawa, with whom I consulted onthe transcript for work on our co-authored study (Delehanty and Oyakawa, "Bilding a Collective Moral Imaginary). I gratefully acknowledge Dr. Oyakawa for her contributions to the arguments in this section and for allowing me to use the transcript in this chapter. The interview excerpt from Alissa provided earlier in this chapter is from a different interview that I conducted.

18. Of course, faith, values, and identity are not always distinct from one another. What I think Alissa meant is that even people who have no religious affiliation can be motivated by values, and that everyone, religious or not, can be motivated by identity.

19. Email received by the author, September 14, 2017.

20. Email received by the author, November 30, 2015.

21. Warren, *Dry Bones Rattling*; Wood, *Faith in Action.*

## Chapter 5

1. Samuel had helped Josiah refinance his loan through a new local nonprofit, run by area churches with help from ELIJAH, that was working to assist victims of predatory lending by paying off the original creditors and issuing no-interest terms to the borrowers for the remaining balance of their loans.

2. CarHop is notorious for never putting a price sticker on a car, instead setting the terms of a sale by adjusting the interest rates on loans. This keeps customers from comparison shopping and obscures the enormous difference between a customer's total financial outlay over the course of the loan and a car's blue book value, as in Josiah's case.

3. Fuist, "'Not Left-Wing, Just Human.'"

4. Williams and Demerath, "Religion and Political Process in an American City."

5. Krull, "Liberal Churches and Social Justice Movements"; Delehanty, "Prophets of Resistance."

6. Lichterman, *How Civic Action Works.*

7. Eliasoph and Lichterman, "Culture in Interaction."

8. Braunstein, *Prophets and Patriots*.

9. Walker and Stepick, "Strength in Diversity?"

10. Lichterman, *How Civic Action Works*, 83.

11. Lichterman, 37.

12. Safe time refers to paid time off for attending to personal or family needs following domestic or sexual violence.

13. This is how I got invited to the planning meeting—a setting that would normally have been closed to an outsider like me: Wendy knew I was excited about the research potential of the campaign, and she was excited about my contributing to the effort. Hence, she invited me to participate but made it clear that I would be expected to work, not just observe.

14. Email received by the author, February 15, 2016.

15. Script obtained during fieldwork. I removed some technical instructions regarding how to mark forms and record information and cleaned up the formatting to make the script more readable in this format.

16. For an insightful analysis of these urban-rural dynamics in state politics, see Cramer, *Politics of Resentment*.

17. ELIJAH is a nonpartisan organization that pushes both Republicans and Democrats to act on issues of concern to its participants. However, it is impossible to deny that Republicans are less favorable to most of these issues, and Alissa did not attempt to deny that in this informal discussion with me.

18. Massengill, *Wal-Mart Wars*; Lakoff, *Moral Politics*.

19. Polletta, *It Was Like a Fever*; Han, *How Organizations Develop Activists*.

20. D. E. Smith, "Standard North American Family SNAF as an Ideological Code"; Lakoff, *Moral Politics*; Massengill, *Wal-Mart Wars*.

21. Massengill, *Wal-Mart Wars*.

## Chapter 6

1. Yukich, *One Family under God*.

2. Adler, *Empathy beyond US Borders*; Della Porta, *Can Democracy Be Saved?*

3. Braunstein, Fuist, and Williams, *Religion and Progressive Activism*; Jenkins, *American Prophets*; C. Smith, *Disruptive Religion*.

4. Fisher and Tamarkin, "Right-Wing Organizers Do This Too"; Lindsay, *Faith in the Halls of Power*.

5. Pew Research Center, "Religious Landscape Study."

6. Lichterman and Williams, "Cultural Challenges for Mainline Protestant Political Progressives"; Swarts, *Organizing Urban America*; Geraty, "Challenges and Opportunities of Community Organizing in Suburban Congregations."

7. Delehanty, "Prophets of Resistance"; Delehanty, "Becoming 'People of Faith.'"

8. Becker, *Congregations in Conflict*.

9. Chaves and Anderson, "Changing American Congregations."

10. Whitehead and Perry, *Taking America Back for God*; Bean, *Politics of Evangelical Identity*; McCarthy, Olson, and Garand, "Religious Right, Religious Left, Both, or Neither?"

11. Wood and Fulton, *Shared Future*, 69–70.

12. Braunstein, *Prophets and Patriots*, 84.

13. Braunstein, 84.

14. C. Smith, *American Evangelicalism*.

15. Communication received by the author, November 14, 2016.

16. Krull, "Liberal Churches and Social Justice Movements."

17. Baker and Martí, "Is the Religious Left Resurgent?"

18. Fetner, *How the Religious Right Shaped Lesbian and Gay Activism*.

19. Hout and Fischer, "Explaining Why More Americans Have No Religious Preference."

20. Krull, "Liberal Churches and Social Justice Movements."

21. The CarHop action was described at the beginning of chapter 5.

22. Cramer, *Politics of Resentment*. "Generic ballot" refers to the number of votes cast for members of each party in total across all legislative or congressional districts in a state in a given election cycle. For example, in the 2012 contests to elect members of the U.S. House of Representatives for Pennsylvania, Republicans gained only 49 percent of the total votes cast yet secured 72 percent of the available seats.

23. Pearce and Denton, *Faith of Their Own*.

24. Eichstedt, "Problematic White Identities"; Ward, "White Normativity."

25. Leondar-Wright, *Missing Class*.

26. Lareau, *Unequal Childhoods*; Eliasoph, *Making Volunteers*.

27. Lareau, *Unequal Childhoods*.

28. DiAngelo, *White Fragility*.

29. Bouie, "Beyond 'White Fragility.'"


## Conclusion

1. Krull, "Liberal Churches and Social Justice Movements"; Stout, *Blessed Are the Organized*.

2. Bretherton, *Resurrecting Democracy*.

3. Williams, "Constructing the Public Good."

4. Davis, "Hopes for 2021?"

5. Mudge, *Leftism Reinvented*; Lichtenstein, "How to Win."

6. Oyakawa, "Building a Movement in the Non-profit Industrial Complex."

7. Wood and Fulton, *Shared Future*; Braunstein, *Prophets and Patriots*; Flores, *Jesus Saved a Ex-Con*.

8. Skocpol, *Diminished Democracy*; Sampson et al., "Civil Society Reconsidered."

9. Speer and Han, "Re-Engaging Social Relationships"; Schradie, *Revolution That Wasn't*; Castells, *Networks of Outrage and Hope*.

10. Stout, *Blessed Are the Organized*; Ganz, *Why David Sometimes Wins*.

11. Language from ELIJAH's web page, retrieved May 14, 2021.

12. Murray, "Child Care Work."

13. Language from ELIJAH's web page, retrieved May 14, 2021.

14. Ammerman, *Studying Lived Religion*.

15. Putnam, *Bowling Alone*; Sampson et al., "Civil Society Reconsidered"; Lee, McQuarrie, and Walker, *Democratizing Inequalities*.

16. Enriquez and Saguy, "Coming out of the Shadows"; Cossyleon, "'Coming Out of My Shell'"; Schlosberg and Collins, "From Environmental to Climate Justice."

17. Flores, *Jesus Saved a Ex-Con*.

18. Cossyleon, "'Coming Out of My Shell.'"

19. Chun, Lipsitz, and Shin, "Intersectionality as a Social Movement Strategy," 918.

20. Wood, *Faith in Action*.

21. Yukich, *One Family under God*.

22. R. M. Smith, *Stories of Peoplehood*.

23. Dreher, *Live Not by Lies*.

24. Riley, "Woke Totemism."

25. Wood and Fulton, *Shared Future*; Lichterman, *Search for Political Community*; Ganz, *Why David Sometimes Wins*; Andrews et al., "Leadership, Membership, and Voice."

26. Tocqueville, *Democracy in America*.

27. Tucker, "Political Is Personal, Expressive, Aesthetic, and Networked."

28. Carroll, "Intersectionality and Identity Politics"; Mandell, Israel, and Schulz, "Breaking Free from Siloes."

## Appendix

1. Michael Burawoy, "The Extended Case Method."

2. Collins, "Social Construction of Black Feminist Thought."

3. Gramsci, *Selections from the Prison Notebooks*.

4. Burawoy, "The Extended Case Method"; Small, "How Many Cases Do I Need?"

5. Sayer, *Method in Social Science*.

6. Small, "How Many Cases Do I Need?," 23.

7. Jerolmack and Murphy, "Ethical Dilemmas and Social Scientific Trade-Offs of Masking in Ethnography."

# References

Adler, Gary. *Empathy beyond US Borders: The Challenges of Transnational Civic Engagement.* Cambridge: Cambridge University Press, 2019.

Alexander, Jeffrey C., and Philip Smith. "The Discourse of American Civil Society: A New Proposal for Cultural Studies." *Theory and Society* 22, no. 2 (April 1, 1993): 151–207.

Alexander, Michelle. *The New Jim Crow: Mass Incarceration in the Age of Colorblindness.* New York: New Press, 2012.

Alinsky, Saul D. *Rules for Radicals: A Practical Primer for Realistic Radicals.* New York: Vintage, 1971.

Ammerman, Nancy T. "Rethinking Religion: Toward a Practice Approach." *American Journal of Sociology* 126, no. 1 (2020): 6–51.

——. *Studying Lived Religion: Contexts and Practices.* New York: New York University Press, 2021.

Andrews, Kenneth T., Marshall Ganz, Matthew Baggetta, Hahrie Han, and Chaeyoon Lim. "Leadership, Membership, and Voice: Civic Associations That Work." *American Journal of Sociology* 115, no. 4 (2010): 1191–242.

Armstrong, Elizabeth A., and Mary Bernstein. "Culture, Power, and Institutions: A Multi-institutional Politics Approach to Social Movements." *Sociological Theory* 26, no. 1 (March 1, 2008): 74–99.

Baker, Joseph O., and Gerardo Martí. "Is the Religious Left Resurgent?" *Sociology of Religion* 81, no. 2 (April 9, 2020): 131–41.

Barber, William J., and Jonathan Wilson-Hartgrove. *The Third Reconstruction: Moral Mondays, Fusion Politics, and the Rise of a New Justice Movement.* Boston: Beacon Press, 2016.

Barnes, Sandra L. "Black Church Culture and Community Action." *Social Forces* 84, no. 2 (December 1, 2005): 967–94.

Bean, Lydia. *The Politics of Evangelical Identity: Local Churches and Partisan Divides in the United States and Canada.* Princeton, NJ: Princeton University Press, 2014.

Becker, Penny Edgell. *Congregations in Conflict: Cultural Models of Local Religious Life.* Cambridge: Cambridge University Press, 1999.

Bellah, Robert N., Richard Madsen, William M. Sullivan, Ann Swidler, and Steven M. Tipton. *Habits of the Heart: Individualism and Commitment in American Life.* 3rd ed. Berkeley: University of California Press, 1985.

Bender, Courtney, Wendy Cadge, Peggy Levitt, and David Smilde, eds. *Religion on the Edge: De-centering and Re-centering the Sociology of Religion.* Oxford: Oxford University Press, 2012.

Billingsley, Andrew. *Mighty Like a River: The Black Church and Social Reform.* Oxford: Oxford University Press, 1999.

Bouie, Jamelle. "Beyond 'White Fragility.'" Opinion, *New York Times*, June 26, 2020. www.nytimes.com/2020/06/26/opinion/black-lives-matter-injustice.html.

Bracey, Glenn E., II. "Black Movements Need Black Theorizing: Exposing Implicit Whiteness in Political Process Theory." *Sociological Focus* 49 (2016): 11–27.

Braunstein, Ruth. "A (More) Perfect Union? Religion, Politics, and Competing Stories of America." *Sociology of Religion* 79, no. 2 (May 19, 2018): 172–95.

——. *Prophets and Patriots: Faith in Democracy across the Political Divide.* Berkeley: University of California Press, 2017.

——. "A Theory of Political Backlash: Assessing the Religious Right's Effects on the Religious Field." *Sociology of Religion*, November 15, 2021. https://doi.org/10.1093/socrel/srab050.

Braunstein, Ruth, Todd Nicholas Fuist, and Rhys H. Williams. *Religion and Progressive Activism: New Stories about Faith and Politics.* New York: New York University Press, 2017.

Braunstein, Ruth, Brad R. Fulton, and Richard L. Wood. "The Role of Bridging Cultural Practices in Racially and Socioeconomically Diverse Civic Organizations." *American Sociological Review* 79, no. 4 (August 1, 2014): 705–25.

Bretherton, Luke. *Resurrecting Democracy: Faith, Citizenship, and the Politics of a Common Life.* Cambridge: Cambridge University Press, 2014.

Brooks, Clem, and Jeff Manza. "A Broken Public? Americans' Responses to the Great Recession." *American Sociological Review* 78, no. 5 (October 1, 2013): 727–48.

Burawoy, Michael. "The Extended Case Method." *Sociological Theory* 16, no. 1 (1998): 4–33.

Carroll, Tamar W. "Intersectionality and Identity Politics: Cross-Identity Coalitions for Progressive Social Change." *Signs: Journal of Women in Culture and Society* 42, no. 3 (February 14, 2017): 600–607.

Castells, Manuel. *Networks of Outrage and Hope: Social Movements in the Internet Age.* New York: John Wiley & Sons, 2012.

Chaves, Mark, and Shawna L. Anderson. "Changing American Congregations: Findings from the Third Wave of the National Congregations Study." *Journal for the Scientific Study of Religion* 53, no. 4 (December 1, 2014): 676–86.

Chun, Jennifer Jihye, George Lipsitz, and Young Shin. "Intersectionality as a Social Movement Strategy: Asian Immigrant Women Advocates." *Signs* 38, no. 4 (2013): 917–40.

Collins, Patricia Hill. "The Social Construction of Black Feminist Thought." *Signs: Journal of Women in Culture and Society* 14, no. 4 (1989): 745–73.

Cossyleon, Jennifer E. "'Coming Out of My Shell': Motherleaders Contesting Fear, Vulnerability, and Despair through Family-Focused Community Organizing." *Socius* 4 (January 1, 2018). https://doi.org/10.1177/2378023117734729.

Cramer, Katherine J. *The Politics of Resentment: Rural Consciousness in Wisconsin and the Rise of Scott Walker.* Chicago: University of Chicago Press, 2016.

Davis, Mike. "Hopes for 2021?" *New Left Review,* January 5, 2021. https://newleftreview.org/sidecar/posts/hopes-for-2021.

Delehanty, Jack. "Becoming 'People of Faith:' Personal Moral Authenticity in the Cultural Practices of a Faith-Based Social Justice Movement." *Sociological Forum* 35, no. 4 (2020): 1228–49.

———. "The Emotional Management of Progressive Religious Mobilization." *Sociology of Religion* 79, no. 2 (May 19, 2018): 248–72.

———. "Prophets of Resistance: Social Justice Activists Contesting Comfortable Church Culture." *Sociology of Religion* 77, no. 1 (2016): 37–58.

Delehanty, Jack, and Michelle Oyakawa. "Building a Collective Moral Imaginary: Personalist Culture and Social Performance in Faith-Based Community Organizing." *American Journal of Cultural Sociology* 6, no. 2 (2018): 266–95.

Della Porta, Donatella. *Can Democracy Be Saved? Participation, Deliberation and Social Movements.* New York: John Wiley & Sons, 2013.

DeSlippe, Dennis. "'As in a Civics Text Come to Life': The East Brooklyn Congregations' Nehemiah Housing Plan and 'Citizens Power' in the 1980s." *Journal of Urban History* 45, no. 5 (2019): 1030–49.

DiAngelo, Robin. *White Fragility: Why It's So Hard for White People to Talk about Racism.* Boston: Beacon Press, 2018.

Doussard, Marc, and Brad R. Fulton. "Organizing Together: Benefits and Drawbacks of Community-Labor Coalitions for Community Organizations." *Social Service Review* 94, no. 1 (March 2020): 36–74.

Dreher, Rod. *The Benedict Option: A Strategy for Christians in a Post-Christian Nation.* New York: Sentinel, 2017.

———. *Live Not by Lies: A Manual for Christian Dissidents.* London: Penguin, 2020.

Du Bois, W. E. B. *Black Reconstruction in America: Toward a History of the Part Which Black Folk Played in the Attempt to Reconstruct Democracy in America, 1860–1880.* New York: Routledge, 2017.

Edgell, Penny. "An Agenda for Research on American Religion in Light of the 2016 Election." *Sociology of Religion* 78, no. 1 (March 1, 2017): 1–8.

———. "A Cultural Sociology of Religion: New Directions." *Annual Review of Sociology* 38, no. 1 (2012): 247–65.

Edwards, Korie Little, and Michelle Oyakawa. *Smart Suits, Tattered Boots: Black Ministers Mobilizing the Black Church in the Twenty-First Century.* New York: New York University Press, 2022.

Eichstedt, Jennifer L. "Problematic White Identities and a Search for Racial Justice." *Sociological Forum* 16, no. 3 (2001): 445–70.

Eliasoph, Nina. *Making Volunteers: Civic Life after Welfare's End.* Princeton, NJ: Princeton University Press, 2011.

Eliasoph, Nina, and Paul Lichterman. "Culture in Interaction." *American Journal of Sociology* 108, no. 4 (2003): 735–94.

Ellingson, Stephen. *The Megachurch and the Mainline: Remaking Religious Tradition in the Twenty-First Century.* Chicago: University of Chicago Press, 2007.

Emerson, Michael O., and Christian Smith. *Divided by Faith: Evangelical Religion and the Problem of Race in America.* Oxford: Oxford University Press, 2001.

Enriquez, Laura E., and Abigail C. Saguy. "Coming Out of the Shadows: Harnessing a Cultural Schema to Advance the Undocumented Immigrant Youth Movement." *American Journal of Cultural Sociology* 4, no. 1 (2016): 107–30.

Ewick, Patricia, and Marc W. Steinberg. *Beyond Betrayal: The Priest Sex Abuse Crisis, the Voice of the Faithful, and the Process of Collective Identity.* Chicago: University of Chicago Press, 2019.

Fetner, Tina. *How the Religious Right Shaped Lesbian and Gay Activism.* Minneapolis: University of Minnesota Press, 2008.

Fisher, Robert, and Sally Tamarkin. "Right-Wing Organizers Do This Too: The Case of the Christian Coalition." *Journal of Community Practice* 19, no. 4 (2011): 403–21.

Flores, Edward Orozco. *Jesus Saved an Ex-Con: Political Activism and Redemption after Incarceration.* New York: New York University Press, 2018.

Fuist, Todd Nicholas. "'Not Left-Wing, Just Human': The Integration of Personal Morality and Structural Critique in Progressive Religious Talk." *Politics and Religion* 11, no. 1 (2017): 169–91.

Fulton, Brad R., Michelle Oyakawa, and Richard L. Wood. "Critical Standpoint: Leaders of Color Advancing Racial Equality in Predominantly White Organizations." *Nonprofit Management and Leadership* 30, no. 2 (2019): 255–76.

Gamson, Joshua. "Must Identity Movements Self-Destruct? A Queer Dilemma." *Social Problems* 42, no. 3 (August 1, 1995): 390–407.

Ganz, Marshall. "Resources and Resourcefulness: Strategic Capacity in the Unionization of California Agriculture, 1959–1966." *American Journal of Sociology* 105, no. 4 (2000): 1003–62.

——. *Why David Sometimes Wins: Leadership, Organization, and Strategy in the California Farm Worker Movement.* Oxford: Oxford University Press, 2009.

Gecan, Michael. *Going Public: An Organizer's Guide to Citizen Action.* New York: Anchor, 2004.

Geraty, Kristin. "Challenges and Opportunities of Community Organizing in Suburban Congregations." In *Religion and Progressive Activism: New Stories about Faith and Politics,* edited by Ruth Braunstein, Todd Nicholas Fuist, and Rhys H. Williams, 161–79. New York: New York University Press, 2017.

Giorgi, Simona, Jean M. Bartunek, and Brayden G. King. "A Saul Alinsky Primer for the 21st Century: The Roles of Cultural Competence and Cultural Brokerage in Fostering Mobilization in Support of Change." *Research in Organizational Behavior* 37 (2017): 125–42.

Goffman, Erving. *Interaction Ritual: Essays on Face-to-Face Behavior.* Garden City, NY: Doubleday, 1967.

Gorski, Philip S. *American Covenant: A History of Civil Religion from the Puritans to the Present.* Princeton, NJ: Princeton University Press, 2017.

Gramsci, Antonio. *Selections from the Prison Notebooks.* Edited by Quintin Hoare and Geoffrey Nowell Smith. London: International, 1971.

Hacker, Jacob S. *The Great Risk Shift: The New Economic Insecurity and the Decline of the American Dream.* Oxford: Oxford University Press, 2008.

Han, Hahrie. *How Organizations Develop Activists: Civic Associations and Leadership in the 21st Century*. Oxford: Oxford University Press, 2014.

Hart, Stephen. *Cultural Dilemmas of Progressive Politics: Styles of Engagement among Grassroots Activists*. Chicago: University of Chicago Press, 2001.

Herberg, Will. *Protestant, Catholic, Jew: An Essay in American Religious Sociology*. Chicago: University of Chicago Press, 1955.

Hoffman, Michael E. S. "The Political Economy of TARP: A Public Opinion Approach." *SSRN*, 2012. https://doi.org/10.2139/ssrn.1998384.

Hout, Michael, and Claude Fischer. "Explaining Why More Americans Have No Religious Preference: Political Backlash and Generational Succession, 1987–2012." *Sociological Science* 1 (2014): 423–47.

——. "Why More Americans Have No Religious Preference: Politics and Generations." *American Sociological Review* 67, no. 2 (April 1, 2002): 165–90.

Hunter, James Davison. *Culture Wars: The Struggle to Define America*. New York: Basic Books, 1991.

Hurwitz, Heather K. "Gender and Race in the Occupy Movement: Relational Leadership and Discriminatory Resistance." *Mobilization: An International Quarterly* 24, no. 2 (2019): 157–76.

Itzigsohn, José, and Karida L. Brown. *The Sociology of W. E. B. Du Bois: Racialized Modernity and the Global Color Line*. New York: New York University Press, 2020.

Jenkins, Jack. *American Prophets: The Religious Roots of Progressive Politics and the Ongoing Fight for the Soul of the Country*. New York: HarperCollins, 2020.

Jerolmack, Colin, and Alexandra K. Murphy. "The Ethical Dilemmas and Social Scientific Trade-Offs of Masking in Ethnography." *Sociological Methods and Research* 48, no. 4 (March 30, 2017): 801–27.

Jones, Robert P. *The End of White Christian America*. New York: Simon and Schuster, 2016.

Kettell, Steven. "Faithless: The Politics of New Atheism." *Secularism and Nonreligion* 2 (November 21, 2013): 61–72.

Klein, Naomi. *This Changes Everything: Capitalism vs. the Climate*. New York: Simon & Schuster, 2015.

Krippner, Greta R. "Democracy of Credit: Ownership and the Politics of Credit Access in Late Twentieth-Century America." *American Journal of Sociology* 123, no. 1 (June 29, 2017): 1–47.

Krull, Laura. "Liberal Churches and Social Justice Movements: Analyzing the Limits of Inclusivity." *Journal for the Scientific Study of Religion* 59, no. 1 (2020): 84–100.

Lakoff, George. *Moral Politics: How Liberals and Conservatives Think*. Chicago: University of Chicago Press, 1996.

Lareau, Annette. *Unequal Childhoods*. Berkeley: University of California Press, 2003.

Layman, Geoffrey. *The Great Divide: Religious and Cultural Conflict in American Party Politics*. New York: Columbia University Press, 2001.

Lee, Caroline W., Michael McQuarrie, and Edward T. Walker. *Democratizing Inequalities: Dilemmas of the New Public Participation.* New York: New York University Press, 2015.

Leondar-Wright, Betsy. *Missing Class: Strengthening Social Movement Groups by Seeing Class Cultures.* Ithaca, NY: Cornell University Press, 2014.

Lichtenstein, Nelson. "How to Win." *Dissent Magazine,* Spring 2019. www .dissentmagazine.org/article/how-to-win.

Lichterman, Paul. "Beyond the Seesaw Model: Public Commitment in a Culture of Self-Fulfillment." *Sociological Theory* 13, no. 3 (1995): 275–300.

——. *Elusive Togetherness: Church Groups Trying to Bridge America's Divisions.* Princeton, NJ: Princeton University Press, 2005.

——. *How Civic Action Works: Fighting for Housing in Los Angeles.* Princeton, NJ: Princeton University Press, 2020.

——. "Religion in Public Action: From Actors to Settings." *Sociological Theory* 30, no. 1 (March 1, 2012): 15–36.

——. *The Search for Political Community: American Activists Reinventing Commitment.* Cambridge: Cambridge University Press, 1996.

——. "Studying Public Religion: Beyond the Beliefs-Driven Actor." In *Religion on the Edge: De-centering and Re-centering the Sociology of Religion,* edited by Courtney Bender, Wendy Cadge, Peggy Levitt, and David Smilde, 115–36. Oxford: Oxford University Press, 2012.

Lichterman, Paul, and Nina Eliasoph. "Civic Action." *American Journal of Sociology* 120, no. 3 (2015): 798–863.

Lichterman, Paul, and Rhys H. Williams. "Cultural Challenges for Mainline Protestant Political Progressives." In *Religion and Progressive Activism: New Stories about Faith and Politics,* edited by Ruth Braunstein, Todd Nicholas Fuist, and Rhys H. Williams, 117–37. New York: New York University Press, 2017.

Lindsay, D. Michael. *Faith in the Halls of Power: How Evangelicals Joined the American Elite.* Oxford: Oxford University Press, 2007.

Madsen, Richard. "The Archipelago of Faith: Religious Individualism and Faith Community in America Today." *American Journal of Sociology* 114, no. 5 (March 1, 2009): 1263–301.

Mandell, Rebecca, Barbara A. Israel, and Amy J. Schulz. "Breaking Free from Siloes: Intersectionality as a Collective Action Frame to Address Toxic Exposures and Reproductive Health." *Social Movement Studies* 18, no. 3 (May 4, 2019): 346–63.

Martí, Gerardo. *American Blindspot: Race, Class, Religion, and the Trump Presidency.* Lanham, MD: Rowman & Littlefield, 2020.

Massengill, Rebekah Peeples. *Wal-Mart Wars: Moral Populism in the Twenty-First Century.* New York: New York University Press, 2013.

McAdam, Doug. "Recruitment to High-Risk Activism: The Case of Freedom Summer." *American Journal of Sociology* 92, no. 1 (1986): 64–90.

McAdam, Doug, and Karina Kloos. *Deeply Divided: Racial Politics and Social Movements in Postwar America.* Oxford: Oxford University Press, 2014.

McAlevey, Jane. *No Shortcuts: Organizing for Power in the New Gilded Age*. Oxford: Oxford University Press, 2016.

McCarthy, Angela F., Laura R. Olson, and James C. Garand. "Religious Right, Religious Left, Both, or Neither? Understanding Religio-Political Identification." *Journal for the Scientific Study of Religion* 58, no. 3 (2019): 547–69.

McRoberts, Omar. "Civil Religion and Black Church Political Mobilization." In *Religion Is Raced: Understanding American Religion in the Twenty-First Century*, edited by Grace Yukich and Penny Edgell, 40–57. New York: New York University Press, 2020.

———. *Streets of Glory: Church and Community in a Black Urban Neighborhood*. Chicago: University of Chicago Press, 2005.

Mills, C. Wright. *The Sociological Imagination*. Oxford: Oxford University Press, 1959.

Morris, Aldon D. *The Origins of the Civil Rights Movement*. New York: Simon and Schuster, 1984.

Mudge, Stephanie L. *Leftism Reinvented: Western Parties from Socialism to Neoliberalism*. Cambridge, MA: Harvard University Press, 2018.

Murray, Susan B. "Child Care Work: Intimacy in the Shadows of Family-Life." *Qualitative Sociology* 21, no. 2 (1998): 149–68.

National Low Income Housing Coalition. *Out of Reach 2019*. 2019. https://reports .nlihc.org/oor/about.

Nepstad, Sharon Erickson. *Convictions of the Soul: Religion, Culture, and Agency in the Central America Solidarity Movement*. Oxford: Oxford University Press, 2004.

O'Brien, John. "Individualism as a Discursive Strategy of Action: Autonomy, Agency, and Reflexivity among Religious Americans." *Sociological Theory* 33, no. 2 (June 1, 2015): 173–99.

———. *Keeping It Halal: The Everyday Lives of Muslim American Teenage Boys*. Princeton, NJ: Princeton University Press, 2017.

O'Brien, John, and Eman Abdelhadi. "Re-examining Restructuring: Racialization, Religious Conservatism, and Political Leanings in Contemporary American Life." *Social Forces* 99, no. 2 (2020): 474–503.

Oliver, Melvin, and Thomas Shapiro. *Black Wealth/White Wealth: A New Perspective on Racial Inequality*. New York: Routledge, 2013.

Olson, Mancur. *The Logic of Collective Action: Public Goods and the Theory of Groups*. Cambridge, MA: Harvard University Press, 2009.

Oyakawa, Michelle. "Building a Movement in the Non-Profit Industrial Complex." Doctoral diss., Ohio State University, 2017.

———. "'Turning Private Pain into Public Action': The Cultivation of Identity Narratives by a Faith-Based Community Organization." *Qualitative Sociology* 38, no. 4 (October 22, 2015): 395–415.

Oyakawa, Michelle, Elizabeth McKenna, and Hahrie Han. "Habits of Courage: Reconceptualizing Risk in Social Movement Organizing." *Journal of Community Psychology* 49, no. 8 (2021): 3101–21.

Pearce, Lisa, and Melinda Lundquist Denton. *A Faith of Their Own: Stability and Change in the Religiosity of America's Adolescents.* Oxford: Oxford University Press, 2010.

Pew Research Center. "In U.S., Decline of Christianity Continues at Rapid Pace." October 17, 2019.

———. "Religious Landscape Study." 2014. www.pewforum.org/religious -landscape-study.

Phipps, Alison. "Whose Personal Is More Political? Experience in Contemporary Feminist Politics." *Feminist Theory* 17, no. 3 (December 1, 2016): 303–21.

Piketty, Thomas, and Emmanuel Saez. "Inequality in the Long Run." *Science* 344, no. 6186 (2014): 838–43.

Polletta, Francesca. "How Participatory Democracy Became White: Culture and Organizational Choice." *Mobilization: An International Quarterly* 10, no. 2 (June 1, 2005): 271–88.

———. *It Was Like a Fever: Storytelling in Protest and Politics.* University of Chicago Press, 2006.

Putnam, Robert D. *Bowling Alone: The Collapse and Revival of American Community.* New York: Simon & Schuster, 2000.

Riley, Alexander. "Woke Totemism: A Sociology of Multicultural Religion." *First Things: A Monthly Journal of Religion and Public Life,* no. 295 (2019): 31–37.

Roediger, David R. *The Wages of Whiteness: Race and the Making of the American Working Class.* New York: Verso, 1999.

Saez, Emmanuel, and Gabriel Zucman. "Wealth Inequality in the United States since 1913: Evidence from Capitalized Income Tax Data." *Quarterly Journal of Economics* 131, no. 2 (May 1, 2016): 519–78.

Sampson, Robert J., Doug McAdam, Heather MacIndoe, and Simón Weffer-Elizondo. "Civil Society Reconsidered: The Durable Nature and Community Structure of Collective Civic Action." *American Journal of Sociology* 111, no. 3 (2005): 673–714.

Sayer, Andrew. *Method in Social Science: A Realist Approach.* 2nd ed. New York: Routledge, 1992.

Schlosberg, David, and Lisette B. Collins. "From Environmental to Climate Justice: Climate Change and the Discourse of Environmental Justice." *Wiley Interdisciplinary Reviews: Climate Change* 5, no. 3 (2014): 359–74.

Schradie, Jen. *The Revolution That Wasn't: How Digital Activism Favors Conservatives.* Cambridge, MA: Harvard University Press, 2019.

Seamster, Louise, and Raphaël Charron-Chénier. "Predatory Inclusion and Education Debt: Rethinking the Racial Wealth Gap." *Social Currents* 4, no. 3 (June 1, 2017): 199–207.

Skocpol, Theda. *Diminished Democracy: From Membership to Management in American Civic Life.* Norman: University of Oklahoma Press, 2003.

Small, Mario Luis. "'How Many Cases Do I Need?' On Science and the Logic of Case Selection in Field-Based Research." *Ethnography* 10, no. 1 (March 1, 2009): 5–38.

Smith, Andrea. *The Revolution Will Not Be Funded: Beyond the Non-profit Industrial Complex*. Boston: South End Press, 2007.

Smith, Christian. *American Evangelicalism: Embattled and Thriving*. Chicago: University of Chicago Press, 1998.

———. *Disruptive Religion: The Force of Faith in Social-Movement Activism*. New York: Routledge, 1996.

———. *Souls in Transition: The Religious and Spiritual Lives of Emerging Adults*. Oxford: Oxford University Press, 2009.

Smith, Dorothy E. "The Standard North American Family SNAF as an Ideological Code." *Journal of Family Issues* 14, no. 1 (March 1, 1993): 50–65.

Smith, Rogers M. "Beyond Tocqueville, Myrdal, and Hartz: The Multiple Traditions in America." *American Political Science Review* 87, no. 3 (September 1, 1993): 549–66.

———. *Stories of Peoplehood: The Politics and Morals of Political Membership*. Cambridge: Cambridge University Press, 2003.

Snow, David A., and Doug McAdam. "Identity Work Processes in the Context of Social Movements: Clarifying the Identity/Movement Nexus." In *Self, Identity, and Social Movements*, edited by Sheldon Stryker, Timothy Joseph Owens, and Robert W. White, 41–67. Minneapolis: University of Minnesota Press, 2000.

Speer, Paul W., and Hahrie Han. "Re-engaging Social Relationships and Collective Dimensions of Organizing to Revive Democratic Practice." *Journal of Social and Political Psychology* 6, no. 2 (2018): 745–58.

Speer, Paul W., and Joseph Hughey. "Community Organizing: An Ecological Route to Empowerment and Power." *American Journal of Community Psychology* 23, no. 5 (1995): 729–48.

Stark, Rodney, and Roger Finke. *Acts of Faith: Explaining the Human Side of Religion*. Berkeley: University of California Press, 2000.

Stout, Jeffrey. *Blessed Are the Organized: Grassroots Democracy in America*. Princeton, NJ: Princeton University Press, 2010.

Swarts, Heidi J. *Organizing Urban America: Secular and Faith-Based Progressive Movements*. Minneapolis: University of Minnesota Press, 2008.

Taylor, Verta, and Nancy Whittier. "Collective Identity in Social Movement Communities: Lesbian Feminist Mobilization." In *Waves of Protest: Social Movements since the Sixties*, edited by Jo Freeman and Victoria Johnson, 169–94. Lanham, MD: Rowman & Littlefield, 1999.

Tocqueville, Alexis de. *Democracy in America*. Edited by Isaac Kramnick. Translated by Gerald Bevan. New York: Penguin Classics, 2003.

Tucker, Kenneth H. "The Political Is Personal, Expressive, Aesthetic, and Networked: Contemporary American Languages of the Self from Trump to Black Lives Matter." *American Journal of Cultural Sociology* 6, no. 2 (2018): 359–86.

Walker, Edward T., and Lina M. Stepick. "Strength in Diversity? Group Heterogeneity in the Mobilization of Grassroots Organizations." *Sociology Compass* 8, no. 7 (July 1, 2014): 959–75.

Ward, Jane. "White Normativity: The Cultural Dimensions of Whiteness in a Racially Diverse LGBT Organization." *Sociological Perspectives* 51, no. 3 (September 1, 2008): 563–86.

Warren, Mark R. *Dry Bones Rattling: Community Building to Revitalize American Democracy.* Princeton, NJ: Princeton University Press, 2001.

——. *Fire in the Heart: How White Activists Embrace Racial Justice.* Oxford: Oxford University Press, 2010.

Weber, Max. *Economy and Society.* Berkeley: University of California Press, 1978.

Whitehead, Andrew L., and Samuel L. Perry. *Taking America Back for God: Christian Nationalism in the United States.* Oxford: Oxford University Press, 2020.

Wilde, Melissa J. "Complex Religion: Interrogating Assumptions of Independence in the Study of Religion." *Sociology of Religion* 79, no. 3 (2018): 287–98.

Wilde, Melissa J., and Sabrina Danielsen. "Fewer and Better Children: Race, Class, Religion, and Birth Control Reform in America." *American Journal of Sociology* 119, no. 6 (2014): 1710–60.

Williams, Rhys H. "Constructing the Public Good: Social Movements and Cultural Resources." *Social Problems* 42, no. 1 (1995): 124–44.

Williams, Rhys H., and N. J. Demerath. "Religion and Political Process in an American City." *American Sociological Review* 56, no. 4 (1991): 417–31.

Wiltfang, Gregory L., and Doug McAdam. "The Costs and Risks of Social Activism: A Study of Sanctuary Movement Activism." *Social Forces* 69, no. 4 (June 1, 1991): 987–1010.

Wong, Janelle S. *Immigrants, Evangelicals, and Politics in an Era of Demographic Change.* New York: Russell Sage Foundation, 2018.

Wood, Richard L. *Faith in Action: Religion, Race, and Democratic Organizing in America.* Chicago: University of Chicago Press, 2002.

Wood, Richard L., and Brad R. Fulton. *A Shared Future: Faith-Based Organizing for Racial Equity and Ethical Democracy.* Chicago: University of Chicago Press, 2015.

Wuthnow, Robert. *Red State Religion: Faith and Politics in America's Heartland.* Princeton, NJ: Princeton University Press, 2012.

——. *The Restructuring of American Religion.* Princeton, NJ: Princeton University Press, 1988.

——. *Rough Country: How Texas Became America's Most Powerful Bible-Belt State.* Princeton, NJ: Princeton University Press, 2014.

——. *Small-Town America: Finding Community, Shaping the Future.* Princeton, NJ: Princeton University Press, 2013.

Yukich, Grace. *One Family under God: Immigration Politics and Progressive Religion in America.* Oxford: Oxford University Press, 2013.

Zald, Mayer N., and John D. McCarthy. "Religious Groups as Crucibles of Social Movements." In *Social Movements in an Organizational Society: Collected Essays,* edited by Mayer N. Zald, 67–96. New York: Routledge, 1987.

# Index

ELIJAH (cont.)
geographical regions in, 40, 188n2; goals of (*see* goals); group style of, 59, 116–18, 127–28, 135 (*see also* social change movements: group styles); immigration reform and, 105–6, 128–34; issue flexibility and, 47, 53–54, 58–59, 138, 148–49; issue teams, in, 49–53; Kids Count on Use initiative, 167–68; Latino Caucus, in, 44, 48, 59; lay leadership in, 41–44; leadership assemblies, 60–61, 104–9; leadership development in, 95, 98, 105, 113, 119, 129–30, 132–34; legislative priorities, 104–5, 118–28; legislative visits (*see* legislative visits); membership, 39, 188n1; non-profit status, 150; organizational structure of, 40–41, 53–59 (*see also* ELIJAH: board of directors, core teams of, lay leadership of, race/ethnic caucuses of, staff organizers); participant observation in, 15–17, 176–79, 181, 191n13; policy proposals of, 28, 53; "power analysis" and, 43; power, debates over, 58–59; predatory lending and, 47–49, 99–100, 111–14, 190n1; Prophetic Resistance rally, 1–2, 5–6, 12–14, 41, 135, 145, 161, 171; racial justice in, 44–45, 71, 74, 159–60 (*see also* ELIJAH: Black churches and; ELIJAH: Latino Caucus, in; racism in (*see* challenges, cultural: race-based); relationship building in, 118–19, 121; religious claims of, 90; religious commitments in, 12; renewable energy task force, 50–53; risk, interpersonal (*see* under Moral vocation); secular spaces, organizing in, 167–70 (*see also* public sphere institutions); self-interest (*see* self-interest); societal significance of, 179–80; staff organizers, 40–41, 46–48, 97, 119–28, 131–34; theology and, 61, 92, 113–14; voting rights and, 94–95, 106; voter turnout operations and, 71–72, 148–50; white evangelicals in, 36, 39; white supremacy in (*see* white supremacy; Working Families Agenda

empathy: cross-racial, 100, 140; development of, 6–7, 30, 69, 166; religious duty, as, 90, 93

empowerment: individuals, of, 55, 56, 65, 76, 167; communities, of, 103–4, 167; political expediency, versus, 55–57, 58

*End of White Christian America, The* (Jones), 35–36

Faith-based community organization (FBCO) federations, 186n3; agenda of, 1–2; composition of, 24, 33; definition of, 1; framing in, 24–25, 29; goals of, 1–2, 170; history of, 1–2; sizes of, 1, 23–24; membership profiles, 24; structures of, 23; white evangelicals in, 36

Faith in Action (FIA), 22–23, 37–38, 186n2

Faith Matters in America summit, 20–23, 28, 36–38

family and community issues, 28–29, 105–7, 118, 134, 136–37

family rhetoric: conservatives' uses of, 29, 133, 136; progressives' uses of, 136–38

Flores, Edward, 170

Fuist, Todd Nichols, 54

Fulton, Brad, 10, 36, 145

Gamaliel Foundation, 23

Gamson, Joshua, 66

Garrison, William Lloyd, 171

George Floyd protests, 32

goals: internal vs. external, 54, 118–28, 129–30, 132–34, 136; short-term vs. long-term, 55–57, 58

Goffman, Erving, 11

Gramsci, Antonio, 179

personal transformation, political
purpose of, 2–3, 66–77, 136
political action: modes of, 54; public
facing, 115; religious practice, as,
135–38
Pope Francis: social justice message of,
38; U.S., visit to, 2015, 16–17, 20
poverty profiteering, 49, 111–15. *See also*
ELIJAH: predatory lending
progressives: faith, discomfort with,
142–45, 159; FBCOs, unfamiliarity
with, 165; secularity and, 17, 27, 31,
151. *See also* religious progressives
public-sphere institutions: decline of,
169–70; faith-based organizing in,
164–70, 172

racial hierarchies, functions of, 25, 90
recession of 2008, effects of, 25–26
relational practices: confessing (*see*
storytelling); cultural dynamics of, 9,
91; definition of, 4–5; faith development and, 75, 88–90; group solidarity formation and, 6–7, 8–9, 30,
78–85, 91, 139, 164; impediments to,
cultural, 153; one-to-one conversations (*see* one-to-ones); phone
banking in, 123–26; political functions of, 6–7, 15, 26–29, 30, 62,
65–66, 69, 78–85, 134–36, 162, 164;
purpose of, 78, 163–64; religious
dynamics of, 10–12, 27–28, 134–36,
164; religious elements in, 10, 38,
80–84, 113–14, 135, 164; racial
consciousness and, 70–71, 74, 79–80,
80–81, 82, 88–89, 152–59; self-
interest and, 87, 89, 91, 96, 162 (*see
also* self-interest)
religious authority. *See* moral authority
religious commitment: associations
with conservatism, 1, 31, 146–48;
collective, 11, 64, 84, 92, 96, 109;
conceptualizations of, 12, 66, 70,
90–91; faith symbols and, 10, 11, 17,
64, 77–78

religious congregations, 29; political
activity, discomfort with, 141–45
religious conservatives, 4–15; denominations, effects on, 33–36; effective-
ness of, 140–41; individualism,
rejection of, 67; religion, association
with, 27. *See also* Religious Right
religious disaffiliation, 31–33, 139,
164, 166
religious landscape, American, since
1960s: Black Americans and, 32–33
(*see also* Black Church); civil rights
movement and (*see* civil rights
movement); cultural assumptions in,
shared, 163; cultural divisions in,
34–35, 141; demographic changes
and, 32, 166; denominational
tensions in, 33; ethnic diversity and,
32; political divisions in, 33–36, 141;
religious practices, collective, 10–11,
96, 100, 109, 135; organizing, as basis
for, 168–70
religious progressives, 14; Black church
and, 32–33; composition of, 36;
inclusive as, 16, 91, 117, 146–47, 148;
opposition to Religious Right and, 31,
146–48; personal transformation in,
2–3, 29, 143–44; public legitimacy of,
17; research questions about, 2, 3, 175
Religious Right, 31, 34, 35–36; "counterfeit" Christianity and, 67 (*see also*
moralistic therapeutic deism);
exclusionary as, 147; "family values"
and, 29, 136; identities in, 143; impact
at state and local levels, 140–41;
pushback against, 31, 33, 147;
religious stereotypes and, 17, 31, 147,
165; religious tradition, 29
Republican Party: civil rights movement and, 34; conservative Christians
and, 31; urban areas, demonization
of, 128
Republicans, 149, 150, 191n17, 192n22
Riley, Alexander, 172
*Roe v. Wade* (1973), 34